PHP 5 Social Networking

Create a powerful and dynamic social networking
website in PHP by building a flexible framework

Michael Peacock

open source

community experience distilled

PUBLISHING

BIRMINGHAM - MUMBAI

PHP 5 Social Networking

First published: October 2010

Production Reference: 1181010

Published by Packt Publishing Ltd.
32 Lincoln Road
Olton
Birmingham, B27 6PA, UK.

ISBN 978-1-849512-38-1

www.packtpub.com

Cover Image by John M. Quick (john.m.quick@gmail.com)

Credits

Author
Michael Peacock

Reviewers
Jason Mayes
Sérgio Serra
Deepak Vohra

Acquisition Editor
Sarah Cullington

Development Editor
Wilson D'souza

Technical Editors
Chris Rodrigues
Ajay Shanker

Indexers
Hemangini Bari
Tejal Daruwale
Rekha Nair

Editorial Team Leader
Aanchal Kumar

Project Team Leader
Priya Mukherji

Project Coordinator
Srimoyee Ghoshal

Proofreader
Aaron Nash

Graphics
Nilesh R. Mohite

Production Coordinator
Melwyn D'sa

Cover Work
Melwyn D'sa

About the Author

Michael Peacock (http://www.michaelpeacock.co.uk) is a web developer and Zend Certified Engineer from Newcastle, UK with a degree in Software Engineering from the University of Durham. After meeting his business partner while studying at Durham, he co-founded Peacock Carter Limited (http://www.peacockcarter.co.uk), a creative agency based in Newcastle, where he helps run the business and manages the development team. Michael presented some of his thoughts on one particular web application architecture at the PHPNW 2010 conference.

Michael loves working on web-related projects and new business ideas and has interests in several companies. At the moment he is working on his latest venture, Central Apps, and its flagship product Invoice Central (http://www.invoicecentral.co.uk/). He also takes part in amateur dramatics in his spare time, volunteering through Juniper Productions (http://www.juniperproductions.org.uk) in Newcastle.

He has been involved with a number of books, having written five books: *PHP 5 Social Networking*, *PHP 5 E-Commerce Development*, *Drupal 6 Social Networking*, *Selling online with Drupal e-Commerce*, *Building websites with TYPO3*, and acted as technical reviewer for two others, *Mobile Web Development* and *Drupal for Education & E-Learning*.

You can follow Michael on Twitter: www.twitter.com/michaelpeacock.

Acknowledgement

I'd like to thank everybody at Packt Publishing, in particular: Douglas Paterson and Sarah Cullington for working with me on building the idea of this book into a suitable structure, Srimoyee Ghoshal for helping to keep the book on track, and Wilson D'souza, the development editor, and of course the technical reviewers, Jason Mayes, Sérgio Serra, and Deepak Vohra who helped improve the quality of the book.

My thanks also go to my friends and family, in particular my fiancée Emma for her support while working on the book.

Finally, I'd like to thank you, the reader; I hope that you enjoy this book and produce a fantastic social network of your own. I look forward to hearing your feedback and seeing what you come up with!

About the Reviewers

Jason Mayes is a Web Developer, Programmer, Technical Consultant, and Strategist, with a creative twist based in the UK.

With a background in Computer Science, it was here that Jason discovered he fitted in to a rare breed of what he likes to call "hybrid developers"—those who equally enjoy being both creative and technical. Combining these two qualities he produces bespoke, usable, and well-implemented digital solutions in a number of areas.

Jason holds a first class MEng degree in Computer Science from The University of Bristol, and is a member of the BCS (British Computing Society). His final year thesis "Reality mining using mobile devices and pseudonymous social networks" was novel in its implementation, and Jason went on to be shortlisted to the final three candidates in the UK for the "Best IT Student" category in the national SET Awards, which was judged by the IET. The SET awards are established as Britain's most important awards for science and engineering undergraduates.

At the time of writing, Jason is Director of Pure42.com—his own company specializing in areas such as web development and design, digital marketing, usability, user experience, graphic design, digital advertising, social media, and technical consultancy.

Jason is also a Senior Web Development Engineer at a global semiconductor company looking after their online developments, implementations, and digital strategy. During his time there he has helped to build the company's successful online presence as it stands today. He has also worked with world leading companies such as Akamai (see `http://bit.ly/d7utAT`) in his quest for optimal solutions, and has been featured in a Computer World article related to "how to improve your website's uptime" (see `http://bit.ly/a3dnPs`).

When not pursuing a new technology or idea, Jason loves taking flying lessons, travelling, or practicing his DSLR photography skills, which he uploads to Flickr.

You can follow Jason on the following sites:

Website: http://www.jasonmayes.com/

Twitter: http://twitter.com/jason_mayes

> I would like to thank all of the staff and lecturers at the University of Bristol Computer Science Department, colleagues, friends, and family who have inspired and stuck with me over the years and contributed to making me the person who I am today.

Sérgio Serra is a software engineer and an expert in business-related applications, especially ERPs.

He started working in software in 1999, first as a developer and later as a systems analyst. Over the years his work has been focused on development and deployment of large industrial applications like ERPs and production planning software. In 2004 he started developing web applications, mainly with PHP and JavaScript. He aims to someday build his own web ERP and put it into the market. In 2010 he, along with a colleague from his Computer Science Graduation, founded their own web company named Sysactum. In the same year they launched a web application for veterinary, which they have called Actumvet.

Deepak Vohra is a consultant and a principal member of the NuBean.com software company. He is a Sun Certified Java Programmer and Web Component Developer, and has worked in the fields of XML, Java programming, and J2EE for over five years. Deepak is the co-author of the Apress book *Pro XML Development with Java Technology* and was the technical reviewer for the O'Reilly book *WebLogic: The Definitive Guide*. He was also the technical reviewer for the Course Technology PTR book *Ruby Programming for the Absolute Beginner* and the technical editor for the Manning Publications book *Prototype and Scriptaculous in Action*. He is also the author of the Packt Publishing books *JDBC 4.0 and Oracle JDeveloper for J2EE Development* and *Processing XML Documents with Oracle JDeveloper 11g*.

Table of Contents

Preface

Social networking has quickly become a very popular activity on the Internet, particularly with sites such as Facebook and MySpace. When it comes to creating social networks there are many options to chose from, including off-the-shelf systems, making use of existing social networks (for example, building a Facebook application or creating a Facebook page), or building something yourself. While it may be easy to find existing solutions, the only way to have one looking and behaving exactly as you want is to build it yourself.

By initially developing a light-weight Model-View-Controller-style framework with PHP, which can easily be extended to give us a stable and solid platform to work with making common tasks easier and giving us a structure for our social networking code, we can rapidly develop a custom, powerful social networking website.

Within the first few chapters, you will have a suite of files that deal with template management, database management, user authentication management, and e-mail sending. Once this is in place, social networking-centric features can be rapidly developed and plugged into the framework, including user registration and dealing with forgotten details, user profiles, building connections with users, sending messages, sharing information, forming groups, a Developer API, and events and birthday calendars.

At the end of this book, you will have a powerful social networking platform that can take the user all the way from the signup process to forming relationships and creating groups of users. The platform is developed in a very flexible way, so the needs of any social networking site can be met, with new features easily and quickly added in as the needs of the site change.

This book doesn't just stop with how to develop a social networking platform; there are many other topics, which any developer should consider such as marketing, search engine optimization, backing up and restoring the site, and how to deal with scaling problems when the site gets popular. All of these topics are discussed too, leaving you not only with a solid social network, but with hints, tips, and advice on how to maintain it in the long term and deal with any challenges on the way.

What this book covers

Chapter 1, PHP Social Networking, looks into the growing popularity of social networking, including popular social networks, different ways to create or utilize social networks, and discusses what we will be creating throughout the course of the book.

Chapter 2, Planning and Developing the Core Framework, discusses several architectural and design patterns, including Model-View-Controller, Registry and Factory, the planning and subsequent development of our skeleton MVC-style framework with template, database, and e-mail management.

Chapter 3, Users, Registration, and Authentication, extends our development framework with user authentication classes, and then walks through development of registration and login features for users, as well as reminders for forgotten details.

Chapter 4, Friends and Relationships, looks at allowing users to connect with one another, either by adding them as friends or establishing custom relationships with one another such as a co-worker or family member.

Chapter 5, Profiles and Statuses, walks through the development of profiles for our users as well as a flexible status system so users can update their friends and contacts with what they are doing.

Chapter 6, Status Stream, discusses how to collate user statuses and activities to show a useful stream of status updates for a user's particular network, as well as for administrators to see how the network is growing.

Chapter 7, Public and Private Messages, enables users to communicate with one another by implementing a simple message system.

Chapter 8, Statuses – Other Media, allows users to share media such as images and videos with other users in their network as status updates and profile posts.

Chapter 9, Events and Birthdays, integrates a calendar to manage and display events created by our users and birthday notifications.

Chapter 10, Groups, allows users to create and maintain groups related to specific topics with their own lists of members, who opt in to be part of the group.

Chapter 11, Developing an API, discusses the development of an API to allow third-party websites and developers to interact with the social network, so that it can gain popularity through other applications too.

Chapter 12, Deployment, Security, and Maintenance, looks at steps to make the framework more secure and protect it from spam, as well as looking at how to back up the site and restoring it from a backup.

Chapter 13, Marketing, SEO, User Retention, and Monetization Strategies, advises on how to market and promote the social network, and gives useful tips to help develop search engine-friendly websites.

Chapter 14, Planning for Growth, goes through a number of potential issues that will occur when the social network becomes more popular, and advises on scalability, deployment and hosting options, caching, and content delivery networks.

What you need for this book

During the course of this book, you will need the following software to try out the various code examples:

- Apache 1.3 or above (2 recommended)
- mod_rewrite module for Apache
- MySQL 5.0 or above
- PHP 5.0 or above (5.2 or above recommended)

When working locally on your own computer, a package such as WampServer 2 for Windows is recommended, as this will install PHP, Apache, and MySQL in one, and make enabling extensions easy.

A text editor is all that is required for editing the code. However, one with syntax highlighting would be beneficial (such as Crimson Editor or Notepad++).

For deployment, an FTP application such as FileZilla will be required, and an SSH client such as PuTTY for some of the backup and restoration options would be useful.

Who this book is for

This book is primarily aimed at PHP developers, but is suitable for any web developer looking to expand their knowledge and understanding of social networking concepts. Intermediate knowledge of PHP and object-oriented programming is assumed, along with a basic knowledge of MySQL.

Conventions

In this book, you will find a number of styles of text that distinguish between different kinds of information. Here are some examples of these styles, and an explanation of their meaning.

Code words in text are shown as follows: "The `delegateControl` method checks that the delegate controller is within the allowed delegates."

A block of code is set as follows:

```
/**
 * Is the profile valid
 * @return bool
 */
public function isValid()
{
  return $this->valid;
}
```

When we wish to draw your attention to a particular part of a code block, the relevant lines or items are set in bold:

```
<form action="relationship/create/{ID}" method="post">
<select name="relationship_type">
<!-- START relationship_types -->
<option value="{type_id}">{type_name}</option>
<!-- END relationship_types -->
</select>
<input type="submit" name="create" value="Connect with {name}" />
</form>
```

New terms and **important words** are shown in bold. Words that you see on the screen, in menus or dialog boxes for example, appear in the text like this: "Now if we click on the **Connect with** button on the relationship form, our relationship is created and we are shown a confirmation message".

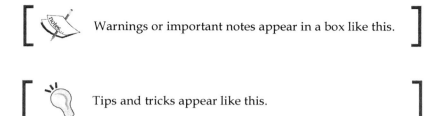

Warnings or important notes appear in a box like this.

Tips and tricks appear like this.

Reader feedback

Feedback from our readers is always welcome. Let us know what you think about this book—what you liked or may have disliked. Reader feedback is important for us to develop titles that you really get the most out of.

To send us general feedback, simply send an e-mail to `feedback@packtpub.com`, and mention the book title via the subject of your message.

If there is a book that you need and would like to see us publish, please send us a note in the **SUGGEST A TITLE** form on `www.packtpub.com` or e-mail `suggest@packtpub.com`.

If there is a topic that you have expertise in and you are interested in either writing or contributing to a book, see our author guide on `www.packtpub.com/authors`.

Customer support

Now that you are the proud owner of a Packt book, we have a number of things to help you to get the most from your purchase.

Downloading the example code for this book

You can download the example code files for all Packt books you have purchased from your account at `http://www.PacktPub.com`. If you purchased this book elsewhere, you can visit `http://www.PacktPub.com/support` and register to have the files e-mailed directly to you.

Errata

Although we have taken every care to ensure the accuracy of our content, mistakes do happen. If you find a mistake in one of our books—maybe a mistake in the text or the code—we would be grateful if you would report this to us. By doing so, you can save other readers from frustration and help us improve subsequent versions of this book. If you find any errata, please report them by visiting http://www.packtpub.com/support, selecting your book, clicking on the **errata submission form** link, and entering the details of your errata. Once your errata are verified, your submission will be accepted and the errata will be uploaded on our website, or added to any list of existing errata, under the Errata section of that title. Any existing errata can be viewed by selecting your title from http://www.packtpub.com/support.

Piracy

Piracy of copyright material on the Internet is an ongoing problem across all media. At Packt, we take the protection of our copyright and licenses very seriously. If you come across any illegal copies of our works, in any form, on the Internet, please provide us with the location address or website name immediately so that we can pursue a remedy.

Please contact us at copyright@packtpub.com with a link to the suspected pirated material.

We appreciate your help in protecting our authors, and our ability to bring you valuable content.

Questions

You can contact us at questions@packtpub.com if you are having a problem with any aspect of the book, and we will do our best to address it.

1
PHP Social Networking

Welcome to PHP social networking! During the course of this book, we are going to build a flexible social networking site and framework using PHP, which we can easily extend to meet the needs of our social network.

In this chapter, you will learn:

- More about social networks
- About existing social networks
- Existing social networking software
- Why and when to roll your own system

We will also discuss the social networking website that we will create during the course of this book: DinoSpace—a social network for keepers of pet dinosaurs.

Introduction to social networks

Social networks are now one of the most widely used aspects of the Web and have really taken off over the past few years. Many businesses, organizations, communities, and families are using social networking to promote themselves, to communicate better with others, and to engage with their audience.

Social networking relies upon users building up their own *network* of contacts on the site. This, in turn, introduces them to new contacts and—on many social networking websites—allows them to be found more easily. Also, this allows new contacts to be recommended or introduced, helping to grow the user's network.

Let's look at an example of how a user's network of contacts can be built up:

This social network representation shows the connections between contacts. It also illustrates how a user may be able to discover friends of a friend and friend recommendations (based on friends in common). This makes it easy for the users to build up their social network, to communicate with new people, or reconnect with lost contacts.

Social networks generally serve two primary functions. Firstly, they allow users to connect with each other and build a contact network, as we have just discussed. They provide a community with collaboration and contribution features as well. This allows the content and information within the social network to be grown by the users themselves. Later in this chapter, we will discuss some of the features available in existing social networks and social networking software, to build up a list of key features we will need to include as well as things we might like to include.

Business logic to social networks

There is some very powerful business logic to using both existing and custom social networks. Creating your own social network or social network tools gives a dedicated customer area, where feedback on products and services can be obtained, for instance, use of support forums to discuss and resolve problems. Areas that allow customers to share tips, resources, and product care tips help promote those products and services.

Examples: Businesses making use of existing social networks and their own social networks

There are some examples of businesses making great use of existing social networks and their own social networking type websites to improve their businesses. Let's have a look at three specific examples.

NameCheap: Twitter

NameCheap is a domain name registrar, and they use Twitter (http://twitter.com/namecheap) for two purposes. Firstly, they collect and respond to feedback from customers mentioning their company, and more prominently, they run various competitions giving away free domain names. These viral competitions encourage more users to follow them, and promote the competition, therefore increasing their brand awareness.

Dell: Twitter

Recently, Dell announced that their Twitter presence (http://twitter.com/delloutlet) generated $6.5 million in revenue, with orders being placed as a result of the links or discounts placed on their Twitter feed. More information is available on the Mashable website: http://mashable.com/2009/12/08/dell-twitter-sales/.

BT: Twitter

British Telecom uses Twitter (http://twitter.com/btcare) to help improve customer service and manage their reputation. In the most instances I've seen this used, it has primarily been in response to customer complaints, to try and assist them with their problems, and escalate matters such as fault testing and engineer call out. This makes them seem more caring (also emphasized by their choice of Twitter username), increases customer satisfaction by resolving problems more quickly.

Netgear: custom

While not strictly a social network, Netgear have various social aspects to their website, both through a dedicated community area (http://www.netgear.com/community/) and the support section of their website (http://kb.netgear.com/app/). The support section integrates community generated content from their discussion forums and brings this into product pages, making it easier for customers to find answers to questions staff have not answered directly. Discussion forum software is also quickly becoming social networking software to an extent, in its own right.

Existing social networks

There are many existing social networks available, some of which are already very popular and have some excellent features. Let's take a look at the most prominent features of some of these more popular sites.

Facebook

Facebook (`www.facebook.com`) is very much a global social networking website for everyone over the age of 13. It started out for students at Harvard University, branching out to all the universities, and now available for everyone. Features available include:

- A customizable profile
- Users can update their statuses
- Users can connect with other users by adding them as "friends"
- Statuses of friends can be commented upon and users can indicate that they *like* a particular status
- Friends can post messages to each other's profiles
- Photos can be posted and shared
- Events can be posted and shared, with attendees sending their RSVPs online
- Groups can be created and joined, promoting specific activities or interests
- Topics can be discussed
- Third-party developers can create their own applications for Facebook, to add more to the platform

LinkedIn

LinkedIn (`www.linkedin.com`) is a social networking site for business contacts, colleagues, and classmates, which primarily encourages business contacts to connect. Features available on LinkedIn include allowing the users to:

- Customize their profile
- Connect with colleagues
- See how users are connected to other
- Recommend other users with respect to a job
- Integrate Twitter with their account profiles
- Create and view business profiles
- Third-party developers can create their own applications too (`http://developer.linkedin.com/index.jspa`)

MySpace

MySpace (www.myspace.com) is a social networking website used primarily by a younger audience. It is very popular with bands, particularly because of how much profiles can be customized with HTML and how music can be embedded within profiles. Features available include:

- Customizable profiles, complete with:
    - HTML customization: allowing users to customize the colors, look, and feel of MySpace
    - Music integration
    - The user's current mood
    - Comments
- Groups: small subsets of users
- MySpace TV: video sharing
- Integration and development of third-party applications via an (a suite of) API(s). We will discuss these further in *Chapter 11, Developing an API*.
- Forums: for discussions.
- Polls: to get user opinion.

Twitter

Twitter (www.twitter.com) is a micro-blogging social networking website, which primarily deals with very short messages of 140 characters or less. Despite this, it has a large number of prominent features, including:

- Profiles can be customized, both in terms of colors and background image
- Users can update their status
- Users can reply to each other's status updates
- Users can repost another user's status update, using the ReTweet function
- Powerful searching based on users replying to each other (@replies) and tagging of tweets with #hashtags

The ease of use and small set of core features have made Twitter very popular.

Existing social networking software

Just like there a number of fantastic social networking sites, there are a number of software systems available as well. These can be used to develop unique social networking sites.

Drupal

Drupal (`http://drupal.org/`) is a popular, freely available, open source content management system. On its own, Drupal can be used to create easy-to-use, easy-to-update websites. By extending this through the thousands of modules that the communities have developed or by creating new modules, we could create almost any type of website we want, ranging from e-commerce to social networking websites.

Drupal does make an excellent candidate for social networking websites, and Packt Publishing has a book published on this subject: *Drupal 6 Social Networking* (`http://www.packtpub.com/build-social-networking-website-with-drupal-6/book`).

Elgg

Elgg (`http://elgg.org/`) is an open source social networking platform, complete with functionality for setting up profiles, sharing files, adding friends, blogging, aggregating RSS, content tagging, and social graphs. Elgg also has an API, allowing developers to extend Elgg by adding additional functionality as well as a RESTful API to allow other applications to interact with the platform.

Joomla!

Joomla! (`http://www.joomla.org/`) is another open source content management system, with a range of built-in social networking features. There is also a commercial add-on, the Jomsocial component (`http://www.jomsocial.com/overview.html`), which turns Joomla! into a truly social network.

Hybrid approaches

There are, of course, options available which combine using an off-the-shelf system and a custom system. However, these mainly facilitate extending the functionality of the existing social networking platform or by integrating some of those social aspects with our own website. Such approaches include:

- Facebook applications: creating applications that are accessed via Facebook's main site, providing additional features to users. For example, a map of dinosaur-friendly restaurants, which are hosted externally by the developer.

- Facebook connect: Allows websites to interact with Facebook, using it as an authentication protocol, pulling friend data from it, as well as pushing, and pulling status updates to and from Facebook.

- Out-of-the-box hosted solutions, such as Ning (`http://www.ning.com/`), that allow users to create and maintain a social network community direct from their web browser.

- Google OpenSocial: A set of common APIs that make applications for social networks interoperable with supporting social networking sites. It also enables site developers to integrate the API so that other developers can build applications for that site, as well.

Rolling your own

Throughout the course of this book, we are going to create our own social networking site from scratch (sometimes referred to as **rolling your own**) using PHP, as opposed to using an existing system, product, or platform (such as Drupal and its social networking modules, Elgg, or leveraging existing social networks such as Facebook).

Why roll your own?

There are a number of very popular and successful social networking websites and social networking products out there, so why would we want to create our own? Some of the benefits for us using our own social networking system are as follows:

- Easier to update and maintain: As we built it, we will know exactly how it works and so we can easily extend and maintain it.

- Licensing: Other products and options have different licenses, which dictate how the software can be used, extended, and shared with our own system. We can decide that for ourselves.

- Enhance knowledge: We can build our own system in order to learn from the process.

- Efficient code: Some existing software packages make use of third-party add-ons, which are not always well optimized for lots of users. By writing our own code, we can ensure we develop in a scalable, efficient way.

- Provide a service.

- Improve business.

- Improve communication.

Easier to update and maintain

Developers who create their own platforms are generally much more familiar with them than with other platforms. As they build them, they know exactly how the platforms work, how to improve, extend, and enhance them. With existing platforms, there is an additional learning curve to developing with them and complications, should the platforms update. With sites such as Facebook, API changes are frequently rolled out, though with existing products, such as Drupal, installing updates is optional.

Licensing

Depending on the platform or product used, there may be different licenses associated with them. Licenses restrict what can and can't be done with the product, how improvements, extensions or modifications can be released, enforcing specific copyright notices or design guidelines, and of course, with many commercial licenses, costing money.

With self-built platforms, the license is up to us. If we want to release our social networking site code to the public, we can, and we can use the license terms we choose.

Enhance knowledge

By creating a social networking website from scratch, you can enhance your knowledge of PHP, social networking, and work with various other third-party APIs along the way to create a fantastic platform.

Provide a service

There are many ways in which websites and social networks provide additional services that are relevant to the social network or the target audience, though these are often through third-party applications. For example, there are features for both Facebook and LinkedIn that can provide a list of books which a user has read. These provide links to book retailers so more information can be discovered, and the books can be purchased. Additionally, some social networks contain knowledge bases of information, which can be improved by the user.

With existing social networks, any additional service provided either directly through the social network or through third-party applications and plugins would, or could, be restricted in a number of ways. The terms and conditions of the social network would be the main restriction, followed by how the features themselves can be added.

For example, if we wanted to add a map of dinosaur-friendly restaurants to an existing social network, it would rely upon:

- Data collection: Use provisions with the social networks terms of service
- Promotion within that social network, which can be a challenge
- Provisions for third-party applications, which would most likely limit and restrict the functionality and design
- Design and user interface guidelines enforced by the social network

Improve business

By tapping into the existing user base of established social networks, we can communicate with a new group of users, increasing awareness, and hopefully, improving business. One slight flaw with existing social networks is providing extra enhancements.

Taking Facebook as an example, third-party developers create additional features and embed them as applications, and some of these applications add business functionality. One example allowed users to book a table at a restaurant. The limitation with using Facebook is that before the information is sent to the application, the user is subjected to several dialogues asking for their confirmation. These dialogues are important to prevent abuse and to ensure user data is used properly. However, it is an obstacle for developers. As more and more applications are available, there is more competition for users' attention, which recently has lead to applications requesting that users invite their friends to use it. These mass invitations have the opposite effect, and discourage users from the applications in question.

With our own social network, the data and functionality would be hosted by ourselves. This gives us the freedom to extend the functionality of the social network to help us improve business as we see fit, leading to a more relevant and user friendly social network!

Improve communication

Social networks remove most barriers to communication, such as geographical location (the only barrier which remains, is Internet access). This is the case for both existing and custom social networks. The primary advantage over using our own system is we are less restricted in how we can communicate with users. With existing social networks, you must be connected to the user and restrictions may be imposed over which communication methods you use within the social network or which external communication details are shown to you.

Why use PHP?

PHP is a popular, open source programming language. Also, unlike some other languages, it isn't a framework in its own right, which means we can structure our application however we wish.

Most modern web hosts support PHP and the database platform we will be using with it (MySQL) and although some other languages are gaining popularity (such as the Ruby on Rails framework), hosting for this isn't as common. Facebook, the world's largest social networking website, is written using PHP (albeit with countless customizations, improvements, and extras), as does Yahoo!, which operates a search engine, news portal websites, and various social websites too. Yahoo! also, until recently, employed Rasmus Lerdorf, the creator of the original PHP engine.

This book assumes we have a reasonable understanding of PHP and some knowledge of object-oriented programming, so another good reason for using PHP is skill level.

When to use something else

As we have discussed earlier, there are already a number of fully featured social networking platforms and products available, written in a variety of different programming languages. Sometimes, it is more appropriate to use one of these, such as:

- When the project has a tight deadline and a base framework isn't already in place. In the interest of time, it would be more appropriate to leverage something else.

- When there are lots of developers on the project with varying skill levels, a project or platform with plenty of existing documentation available would allow the whole team to be able to get started right away.

- If the project is for a client and they have a preferred platform.

- If an existing product has the required features and works in the way required for the project.

Our site: DinoSpace

Throughout the course of this book we are going to develop a social networking site for keepers of pet dinosaurs (of course nobody owns a real pet dinosaur, it would be too expensive, but for the sake of this book, let's pretend!), which we will call DinoSpace. The social network will enable:

- Keepers of pet dinosaurs to connect with one another

- Friendships and other custom relationships (for example, walking buddy) to be maintained with other members of the site

- Users to share stories about their pets

- Profiles of pet dinosaurs to be created:
    ○ Statuses to be updated

- Dinosaur-friendly places to visit to be promoted:
    ○ Non-keepers of dinosaurs to use the site to promote businesses and events that dinosaur keepers may find useful or interesting

- Help and support to be provided to fellow Dinosaur keepers in an interactive way

At the end of this book, we will have a flexible social network for owners of pet dinosaurs. Some screens of the final product are shown. First, we have a basic profile page:

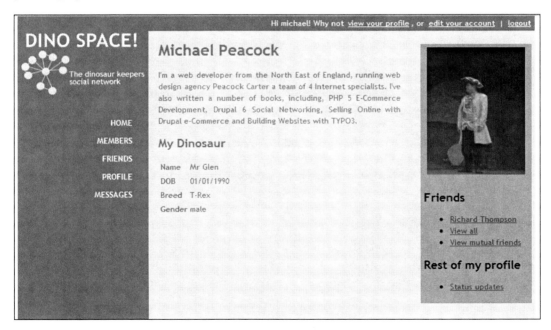

Complete with a customizable user status stream:

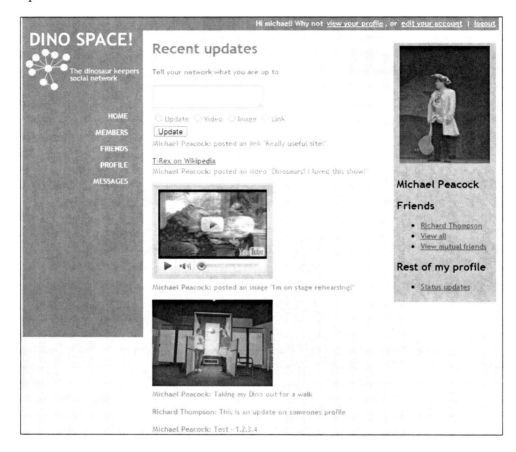

As well as a range of other features, which we will discuss now.

Feature list

From looking at the features available in existing social networking platforms and products, the following features seem standard throughout most of them, and so we shall try and incorporate them into our social networking website:

- Status updates: So that users can update their network with their current status

- Commenting on status updates: So that friends and connections can comment on these status changes

- Status stream: So that changes to many contacts statuses can be viewed at a glance
- Friends and relationships: So that users can connect with one another and define the context of the connection, for example, friend, colleague, or even Dino-walking partner
- Customizable profiles: So that users can build a profile of themselves with custom information about them
- Groups: So that smaller subsets can be created and nurtured within the site, focusing on specific interests or discussions
- Messages: So that users can keep in touch with one another
- Discussions: Encouraging open discussion amongst users
- Image sharing
- Video integration and sharing
- Calendars, events and birthdays: So that users can see upcoming events, create events, and invite friends, perhaps to promote a local T-Rex immunization day at a health center

Limitations

Users of large social networks such as Facebook typically have a large network of friends (or contacts) and subsequently a large number of updates, particularly when combined with the third-party applications, which can also post status updates on their behalf. To ensure that feeds of updates don't become too cluttered, these updates go through a special service that they have developed, which allows certain applications to be filtered out and tries to ensure the user's stream is more relevant.

This is something we won't be able to implement ourselves. However, Facebook has released a number of their components as open source projects, which could be integrated into our framework, should we wish to make use of some of their solutions to large scale social networking problems.

More information can be found on the Facebook open source page: `http://developers.facebook.com/opensource.php`.

Summary

In this chapter, we have looked into what social networking is and why we might wish to use it. Also, we discussed why we created our own site from scratch, as opposed to using an existing system. We have also discussed various existing systems and looked at their features to build a list of features, which we want to use in our site, DinoSpace!

In Chapter 2 we will plan and develop our basic development framework, which we will slowly expand over the course of the book to create a powerful social networking website.

2
Planning and Developing the Core Framework

Now that we know exactly what we are going to do in this book, and why we are going to do it, we can start building our social networking site. To ensure a speedy development process, we are going to invest some time in this chapter to carefully plan and develop a micro-framework, which will take the hassle out of many common development tasks. This will be a small, light-weight framework, as our focus is on social networking, and the purpose of the framework is purely to help us do this.

In this chapter, you will learn:

- About some common design and architectural patterns that solve common programming problems, including:
  - MVC: The Model-View-Controller architecture
  - The Registry pattern
  - The Factory pattern
  - The Front Controller pattern
- How to effectively structure files within a development framework
- How to build the framework, including:
  - How to handle user authentication
  - How to abstract database access functions
  - Template management
- Providing a single point of access to the site

Designing the framework

Before we jump in and start programming, it is important that we take some time to plan and properly design the framework.

Patterns—making life easier

Design and architectural patterns are solutions to common programming problems, and their appropriate use can help ensure that a system is well-designed, easy to build upon, and easy for others to work with.

MVC: Model-View-Controller

The Model-View-Controller pattern is an architectural design pattern designed to separate the user interface from the business logic of an application. The user interface (view) uses the controller to interact with the logic and data of the application (model).

Let's think about our Dino Space social networking site, to see how this will work. If a user adds another user as a friend—they see the **Add as a friend** view. When they click the appropriate button to add the user as a friend, the controller processes this request from the user, and passes the request to the model, which updates the user's friends list, and where appropriate, sends any notifications. The view then updates, via instructions from the controller, to inform the user of the outcome of their request.

The following figure shows the components of the MVC architectural design pattern:

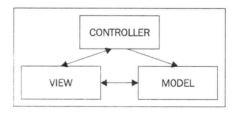

Our use of MVC won't be a religions implementation of the pattern. However, it will be an MVC style; there are numerous debates and discussions within the industry about exactly what MVC is within websites and web-frameworks, and if it is even truly applicable to web-based applications.

Model

Within our framework, the models will be PHP classes that store, manage, and process data and business logic. Access to the underlying database of data will be handled by a database access layer, which the model will make use of. The models will link closely with the database behind our social networking site, representing the data in a more suitable way, which is easier to access and manipulate than accessing the database directly. *Models work with db mostlly*

View

In our framework, the view will be made up of a combination of template files (which will contain HTML and placeholders for dynamic data), images, CSS files, and JavaScript. The templates will be merged and outputted to the user's browser on the fly by the controller.

Controller *process user request.*

The controllers will be a series of PHP classes, which process the user's request, and interact with the model, as well as generate views. Technically, some of our JavaScript (particularly where AJAX is used) also makes up a part of the controller, as it interacts between the view, and the model; these instances are extensions of the controller.

Because we are using the MVC pattern in a web-based environment, the architecture shown earlier can be illustrated in more detail with its interaction with the web-browser and the database. The following figure shows how the web browser and the database fit into the MVC architecture (extended MVC architecture interacting with the browser and the database):

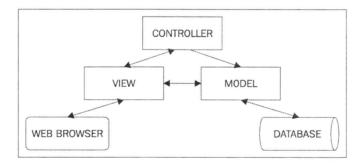

The Front Controller pattern

The Front Controller pattern is a single file, through which all requests are routed (in our case, using Apache's `mod_rewrite`). In our case, this will almost definitely be the `index.php` file. This file will process the user's request, and pass the request to the appropriate controller.

By using a single front controller, our core includes files, core settings, and other common requirements that can all be performed, so that we know regardless of the user request these will have taken place.

If we used specific files for users to request, for example `friends.php` for friend actions, we would either have to "copy and paste" these standard features, functions, and settings, or ensure that we included a specific file that does this for us, which can be an issue if we need to re-factor the code and remove or rename this file — as we would need to ensure that we updated all the references to it.

Registry

Within most web application frameworks, there are numerous core objects, or objects containing core functionality that every aspect of the application will need to have access to. The registry pattern provides us with a means to store all of these core objects within one central object, and access them from within.

Dependency injection

The registry pattern also makes dependency injection easier, as instead of making the object, or the objects it contains globally available — for example, through being a Singleton (which is often seen as a bad practice) — we would need to pass these objects to each of our models and controllers when we instantiate them. By storing all of the core objects within a single registry object, we only need to pass the registry object to these other objects, as opposed to having to pass six or seven objects, along with arrays of system-wide settings.

Within our social networking website, there are going to be a number of tasks that we frequently need to do, such as:

- Check to see if a user is logged in
- Get the logged in user's data
- Query the database, and perform other database-related functions
- Send e-mail notifications, for example, when a user adds another user as a friend

- Manage templates, by sending data to the views to be outputted to the user's browser

- Process the URL the user is accessing the site through, to determine which action should be performed, which controller should be used, and which method should be called

These functions will be abstracted into their own object that will be stored centrally within our registry. The rest of our social networks code can access all of these objects and features directly from our registry. The architecture of the registry is illustrated in the following screenshot:

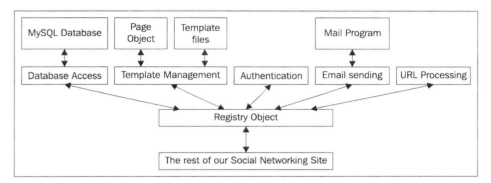

Factory within our registry

Another design pattern that we will make use of is the Factory pattern. To save the need of creating all of the objects that our registry is going to manage, and passing them to the registry, we will simply tell the registry the name of the object we wish to create. The registry will then include the necessary class for us, and create (instantiate) the object for us. The registry then stores the newly created object in its array of objects. It is called a factory because the factory object (in our case, the registry) creates other objects.

A note on the Singleton pattern

Another pattern worth discussing is the Singleton pattern. This pattern generally involves creating a static object, for which only one instance is ever created within the application. Generally, the static nature of the Singleton means that it can be called from anywhere within our social networks code.

Using a Singleton for this purpose is bad practice, as it would mean our code and other objects would need to know details of the Singleton object itself. As we discussed earlier, our registry object should be passed directly to the objects in our social networks code, through their constructors, eliminating the need for the object to be globally available.

Although the registry would be useful as a Singleton, as we would only want one instance of the object to exist, we don't need to worry about this because with PHP 5 by default objects are passed by reference. This means if we pass an object to another object, instead of getting a new copy of the object (as with PHP 4), a reference to the single instance of the object is created, updating the central object, unless we were to clone the object or create a new instance of the registry class.

This is akin to pointers in the C programming language, where a pointer simply points to the space in memory used by an object or variable. When the object or variable needs to be updated, it is accessed via the pointer, saving concern for updating copies or clones of the variable or object by mistake.

Registry + MVC

By combining the MVC architecture with the registry and front controller pattern, we now have a framework where all the requests come through a central file, which creates the registry, and creates the necessary controllers. The controllers create various models where appropriate, and in some cases, pass control to other controllers, before generating and manipulating the templates to generate the views as appropriate. The following diagram shows all of these components working together:

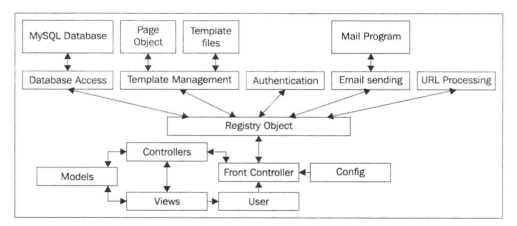

Folder structure

Another important part of the system planning process is the directory structure that we are going to use. This will help us ensure that our files are properly organized, so that when we want to find or edit a particular file, we know exactly where to look.

Our proposed use of the MVC and Registry patterns give us a way to separate certain files, by classifying them as models, views, controllers or related to the registry; so, let's start with those folders:

- Controllers
- Models
- Registry
- Views

Within the views folder, we will have some template files, some images, some CSS, and some JavaScript. We may also allow users to switch between designs, so we would want to keep all of these, for one particular design, within a particular sub-folder. We may also utilize JavaScript libraries, as well as specific JavaScript within a particular view, so we would want to keep these separate too. If we bring this together, we get:

- Controllers
- Models
- Registry
- Views:
    - ° MainView
    - ° CSS
    - ° Images
    - ° JavaScript
    - ° Templates

We are also likely to have two types of uploaded files; files that we, as the administrator, upload to the site once it is live (resources), and files that users upload (uploads) — different aspects of the social network may utilize user uploads, so we should categorize this further:

- Controllers
- Models
- Registry
- Resources:
    - ° Images
        - ° Small
        - ° Large

- ° Original:
- ° Files
- Uploads:
  - ° ProfilePics
    - ° Small
    - ° Large:
  - ° Photos
    - ° Small
    - ° Large:
  - ° Files
- Views:
  - ° MainView
  - ° CSS
  - ° Images
  - ° JavaScript
  - ° Templates

Building the framework

Now that we know the best practices to use when building the framework for our social network, we can start to build it!

Registry

Let's start with our registry as this will be a very important aspect to our framework. The registry is made up of the registry object itself, and the various objects that we will store within it.

The registry object

The registry object itself is very straightforward; it needs to contain two arrays, one to store any settings and data we wish to centrally store within the registry, and one to store the core objects that we wish to access via the registry.

```php
<?php
/**
 * PHP Social Networking
```

```
 * @author Michael Peacock
 * Registry Class
 */
class Registry {

/**
 * Array of objects
 */
private $objects;

/**
 * Array of settings
 */
private $settings;

    public function __construct() {
    }
```

For each of these two arrays, we need two methods: one to store data or an object within the relevant array, and another to retrieve the data or object. Because we are going to use a Factory Method for storing objects, this code will be different from the code for storing settings.

```
/**
 * Create a new object and store it in the registry
 * @param String $object the object file prefix
 * @param String $key pair for the object
 * @return void
 */
public function createAndStoreObject( $object, $key )
{
    require_once( $object . '.class.php' );
```

As we discussed earlier, most of our objects require access to the registry object, and this includes objects stored within the registry. To provide it access, we pass the registry object as a parameter to the objects constructor. Remember: this allows that object to *reference* this instance of the registry (as per the notes on Singleton earlier).

```
    this->objects[ $key ] = new $object( $this );
}
```

When storing settings, however, we simply need to take the data and store it directly in the array.

```
/**
 * Store Setting
 * @param String $setting the setting data
 * @param String $key the key pair for the settings array
 * @return void
 */
public function storeSetting( $setting, $key )
{
    $this->settings[ $key ] = $setting;
}
```

Retrieving data or objects from the registry both work in the same way, as illustrated by the getSetting and getObject methods; they consist of the same code, acting on their respective arrays.

```
/**
 * Get a setting from the registries store
 * @param String $key the settings array key
 * @return String the setting data
 */
public function getSetting( $key )
{
    return $this->settings[ $key ];
}


/**
 * Get an object from the registries store
 * @param String $key the objects array key
 * @return Object
 */
public function getObject( $key )
{
    return $this->objects[ $key ];
}
}


?>
```

Registry objects

The registry object itself is the easy bit; its purpose is to hold data and other objects. It is the objects that will be held in here that will be more complicated. The objects that the registry will use will include:

- Database access
- User authentication
- Template management
- E-mail sending
- URL processing

Database

Our database access class (`registry/mysqldb.class.php`) should provide us with a basic level of abstraction when accessing the database; this also allows us to simplify certain tasks such as inserting records into a database, performing updates, and if we wanted to, even tasks such as creating and editing database tables.

The class needs to be able to:

- Connect to at least one database
- Manage connections to multiple databases where more than one have been connected to
- Execute queries
- Return result sets from executed queries
- Return information from executed queries, such as the ID of the record that was last inserted into the database
- Cache the results of queries (the main use of this is to integrate a result set with the view; this would be done by caching the results, and associating it with a section in the templates)

Many of the functions of this class will be simple wrappers for existing MySQL database functions, with some additions, and allow us to include more error handling should we wish.

Connecting to the database and managing connections

In order to connect to multiple databases, we need to maintain a record of the different connections. This can be done by storing each connection resource in an array, keeping a record as to which of the items in this array is the active connection. When a query is executed, it will perform the query against the currently active connection.

```php
<?php
/**
 * Database management / access class: basic abstraction
 *
 * @author Michael Peacock
 * @version 1.0
 */
class Mysqldb {

  /**
    * Allows multiple database connections
    * each connection is stored as an element in the array, and the
      active connection is maintained in a variable (see below)
    */
  private $connections = array();

  /**
    * Tells the DB object which connection to use
    * setActiveConnection($id) allows us to change this
    */
  private $activeConnection = 0;
  /**
    * Queries which have been executed and the results cached for
      later, primarily for use within the template engine
    */
  private $queryCache = array();

  /**
    * Data which has been prepared and then cached for later usage,
      primarily within the template engine
    */
  private $dataCache = array();

  /**
    * Number of queries made during execution process
    */
  private $queryCounter = 0;
```

```
/**
 * Record of the last query
 */
private $last;

/**
 * Reference to the registry object
 */
private $registry;

/**
 * Construct our database object
 */
public function __construct( Registry $registry )
{
    $this->registry = $registry;
}
```

To connect to the database, we pass the database server host, username, and password and of course the name of the database we wish to connect to. The resulting connection is stored in our connections array, and the connection ID (Array key) is returned.

```
/**
 * Create a new database connection
 * @param String database hostname
 * @param String database username
 * @param String database password
 * @param String database we are using
 * @return int the id of the new connection
 */
public function newConnection( $host, $user, $password, $database )
{
    $this->connections[] = new mysqli( $host, $user, $password,
        $database );
    $connection_id = count( $this->connections )-1;
    if( mysqli_connect_errno() )
    {
        trigger_error('Error connecting to host. '.$this-
            >connections[$connection_id]->error, E_USER_ERROR);
    }


    return $connection_id;
}
```

When we need to swap between connections, for example, to look up data from an external source, or authenticate against another system, we need to tell the database object to use this different connection. This is achieved through the `setActiveConnection` method.

```
/**
 * Change which database connection is actively used for the next
   operation
 * @param int the new connection id
 * @return void
 */
public function setActiveConnection( int $new )
{
    $this->activeConnection = $new;
}
```

Executing queries

After a query is executed, we may wish to get the rows from the result of the query; to allow us to do this, we simply store the result of the query in the classes `$last` variable, so that it can be accessed by other methods.

```
/**
 * Execute a query string
 * @param String the query
 * @return void
 */
public function executeQuery( $queryStr )
{
    if( !$result = $this->connections[$this->activeConnection]-
      >query( $queryStr ) )
    {
        trigger_error('Error executing query: ' . $queryStr .' -
          '.$this->connections[$this->activeConnection]->error,
          E_USER_ERROR);
    }
    else
    {
        $this->last = $result;
    }

}
```

When we do need to get the results from a query, we simply call the MySQLi `fetch_array` method on the result stored in the last variable.

```
/**
 * Get the rows from the most recently executed query, excluding
   cached queries
 * @return array
 */
public function getRows()
{
    return $this->last->fetch_array(MYSQLI_ASSOC);
}
```

Simplifying common queries

Common queries such as INSERT, UPDATE, and DELETE are often very repetitive; however, they are quite easy to abstract the basics of into our database management class. This won't work for all situations, but should make our lives easier for the bulk of these operations. We can abstract select queries to this class too. However, these are much more complicated, particularly, as we will more often than not, need to utilize more complicated logic, such as sub-queries, joins, and aliases. This more complicated logic would need to be developed into the code.

Deleting records can be done simply using the table name, conditions, and a limit. In some cases, a limit may not be required, so if a non-empty string is passed, we need to add the LIMIT keyword to the query.

```
/**
 * Delete records from the database
 * @param String the table to remove rows from
 * @param String the condition for which rows are to be removed
 * @param int the number of rows to be removed
 * @return void
 */
public function deleteRecords( $table, $condition, $limit )
{
    $limit = ( $limit == '' ) ? '' : ' LIMIT ' . $limit;
    $delete = "DELETE FROM {$table} WHERE {$condition} {$limit}";
    $this->executeQuery( $delete );
}
```

Updating and inserting records are tasks I find to be the most cumbersome; however, we can easily abstract these simply by passing the table name, an array of field names and field value pairs, and in the case of update operations, a condition.

```php
/**
 * Update records in the database
 * @param String the table
 * @param array of changes field => value
 * @param String the condition
 * @return bool
 */
public function updateRecords( $table, $changes, $condition )
{
    $update = "UPDATE " . $table . " SET ";
    foreach( $changes as $field => $value )
    {
        $update .= "`" . $field . "`='{$value}',";
    }

    // remove our trailing ,
    $update = substr($update, 0, -1);
    if( $condition != '' )
    {
        $update .= "WHERE " . $condition;
    }
    $this->executeQuery( $update );

    return true;

}

/**
 * Insert records into the database
 * @param String the database table
 * @param array data to insert field => value
 * @return bool
 */
public function insertRecords( $table, $data )
{
    // setup some variables for fields and values
    $fields = "";
    $values = "";

    // populate them
```

```
foreach ($data as $f => $v)
{

    $fields  .= "`$f`,";
    $values .= ( is_numeric( $v ) && ( intval( $v ) == $v ) ) ?
      $v."," : "'$v',";

}

// remove our trailing ,
$fields = substr($fields, 0, -1);
// remove our trailing ,
$values = substr($values, 0, -1);

$insert = "INSERT INTO $table ({$fields}) VALUES({$values})";
//echo $insert;
$this->executeQuery( $insert );
return true;
}
```

Sanitizing data

Depending on the exact PHP setup, data needs to be sanitized slightly differently, to prevent characters being escaped too many times. This is often the result of `magic_quotes_gpc` setting. To make things easier, and to provide a single place for changes to be made depending on our server's configuration, we can centralize our data sanitization.

```
/**
 * Sanitize data
 * @param String the data to be sanitized
 * @return String the sanitized data
 */
public function sanitizeData( $value )
{
    // Stripslashes
    if ( get_magic_quotes_gpc() )
    {
        $value = stripslashes ( $value );
    }

    // Quote value
    if ( version_compare( phpversion(), "4.3.0" ) == "-1" )
    {
        $value = $this->connections[$this->activeConnection]-
```

```
      >escape_string( $value );
   }
   else
   {
      $value = $this->connections[$this->activeConnection]-
         >real_escape_string( $value );
   }
   return $value;
}
```

Wrapping other MySQLi functions

This leaves us with a few other common MySQLi functions to wrap into our class, including fetching the data from the executed query, fetching the number of rows returned by a query, and getting the number of rows affected by a query.

```
/**
 * Get the rows from the most recently executed query, excluding
   cached queries
 * @return array
 */
public function getRows()
{
   return $this->last->fetch_array(MYSQLI_ASSOC);
}


public function numRows()
{
    return $this->last->num_rows;
}


/**
 * Gets the number of affected rows from the previous query
 * @return int the number of affected rows
 */
public function affectedRows()
{
   return $this->last->affected_rows;
}
```

Disconnecting

When the database object is no longer required, we should disconnect from all of the connections we have made to various databases. This can be done through a simple `foreach` loop in the deconstructor.

```
/**
 * Deconstruct the object
 * close all of the database connections
 */
public function __deconstruct()
{
    foreach( $this->connections as $connection )
    {
        $connection->close();
    }
}
}
?>
```

Template management

Template management is another set of core tasks that will need to be accessed by almost every aspect of our social network code. Every page request needs to display something to the user, and for each user the page will normally be different, and contain dynamic data from our database.

For example, when any user views their friends list, they will all see the same page layout; however, the list of friends will be different. When they view a profile, all profiles will have the same layout, with different data, and in some cases, some additional sections to the page, depending on how complete their profile is.

Our template manager should take a series of template files, which contain the HTML to be sent to the browser, and manage data, which should be inserted into it, as well as process this dynamic replacement of data.

Additional templates should be able to be included within a template, should they be required—for instance when viewing the profile of a user who has comments enabled, a comments list and form should be displayed, whereas a user without this would not see a list of a comments form.

The data and template contents will be stored in a Page object; the management of this object and its processing will be handled by the template object. Let's go through what we need in our template class (`registry/template.class.php`).

Firstly, we need to create the object, which involves assigning our registry to a variable, including the page class, and instantiating a page object.

```
/**
 * Include our page class, and build a page object to manage the
   content and structure of the page
 * @param Object our registry object
 */
public function __construct( Registry $registry )
{
   $this->registry = $registry;
    include( FRAMEWORK_PATH . '/registry/page.class.php');
    $this->page = new Page( $this->registry );
}
```

Since the views are made up of a number of template files, we need to be able to include these files and send them to our page object. Certain pages might be made up of two templates, others may be made up of three or more. To make this flexible, instead of defining parameters for this method, we instead take however many templates are passed as parameters and include them, in order, to our page object.

```
/**
 * Set the content of the page based on a number of templates
 * pass template file locations as individual arguments
 * @return void
 */
public function buildFromTemplates()
{
    $bits = func_get_args();
    $content = "";
    foreach( $bits as $bit )
    {

        if( strpos( $bit, 'views/' ) === false )
        {
           $bit = 'views/' . $this->registry->getSetting('view') . '/
              templates/' . $bit;
        }
        if( file_exists( $bit ) == true )
        {
           $content .= file_get_contents( $bit );
        }

    }
    $this->page->setContent( $content );
}
```

Within our template files, we may need to insert other templates. For instance, as we mentioned earlier, if one user has comments enabled on their profile, and another doesn't, then they will use the same main template, however, different templates will be inserted dynamically into them.

We can do this by taking a `$tag` (which is something contained within the template already included), and a template `$bit`, which is included and placed within the main template where the `$tag` was found.

```
/**
 * Add a template bit from a view to our page
 * @param String $tag the tag where we insert the template e.g.
   {hello}
 * @param String $bit the template bit (path to file, or just the
   filename)
 * @return void
 */
public function addTemplateBit( $tag, $bit )
{
    if( strpos( $bit, 'views/' ) === false )
    {
        $bit = 'views/' . $this->registry->getSetting('view') . '/
          templates/' . $bit;
    }
    $this->page->addTemplateBit( $tag, $bit );
}
```

These templates bits that we insert into our page object need to actually be replaced into the current page, which is where the `replaceBits` method comes in. This iterates through the list of template bits, and performs the replacement. The replacement is done in order, so if we wanted to insert a template into a page, and then insert another template into that one, we can do, so long as they were added in order.

The replacement is a simple `str_replace` to find the tag, and replace it with the contents from the template.

```
/**
 * Take the template bits from the view and insert them into our page
   content
 * Updates the pages content
 * @return void
 */
private function replaceBits()
{
    $bits = $this->page->getBits();
    // loop through template bits
```

```
    foreach( $bits as $tag => $template )
    {
        $templateContent = file_get_contents( $template );
        $newContent = str_replace( '{' . $tag . '}', $templateContent,
            $this->page->getContent() );
        $this->page->setContent( $newContent );
    }
}
```

Data that we wish to have placed into our templates works in a similar way to template bits, except that we can simply replace the tag with the data passed, as opposed to the contents of another file.

There are two exceptions, which require a little more work from us, both of which involve iterating through data. If we have a list of friends of a user for instance, which we have found via a database query, we would want to loop through and place these in the page. Similarly, if we were to build our own array of custom data, we may wish to iterate through these and place them on the page.

To facilitate this, the replaceTags method also accepts data as an array; if it is an array, the first item of the array indicates the type of data (Query or Array) and the second array points to a cache reference, which indicates where it is stored in the database object. Control is then passed to a suitable method to perform more advanced replacements.

The $pp parameter indicates whether we are processing "Post Parse Tags"; these are tags that only appear after we have performed our first set of tag replacements (for example, tags defined within database content that is placed into the template). We may wish to insert data into this, so we can perform the replaceTags function a second time, instructing it to use the array of Post Parse tags as opposed to standard tags. To review:

- Our templates use template tags (such as {heading}) to indicate where dynamically generated data should be inserted.
- Sometimes, these template tags are placeholders for other files.
- Templates are parsed by the replaceTags method.
- Templates are inserted into template tags via the replaceBits method.
- If the replacement for a template tag contains another tag (for example, if we have data in the database for a "CMS" style page, where we wish to insert the username), there may be some template tag replacements that we need to do after the first replacements. These tags are defined as post parse tags, and are replaced by the replaceTags method, with a true parameter to indicate that it should use the post parse tags array.

```
/**
 * Replace tags in our page with content
 * @return void
 */
private function replaceTags( $pp = false )
{
    // get the tags in the page
    if( $pp == false )
    {
        $tags = $this->page->getTags();
    }
    else
    {
        $tags = $this->page->getPPTags();
    }

    // go through them all
    foreach( $tags as $tag => $data )
    {
        // if the tag is an array, then we need to do more than a
          simple find and replace!
        if( is_array( $data ) )
        {
            if( $data[0] == 'SQL' )
              {
                // it is a cached query...replace tags from the database
                $this->replaceDBTags( $tag, $data[1] );
              }
            elseif( $data[0] == 'DATA' )
            {
                 // it is some cached data...replace tags from cached
                  data
                $this->replaceDataTags( $tag, $data[1] );
            }
        }
        else
        {
            // replace the content
            $newContent = str_replace( '{' . $tag . '}', $data, $this-
              >page->getContent() );
            // update the pages content
            $this->page->setContent( $newContent );
        }
    }
}
```

When replacing a part of a template with a loop of data, the replacement is shown in the template slightly differently, normally starting with `<!-- START tagname -->` and ending with `<!-- END tagname -->`, containing a number of `{tags}` within. An additional feature included here is APD—this stands for additional parsing data. This is particularly useful in drop-down lists. If we generate a drop-down list from a list of data, we may wish to set one of them as selected. This is done through additional parsing data, for a particular block of template replacements; we can set a particular tag, and indicate that if it equals a certain value, another tag should be set.

An example of this in use would be viewing a list of a user's friends: we can use APD to highlight ourselves in the list. We would inform the APD array that within the friends loop we wish to compare the `user_id` of the friend, to our `user_id`, and if they match, set another tag to `"this is you!"`. We will go through some code examples of this feature later in the book.

Loops of data that are processed by the template engine fall into one of three categories:

- The (cached) results of a database query—and we want to loop through the results, putting them into the template.

- The (cached) results of some data processing stored in an array. More often than not, this would be if we query the database, and then modify the data afterwards. We would cache it, and send it to the template engine.

- An array of data.

- If a template tag is to be replaced with the contents of a cached database query, then the `replaceDBTags` method will be called. This method takes the tag (denoting the loop, that is, tagname from `<!--START tagname -->` from above), and the ID of the cached results set.

```
/**
 * Replace content on the page with data from the database
 * @param String $tag the tag defining the area of content
 * @param int $cacheId the queries ID in the query cache
 * @return void
 */
private function replaceDBTags( $tag, $cacheId )
{
    $block = '';
    $blockOld = $this->page->getBlock( $tag );
    $apd = $this->page->getAdditionalParsingData();
    $apdkeys = array_keys( $apd );
    // foreach record relating to the query...
```

The code iterates through the results of the database cache, and processes it.

```
while ($tags = $this->registry->getObject('db')-
  >resultsFromCache( $cacheId ) )
{
    $blockNew = $blockOld;
```

Checking to see if the loop relates to any "additional parsing data" we might have set, if it does, then it performs some checks on the data to see if the relevant field in the current record relates to the condition set in the APD.

```
// Do we have APD tags?
if( in_array( $tag, $apdkeys ) )
{
    // YES we do!
      foreach ($tags as $ntag => $data)
        {
         $blockNew = str_replace("{" . $ntag . "}", $data,
           $blockNew);
         // Is this tag the one with extra parsing to be done?
         if( array_key_exists( $ntag, $apd[ $tag ] ) )
         {
           // YES it is
           $extra = $apd[ $tag ][$ntag];
           // does the tag equal the condition?
          if( $data == $extra['condition'] )
           {
```

If the field in the record relates to the APD data, then we add the extra parsing data to the template, but only for this loop. For example, this could be to indicate that the current item in a drop-down list (generated from a database query) is the one that should be selected.

```
           // Yep! Replace the extratag with the data
           $blockNew = str_replace("{" . $extra['tag'] . "}",
             $extra['data'], $blockNew);
         }
         else
         {
           // remove the extra tag - it aint used!
           $blockNew = str_replace("{" . $extra['tag'] . "}",
             '', $blockNew);
         }
        }
      }
}
else
{
    // create a new block of content with the results replaced
      into it
```

If there isn't any APD set for this loop, we simply take each field in the record, find the tags in the template loop that relate to it, and replace them with the fields value.

```
foreach ($tags as $ntag => $data)
    {
      $blockNew = str_replace("{" . $ntag . "}", $data,
        $blockNew);
    }
}
```

Each iteration through the database cache is added to a variable, which is then, once all the processing is completed, replaced directly into the template, as shown in the highlighted code below:

```
    $block .= $blockNew;
}
$pageContent = $this->page->getContent();
// remove the seperator in the template, cleaner HTML
$newContent = str_replace( '<!-- START ' . $tag . ' -->' .
  $blockOld . '<!-- END , . $tag ., -->', $block, $pageContent );
// update the page content
$this->page->setContent( $newContent );
}
```

Replacing data from cached (non-database) data works in the same way; the only differences here are that APD isn't accounted for, and that the cache reference relates to cached data not a cached query.

```
/**
 * Replace content on the page with data from the cache
 * @param String $tag the tag defining the area of content
 * @param int $cacheId the datas ID in the data cache
 * @return void
 */
private function replaceDataTags( $tag, $cacheId )
{

    $blockOld = $this->page->getBlock( $tag );
    $block = '';
    $tags = $this->registry->getObject('db')->dataFromCache( $cacheId
);

    foreach( $tags as $key => $tagsdata )
    {
        $blockNew = $blockOld;
        foreach ($tagsdata as $taga => $data)
```

```
        {
          $blockNew = str_replace("{" . $taga . "}", $data,
            $blockNew);
        }
        $block .= $blockNew;
    }


    $pageContent = $this->page->getContent();
    $newContent = str_replace( '<!-- START '.$tag.'-->'.
      $blockOld.'<!-- END '.$tag.' -->', $block, $pageContent );
    $this->page->setContent( $newContent );
}
```

If we had a single row of data from a database, or an array of data fields from one of our models, such as a user's profile data, we would probably want to be able to quickly convert all of this data into template tag variables. The following method does this for us, and to prevent overlap with existing tags, we can also pass a prefix that is added to the tag.

```
/**
  * Convert an array of data into some tags
  * @param array the data
  * @param string a prefix which is added to field name to create the
    tag name
  * @return void
  */
public function dataToTags( $data, $prefix )
{
    foreach( $data as $key => $content )
    {
        $this->page->addTag( $prefix.$key, $content);
    }
}
```

Because the title of a page is a variable within our page object, we need to extract this and replace it within our template when required.

```
/**
  * Take the title we set in the page object, and insert them into
    the view
  */
public function parseTitle()
{
    $newContent = str_replace('<title>', '<title>'. $this->page-
      >getTitle(), $this->page->getContent() );
    $this->page->setContent( $newContent );
}
```

Finally, just before sending the output to the browser, we need to perform all of our replacements.

```
/**
 * Parse the page object into some output
 * @return void
 */
public function parseOutput()
{
    $this->replaceBits();
    $this->replaceTags(false);
    $this->replaceBits();
    $this->replaceTags(true);
    $this->parseTitle();
}
```

This templating system replaces template tags formatted as {templatetag}, as opposed to $templatetag, {$templatetag}, or {$template->tag}. The main reason for this comes down to personal preference, though there are methods that can make taking data stored in an array and pushing it into the PHP variables defined within the template.

Personally, I prefer to have the views not do any processing themselves (the template engine instead has to push them to the template, as opposed to the template file being executed). There are also alternative template engines available, such as Smarty, which is used in a range of applications, and works in a different way. If you find that this method doesn't suit your requirements, feel free to experiment with other template engines, or alternatively, modify this system to better match your needs.

Page

The actual content from the templates and replacement data will be stored in our page object, so let us see what we need in our page class (registry/page. class.php).

Firstly, we need some variables to store the replacement data, such as tags, post-parse tags, additional parsing data, and of course, the content of the page as defined by the templates it is built from.

```
// page title
private $title = '';
// template tags
private $tags = array();
// tags which should be processed after the page has been parsed
// reason: what if there are template tags within the database
   content, we must parse the page, then parse it again for post parse
```

```
tags
private $postParseTags = array();
// template bits
private $bits = array();
// the page content
private $content = "";
private $apd =  array();

/**
 * Create our page object
 */
function __construct( Registry $registry )
{
    $this->registry = $registry;
}
```

We need to set our page title variable and get it, so we need a getter and setter for this.

```
/**
 * Get the page title from the page
 * @return String
 */
public function getTitle()
{
    return $this->title;
}

/**
 * Set the page title
 * @param String $title the page title
 * @return void
 */
public function setTitle( $title )
{
    $this->title = $title;
}
```

We need to be able to update the content variable, for instance, after adding a new template bit, or performing some replacement on the content.

```
/**
 * Set the page content
 * @param String $content the page content
 * @return void
```

```
 */
public function setContent( $content )
{
    $this->content = $content;
}
```

We need to be able to add tags to our replacement array.

```
/**
 * Add a template tag, and its replacement value/data to the page
 * @param String $key the key to store within the tags array
 * @param String $data the replacement data (may also be an array)
 * @return void
 */
public function addTag( $key, $data )
{
    $this->tags[$key] = $data;
}
```

If through some conditional logic in our code, we no longer use a tag or group of tags, and there are no placeholders for them in the content, we will want to remove it from the array.

```
public function removeTag( $key )
{
    unset( $this->tags[$key] );
}
```

We also need to get the tags we wish to replace, so that our template object can perform the replacements.

```
/**
 * Get tags associated with the page
 * @return void
 */
public function getTags()
{
    return $this->tags;
}
```

In addition to adding and getting tags from above, we also need to add and get Post Parse tags.

```
/**
 * Add post parse tags: as per adding tags
 * @param String $key the key to store within the array
 * @param String $data the replacement data
```

```
 * @return void
 */
public function addPPTag( $key, $data )
{
    $this->postParseTags[$key] = $data;
}


/**
 * Get tags to be parsed after the first batch have been parsed
 * @return array
 */
public function getPPTags()
{
    return $this->postParseTags;
}


/**
 * Add a template bit to the page, doesnt actually add the content
   just yet
 * @param String the tag where the template is added
 * @param String the template file name
 * @return void
 */
public function addTemplateBit( $tag, $bit )
{
    $this->bits[ $tag ] = $bit;
}
```

This addAdditionalParsingData method sets when additional parsing data lookups should be performed, by defining the $block of code within the template where the parsing should be done, the $tag to compare the $condition. The $extratag that is replaced with $data should $tag equal $condition.

```
/**
 * Adds additional parsing data
 * A.P.D is used in parsing loops.  We may want to have an extra bit
   of data depending on on iterations value
 * for example on a form list, we may want a specific item to be
  "selected"
 * @param String block the condition applies to
 * @param String tag within the block the condition applies to
 * @param String condition : what the tag must equal
 * @param String extratag : if the tag value = condition then we have
   an extra tag called extratag
```

```
 * @param String data : if the tag value = condition then extra tag
      is replaced with this value
 */
public function addAdditionalParsingData($block, $tag, $condition,
   $extratag, $data)
{
   $this->apd[$block] = array($tag => array('condition' => $condition,
      'tag' => $extratag, 'data' => $data));
}
```

We will want to get a list of all the template bits we need to process into the page (processing is done by the template object).

```
/**
 * Get the template bits to be entered into the page
 * @return array the array of template tags and template file names
 */
public function getBits()
{
    return $this->bits;
}
```

We also need to get our array of additional parsing data for the template handler to process.

```
public function getAdditionalParsingData()
{
   return $this->apd;
}
```

We often need to just access a specific loop block within our page; this method makes this easy, by searching for us using regular expressions, and returning it.

```
/**
 * Gets a chunk of page content
 * @param String the tag wrapping the block ( <!-- START tag -->
   block <!-- END tag --> )
 * @return String the block of content
 */
public function getBlock( $tag )
{
   //echo $tag;
   preg_match (,#<!-- START ,. $tag . , -->(.+?)<!-- END ,.
      $tag . , -->#si', $this->content, $tor);
   $tor = str_replace (,<!-- START ,. $tag . , -->', „", $tor[0]);
   $tor = str_replace (,<!-- END ,  . $tag . , -->', „", $tor);

   return $tor;
}
```

Obviously, we need to get the content from the page, so we use the
getContent method.

```
public function getContent()
{
    return $this->content;
}
```

Finally, when we are ready to output the content to the browser, we do some final
replacements. These are of template tags that we want to have in a template, but may
not always replace. One example is a registration form; if the submission has errors,
we would replace the form fields with the user's submission attempt. If, however,
the user is viewing the form for the first time, they wouldn't want to see anything, so
we would either have to explicitly remove the template tags, or instead, prefix them
with form_, and any leftovers are auto removed.

Once this is done, the content is returned to be output to the browser.

```
public function getContentToPrint()
{
    $this->content = preg_replace ('#{form_(.+?)}#si', '',
       $this->content);
    $this->content = preg_replace ('#{nbd_(.+?)}#si', '',
       $this->content);
    $this->content = str_replace('</body>', '<!-- Generated by our
       Fantastic Social Netowk -->
</body>', $this->content );
      return $this->content;
}
```

Authentication

In *Chapter 3, Users, Registration, and Authentication*, we will discuss how our user's
database will be structured, how we will manage the login and sign up process,
and how user authentication will work in general.

For now, we will leave this aspect out of our registry, and come back to it in the
next chapter.

URL processing

Since we are using a single frontend controller, we need to process the incoming
URL, in particular the page $_GET variable, to work out how to handle the users
request. This is generally done by breaking the variable down in parts, separated
by a forward slash.

Manually setting the URL path is something we may need to do, so a simple setter method is needed.

```
/**
 * Set the URL path
 * @param String the url path
 */
public function setURLPath($path)
{
    $this->urlPath = $path;
}
```

The getURLData method processes the incoming URL, and breaks it down into parts, building up an array of "URL bits".

```
/**
 * Gets data from the current URL
 * @return void
 */
public function getURLData()
{
    $urldata = ( isset( $_GET['page'] ) ) ? $_GET['page'] : '' ;
    $this->urlPath = $urldata;
    if( $urldata == '' )
    {
        $this->urlBits[] = '';
        $this->urlPath = '';
    }
    else
    {
        $data = explode( '/', $urldata );
        while ( !empty( $data ) && strlen( reset( $data ) ) === 0 )
        {
            array_shift( $data );
        }
        while ( !empty( $data ) && strlen( end( $data ) ) === 0)
        {
            array_pop($data);
        }
        $this->urlBits = $this->array_trim( $data );
    }
}
```

The rest of our social networks code needs to access the URL bits to determine what they need to do, so we need a suitable get method.

```
public function getURLBits()
{
    return $this->urlBits;
}
```

Similarly, we may need to have easy access to a specific bit. For example, if the request is friends/view/ID, the first bit would indicate that we use the friend's controller; the friends controller would then use a switch statement against the second URL bit, to work out what it needs to do.

```
public function getURLBit( $whichBit )
{
    return ( isset( $this->urlBits[ $whichBit ] ) ) ?
        $this->urlBits[ $whichBit ]   : 0 ;
}
```

Another getter we need is to get the URL path.

```
public function getURLPath()
{
    return $this->urlPath;
}
```

If we need to generate a URL, for instance, to build a link, or redirect the user, we can make this easier with a helper function, which takes an array or URL $bits, any additional information to go in the query string of the URL, $qs, and if the URL is an administrative URL, $admin, (if it is, then it appends the administration directory to the URL).

```
public function buildURL( $bits, $qs, $admin )
{
    $admin = ( $admin == 1 ) ? $this->registry->getSetting('admin_
        folder') . '/' : '';
    $the_rest = '';
    foreach( $bits as $bit )
    {
        $the_rest .= $bit . '/';
    }
    $the_rest = ( $qs != '' ) ? $the_rest . '?&' .$qs : $the_rest;
    return $this->registry->getSetting('siteurl') . $admin . $the_rest;

}
```

Extending the registry: potential new objects

There are many other features that we could add to our registry if we needed to make it more powerful, including:

- Accessing the file system
- Enhancing security:
    - Checking against a banned list
    - Checking the format of certain data

- Generating and processing RSS feeds

Front Controller: single point of access

As we discussed earlier, we are going to implement the Front Controller pattern. This will provide us with a single point of access to the framework powering Dino Space.

index.php

Our front controller is our `index.php` file. The first thing we should do is call `session_start`, as this needs to be done before anything is sent to the browser, so by calling it first, we know this will be the case.

```
session_start();
```

We should also define a framework path constant, so if we are in another file elsewhere, and we need to access a file relative to the framework path, we can use this constant. Overuse of constants isn't recommended, however, and we are only going to use them on occasions where appropriate.

```
DEFINE("FRAMEWORK_PATH", dirname( __FILE__ ) ."/" );
```

Next, we need to build our registry, and tell it which objects to create. As you can see, the authenticate object is commented out, until we discuss this in Chapter 3.

```
require('registry/registry.class.php');
$registry = new Registry();
// setup our core registry objects
$registry->createAndStoreObject( 'template', 'template' );
$registry->createAndStoreObject( 'mysqldb', 'db' );
//$registry->createAndStoreObject( 'authenticate', 'authenticate' );
$registry->createAndStoreObject( 'urlprocessor', 'url' );
```

Next, we can include our configuration file, and connect to the database.

```
// database settings
include(FRAMEWORK_PATH . 'config.php');
// create a database connection
$registry->getObject('db')->newConnection( $configs['db_host_sn'],
  $configs['db_user_sn'], $configs['db_pass_sn'],
  $configs['db_name_sn']);
```

Now that we are connected to the database, we can look up any settings we have in a suitable settings table, and store them in our registries settings array. This should be for things like: administrators notification e-mail address, default view, if certain features are enabled, and any API keys that we may need if we connect to third-party services.

```
// store settings in our registry
$settingsSQL = "SELECT `key`, `value` FROM settings";
$registry->getObject('db')->executeQuery( $settingsSQL );
while( $setting = $registry->getObject('db')->getRows() )
{
    $registry->storeSetting( $setting['value'], $setting['key'] );
}
```

The next stage would be to check if the user is logged in, build the default template, and include the appropriate controller. We don't have any controllers at the moment, and we haven't discussed how our models and controllers will work, so we will leave those commented out for now, and return to them in Chapter 3.

```
// process authentication
// coming in chapter 3

/**
 * Once we have some template files, we can build a default template
$registry->getObject('template')->buildFromTemplates('header.tpl.php',
  'main.tpl.php', 'footer.tpl.php');

$registry->getObject('template')->parseOutput();
print $registry->getObject('template')->getPage()-
>getContentToPrint();
*/

?>
```

.htaccess

We are routing all of our requests through our `index.php` file, and by passing further information as the page `$_GET` parameter, this results in URLs which look like: `http://test.com/?page=friends/view/1/Michael_Peacock`. This isn't a particularly nice looking URL, so we use the Apache `mod_rewrite` module (which most hosts have installed by default—if you use WAMPServer for development, you may need to enable it in the Apache Modules menu), to take a nicer URL such as `http://test.com/friends/view/1/Michael_Peacock`, which eliminates the need for `?page=`, and translates it into the other format. This is rewritten by defining a rewrite rule in a `.htaccess` file within our code.

```
ErrorDocument 404 /index.php
DirectoryIndex index.php
<IfModule mod_rewrite.c>
  RewriteEngine on
  RewriteCond %{REQUEST_FILENAME} !-f
  RewriteCond %{REQUEST_FILENAME} !-d
  RewriteRule ^(.*)$ index.php?page=$1 [L,QSA]
</IfModule>
```

Let's go through this file, line by line.

1. First, we tell Apache that the `index.php` file should deal with any 404 errors (file not found).

2. The `index.php` file is the default file in the directory, so if someone visits the folder on the web server with our site in, and doesn't specify a file, `index.php` is called automatically.

3. The `IfModule` block is conditional: the rules only apply if the module `mod_rewrite` is installed.

4. If it is installed, we enable the rewrite engine.

5. If the user is trying to request a file, don't follow the rewrite rule (without this, uploaded files and images wouldn't be displayed as even these requests would be routed through our `index.php` file).

6. If the user is trying to access a directory that exists, then the rule isn't followed again.

7. Finally, we have the rewrite rule, which takes the users request, and interoperates it as the page `$_GET` parameter for our `index.php` file to process. The rule takes everything from the URL (apart from the domain, and any folders our site may be stored within) and appends it to the page get variable. This line also takes any user-specified query strings (for example, *&somefield=somevalue*) and appends it to the URL (QSA), and then ignores other rules if that rule was used (L).

Summary

In this chapter, we have discussed a number of best practice techniques for designing a framework to facilitate rapid development of our social networking website. This included the Model-View-Controller architectural design pattern, the Registry pattern, the Front Controller pattern, the Factory pattern, and we also discussed the Singleton pattern.

We also discussed a suitable directory structure for our social networking site to use, before building the core objects for our registry, and our front controller.

We now have a simple, lightweight framework that can help us rapidly develop the rest of our social networking site. In the next chapter, we will look at user registration, logging in, authentication (which will involve creating our authentication registry object), and a controller to facilitate user registration.

3
Users, Registration, and Authentication

With our basic framework in place, we are now able to start developing our social networking site. The most important aspect of a social networking website is the users; without users, we don't have a social network. In order to have users who can use the site (overlooking marketing, and getting users to the site for the moment), we need to be able to allow users to sign up, log in, and get the details of a user who is currently logged in. We will also want to be able to manage permissions of users, to see what they are permitted to do, and what they are prohibited from doing on the site.

In this chapter, you will learn:

- Why privacy policies are important
- What core user data to store in the database
- How to extend user data to include profile data, without interfering too much with our users table in the database
- Why you would want to implement a CAPTCHA system to prevent automated signups
- The importance of privacy policies
- How to verify a user's e-mail address to prevent users signing up with invalid e-mail addresses
- How to process user sign ups and logins, and to check whether a user is a logged in user
- What to do when a user forgets their username or password

With this in place, we will have the first major building block to our social networking website—users!

Privacy policies

When users sign up to any website, they generally agree to the terms and conditions of the website, and the privacy policy. While the terms and conditions generally set out information about liability, conduct on the site, and so on, the privacy policy explains what will be done with the users' data.

It is important to be clear and honest with users about their data, and reassuring about the security of their data. Facebook has had a lot of bad press recently relating to its privacy policy and the tools available to their users to protect their data. In particular, one of their recent changes resulted in a document that was over 5,800 words long—something that most users won't read or understand (`http://www.huffingtonpost.com/2010/05/12/facebook-privacy-policy-s_n_574389.html`). When stating your privacy policies:

- Be clear and concise
- Make it clear who can access the data they add to the site:
  - Are all profiles public?
  - How much information is available to what type of user?
  - How can the information be restricted?
- Explain who owns the data—does the user retain ownership or do they grant a licence of use to us?

It is also important for us to think about how we might allow users to change their own privacy settings, including which profile information they would like to make public, public only to their network, or completely private—particularly with regards to contact details and dates of birth.

Some countries also have legislation in place governing the management of user data, such as the Data Protection Act in the UK. This covers issues such as:

- Security—ensuring data is held securely, and isn't easy for others to access, unless the user's permission has been given
- Relevancy—ensuring data held is kept up to date and is relevant
- Removal—allowing users to request full removal of their data
- Access—allowing users to request copies of all data held about them

Users

At their core, users can be represented by a few simple pieces of information:

- A unique identifier such as a user ID

- A unique identifier that the user themselves can easily remember, such as their chosen username or their e-mail address

- A password, which is used to authenticate the user — to prove they are who they say they are

As far as our authentication system is concerned, this will be a user. We will of course extend this with a user profile, but in terms of authentication, this is all the information we need.

Our user object

Our user object is created when a user tries to log in, either based on submitting a login form supplying their username and password, or based on session data for the user ID.

If username and password are supplied, then it checks the credentials and populates its variables if such a user exists. If only an ID is supplied, then it populates based on whether there is a user of that ID. Since the authentication class controls whether the current user is logged in or not, we can use this object to view or perform actions on other users if we wished, as by separating the two we won't be automatically logged in as the user populated within this object. As a result, we can extend this object to reset the user's password, edit the user, deactivate the user, and so on.

The constructor takes four arguments, the registry (dependency injection, so it can communicate with the rest of the framework), a user ID, a username, and a password, the latter three being optional, and used as described above.

```
public function __construct( Registry $registry, $id=0,
  $username='', $password='' )
    {
        $this->registry = $registry;
```

If we haven't set a user ID (that is, $id is 0) and we have set a username and a password, we should look up the user to see whether these are valid credentials:

```
if( $id=0 && $username != '' && $password != '' )
    {
        $user = $this->registry->getObject('db')-
          >sanitizeData( $username );
```

As our passwords are hashed in the database, we need to hash the password we were supplied. We can hash the password directly in the query (by using the MySQL function MD5), however, this exposes the password in plain text more than required, as it would be processed and accessed by both PHP and the MySQL server (which may be stored on a remote machine):

```
$hash = md5( $password );
$sql = "SELECT * FROM users WHERE username='{$user}' AND
  password_hash='{$hash}' AND deleted=0";
$this->registry->getObject('db')->executeQuery( $sql );
if( $this->registry->getObject('db')->numRows() == 1 )
{
```

We have a record in the database, so the user is valid, so we set the various properties of our user object:

```
    $data = $this->registry->getObject('db')->getRows();
    $this->id = $data['ID'];
    $this->username = $data['username'];
    $this->active = $data['active'];
    $this->banned = $data['banned'];
    $this->admin = $data['admin'];
    $this->email = $data['email'];
    $this->pwd_reset_key = $data['pwd_reset_key'];
    $this->valid = true;
    }
}
elseif( $id > 0 )
{
```

If we supplied a user ID, then we look up the user with that ID and populate the object with their details. As discussed above, we don't want to set them as logged-in here, because we may use this object to edit, delete, and create users, and integrating authentication would log out the administrator and log them in as someone else if they tried to edit an existing user.

```
    $id = intval( $id );
    $sql = "SELECT * FROM users WHERE ID='{$id}' AND deleted=0";
    $this->registry->getObject('db')->executeQuery( $sql );
    if( $this->registry->getObject('db')->numRows() == 1 )
    {
        $data = $this->registry->getObject('db')->getRows();
        $this->id = $data['ID'];
        $this->username = $data['username'];
        $this->active = $data['active'];
        $this->banned = $data['banned'];
```

```
        $this->admin = $data['admin'];
        $this->email = $data['email'];
        $this->pwd_reset_key = $data['pwd_reset_key'];
        $this->valid = true;
    }
  }

}
```

Our authentication registry object

One of the first things our framework needs to do, once it is connected to the database, and some core settings are loaded, is to check whether the current user is logged in. This is simply done by checking for an active session, and if one exists, building the user object from that, or checking to see if a username and password have been supplied, and building the user from that.

This will make up part of our authentication object (registry/authentication. class.php), which will reside in our registry and interact with the user object.

The checkForAuthentication method checks both for an active session and user credentials being passed in POST data, and calls additional methods to build the user object if appropriate.

```
public function checkForAuthentication()
    {
```

Initially, we remove any error template tags on the page (which we would use to inform the user of an invalid login):

```
$this->registry->getObject('template')->getPage()-
  >addTag('error', '');

if( isset( $_SESSION['sn_auth_session_uid'] ) && intval( $_
  SESSION['sn_auth_session_uid'] ) > 0 )
  {
```

If session data is set, we call the sessionAuthenticate method:

```
$this->sessionAuthenticate( intval( $_SESSION['sn_auth_
    session_uid'] ) );
```

The `sessionAuthenticate` method then sets the `loggedIn` property to indicate whether the user is logged in or not:

```
if( $this->loggedIn == true )
{
   $this->registry->getObject('template')->getPage()-
      >addTag('error', '');

}
else
{
```

If the user is not logged in, and we have a valid session, then something went wrong somewhere, so we should inform the user their login attempt was not successful:

```
$this->registry->getObject('template')->getPage()-
   >addTag('error', '<p><strong>Error: Your username or
   password was not correct,
   please try again</p><strong>');
}
}
```

If session data was not set, we check for post data, and call the `postAuthenticate` method if appropriate, following the same steps as above.

```
elseif( isset(  $_POST['sn_auth_user'] ) &&
  $_POST['sn_auth_user'] != '' && isset(
  $_POST['sn_auth_pass'] ) && $_POST['sn_auth_pass'] != '')
{
   $this->postAuthenticate( $_POST['sn_auth_user'] , $_
     POST['sn_auth_pass'] );
   if( $this->loggedIn == true )
   {
      $this->registry->getObject('template')->getPage()-
         >addTag('error', '');

   }
   else
   {

      $this->registry->getObject('template')->getPage()-
         >addTag('error', '<p><strong>Error: Your username or
         password was not correct,
         please try again</p><strong>');
   }
}
elseif( isset( $_POST['login']) )
{
```

If the login post variable has been set, but neither session data or POST login data has been submitted, then the user didn't enter a username or a password, so we should tell them this:

```
$this->registry->getObject('template')->getPage()-
   >addTag('error', '<p><strong>Error:
   Your must enter a username and a password</p><strong>');
}


}
```

This method also sets suitable template tag variables for standard errors if there was a problem authenticating the user.

POST authentication

In the code above, if the user has tried to log in by submitting a login form, the `postAuthenticate` method is called. This method is shown below. It utilizes the user object to query the database, if the user exists and is logged in, then it sets the appropriate session data, as highlighted below:

```
private function postAuthenticate( $u, $p )
   {
      $this->justProcessed = true;
      require_once(FRAMEWORK_PATH.'registry/user.class.php');
      $this->user = new User( $this->registry, 0, $u, $p );

      if( $this->user->isValid() )
      {
         if( $this->user->isActive() == false )
         {
            $this->loggedIn = false;
            $this->loginFailureReason = 'inactive';
         }
         elseif( $this->user->isBanned() == true )
         {
            $this->loggedIn = false;
            $this->loginFailureReason = 'banned';
         }
         else
         {
            $this->loggedIn = true;
            $_SESSION['sn_auth_session_uid'] = $this->user-
               >getUserID();
         }
```

```
        }
        else
        {
            $this->loggedIn = false;
            $this->loginFailureReason = 'invalidcredentials';
        }
    }
```

SESSION authentication

If the user hasn't tried to log in by submitting a form, but has some session data set, we try and authenticate them based on the session data:

```
private function sessionAuthenticate( $uid )
    {
        require_once(FRAMEWORK_PATH.'registry/user.class.php');
        $this->user = new User( $this->registry, intval( $_SESSION['sn_
          auth_session_uid'] ), '', '' );

        if( $this->user->isValid() )
        {
            if( $this->user->isActive() == false )
            {
                $this->loggedIn = false;
                $this->loginFailureReason = 'inactive';
            }
            elseif( $this->user->isBanned() == true )
            {
                $this->loggedIn = false;
                $this->loginFailureReason = 'banned';
            }
            else
            {
                $this->loggedIn = true;
            }

        }
        else
        {
            $this->loggedIn = false;
            $this->loginFailureReason = 'nouser';
        }
        if( $this->loggedIn == false )
        {
            $this->logout();
        }


    }
```

Salt your passwords!

Our passwords are stored in the database as an MD5 one-way hash. This means we don't keep a copy of the user's password; instead, we hash the password when they try to log in, and compare the hash to the password in the database. If our database was compromised, our users' passwords should be safe. This hashing cannot be reversed, but there are dictionaries available for common words or phrases, which means it is possible to work out some passwords from the hashes. We can prevent this further by salting the password; this involves adding a "salt" to the password and then hashing it. This is typically done by creating a random string for each user and storing it in their row in the users table. Passwords in the Dino Space code are currently not salted, to make it easier should you wish to change how the passwords are hashed, or integrate with other login systems.

Structuring the database

For our users table (without social profile data), we need the following fields:

Field	Type	Description
ID	Integer, Primary Key, Auto-increment	The unique user ID
Username	Varchar	The username
Password_hash	Varchar	The MD5 hash of the user's password
Password_salt	Varchar(5)	If we decide to salt our passwords
Email	Varchar	The user's e-mail address
Active	Bool	Defines whether the user account is active or not
Admin	Bool	Defines whether the user account is an administrator or not
Banner	Bool	Defines whether the user account has been banned
reset_key	Varchar	Random string used for resetting the password when the user forgets it
Reset_expires	Timestamp	Time at which that reset string expires— preventing someone spamming a user by constantly requesting a new key

Registration

We currently have two primary database tables for our users. A users table, containing the core user data, and a `users_profile` table, containing other (non-essential) information.

Standard details

Our core registration fields are defined in our registration controller; they are stored as array pairs, referencing the field name with a more descriptive name (the more descriptive name is used for error messages).

```
/**
 * Standard registration fields
 */
private $fields = array( 'user' => 'username', 'password' =>
'password', 'password_confirm' => 'password confirmation',
'email' => 'email address');

/**
 * Any errors in the registration
 */
private $registrationErrors = array();

/**
 * Array of error label classes - allows us to make a field a
   different color, to indicate there were errors
 */
private $registrationErrorLabels = array();

/**
 * The values the user has submitted when registering
 */
private $submittedValues = array();

/**
 * The santized versions of the values the user has submitted -
   these are database ready
 */
private $sanitizedValues = array();

/**
 * Should our users automatically be "active" or should they
     require email verification?
 */
```

```
   private $activeValue = 1;
private function checkRegistration()
   {
```

We set an `allClear` variable, to indicate that the values submitted are all acceptable. Each time an error is encountered, this is set to `false`, so that we can report the error back to the user:

```
   $allClear = true;
```

The first stage is to check whether the user has actually submitted all of the required fields, if any of them are blank, then we flag these errors to the user.

```
// blank fields
foreach( $this->fields as $field => $name )
{
   if( ! isset( $_POST[ 'register_' . $field ] ) ||
     $_POST[ 'register_' . $field ] == '' )
{
```

If any are blank, our `allClear` variable is set to false, and we generate error strings, and store them in our errors array:

```
      $allClear = false;
      $this->registrationErrors[] = 'You must enter a ' . $name;
      $this->registrationErrorLabels['register_' . $field . '_
        label'] = 'error';
   }
}
```

Next, we can check the values in more detail. Let's start with the password!

We will want the password to be at least seven characters, to help ensure it is secure. To prevent issues of a user not knowing their password because they entered it incorrectly, we ask the user to verify their password, so we must also check the password and its verification match:

```
// passwords match
if( $_POST[ 'register_password' ] != $_POST[ 'register_password_
  confirm' ] )
{
   $allClear = false;
   $this->registrationErrors[] = 'You must confirm your
     password';
   $this->registrationErrorLabels['register_password_label'] =
     'error';
   $this->registrationErrorLabels['register_password_confirm_
     label'] = 'error';
```

```
   }

   // password length
   if( strlen( $_POST['register_password'] ) < 6 )
   {
      $allClear = false;
      $this->registrationErrors[] = 'Your password is too short, it
         must be at least 6 characters';
      $this->registrationErrorLabels['register_password_label'] =
         'error';
      $this->registrationErrorLabels['register_password_confirm_
         label'] = 'error';
   }
```

Next, we have the e-mail address—we need to check it for header injection, and that the format of the e-mail address is correct. The first highlighted section of code shows the header injection check, and the second shows the format check.

```
   // email headers
   if( strpos( ( urldecode( $_POST[ 'register_email' ] ) ), "\r" )
      === true || strpos( ( urldecode( $_POST[ 'register_email' ]
      ) ), "\n" ) === true )
   {
      $allClear = false;
      $this->registrationErrors[] = 'Your email address is not
         valid (security)';
      $this->registrationErrorLabels['register_email_label'] =
         'error';
   }

   // email valid
   if( ! preg_match( "^[_a-z0-9-]+(\.[_a-z0-9-]+)*@[a-z0-9-]+(\.[a-
      z0-9-]+)*(\.[a-z]{2,4})^", $_POST[ 'register_email' ] ) )
   {
      $allClear = false;
      $this->registrationErrors[] = 'You must enter a valid email
         address';
      $this->registrationErrorLabels['register_email_label'] =
         'error';

   }
```

To help protect us from a legal perspective, we should get legal advice on the policies and terms and conditions we need to enforce on our social network. When we have such terms in place, we will want our users to accept these before allowing them to join—let's ensure they ticked the appropriate box on our registration form template:

```
// terms accepted
if( ! isset( $_POST['register_terms'] ) || $_POST['register_
  terms'] != 1 )
{
    $allClear = false;
    $this->registrationErrors[] = 'You must accept our terms and
      conditions.';
    $this->registrationErrorLabels['register_terms_label'] =
      'error';
}
```

If a user signs up with the e-mail address or username of an existing user, we will have some problems—particularly when they come to log in, or request an e-mail to reset their password. To prevent this, we need to check that the username and e-mail address are not currently in use by another user, which can be done with a simple database query:

```
// duplicate user+email check
$u = $this->registry->getObject('db')->sanitizeData( $_
    POST['register_user'] );
$e = $this->registry->getObject('db')->sanitizeData( $_
    POST['register_email'] );
$sql = "SELECT * FROM users WHERE username='{$u}' OR
  email='{$e}'";
$this->registry->getObject('db')->executeQuery( $sql );
if( $this->registry->getObject('db')->numRows() == 2 )
{
    $allClear = false;
    // both
    $this->registrationErrors[] = 'Both your username and email
      address are already in use on this site.';
    $this->registrationErrorLabels['register_user_label'] =
        'error';
    $this->registrationErrorLabels['register_email_label'] =
        'error';
}
elseif( $this->registry->getObject('db')->numRows() == 1 )
{
    // possibly both, or just one
    $u = $this->registry->getObject('db')->sanitizeData( $_
      POST['register_user'] );
    $e = $this->registry->getObject('db')->sanitizeData( $_
      POST['register_email'] );
    $data = $this->registry->getObject('db')->getRows();
    if( $data['username'] == $u && $data['email'] == $e )
    {
```

```
                    $allClear = false;
                    $this->registrationErrors[] = 'Both your username and
                        password are already in use on this site.';
                    $this->registrationErrorLabels['register_user_label'] =
                      'error';
                    $this->registrationErrorLabels['register_email_label'] =
                        'error';
                    // both
                }
                elseif( $data['username'] == $u )
                {
                    $allClear = false;
                    // username
                    $this->registrationErrors[] = 'Your username is already
                      in use on this site.';
                    $this->registrationErrorLabels['register_user_label'] =
                        'error';

                }
                else
                {
                    $allClear = false;
                    // email address
                    $this->registrationErrors[] = 'Your email address is
                        already in use on this site.';
                    $this->registrationErrorLabels['register_email_label'] =
                        'error';
                }
            }
```

Finally, before we go onto profile fields, we check to see if we have enabled CAPTCHA. If we have, then we should do a check that the user is a human and not an automated spam bot. We will discuss CAPTCHA implementation later in this chapter.

```
            // captcha
            if( $this->registry->getSetting('captcha.enabled') == 1 )
            {
                // captcha check
            }
```

Now that we have checked all of the core fields, we pass control to our registration extension, which will process all of the profile related fields:

```
// hook
if ( $this->registrationExtention->checkRegistrationSubmission()
    == false )
{
    $allClear = false;
}
```

If all is clear (that is, there were no errors either from this function, or the registration controller extension), then we store our sanitized data, and return `true` — so that another method can create the user account and profile:

```
if( $allClear == true )
{
    $this->sanitizedValues['username'] = $u;
    $this->sanitizedValues['email'] = $e;
    $this->sanitizedValues['password_hash'] = md5( $_
        POST['register_password'] );
    $this->sanitizedValues['active'] = $this->activeValue;
    $this->sanitizedValues['admin'] = 0;
    $this->sanitizedValues['banned'] = 0;

    $this->submittedValues['register_user'] = $_POST['register_
        user'];
    $this->submittedValues['register_password'] = $_
        POST['register_password'];
    return true;
}
else
{
    $this->submittedValues['register_user'] = $_POST['register_
        user'];
    $this->submittedValues['register_email'] = $_POST['register_
        email'];
    $this->submittedValues['register_password'] = $_
        POST['register_password'] ;
    $this->submittedValues['register_password_confirm'] = $_
        POST['register_password_confirm'] ;
    $this->submittedValues['register_captcha'] = ( isset( $_
     POST['register_captcha'] ) ?
     $_POST['register_captcha']   : '' );
    return false;
}


}
```

Hooking additional fields on

Depending on the social network we were developing, we will have different profile fields. To make our code flexible, these fields are abstracted to a registration extension, so if we reuse our code, we simply need to change this one file to process these additional fields, and we know that it won't interfere with our core fields. In Dino Space land, citizens are only permitted to keep one Dinosaur, after all, who could cope with looking after more than one! This would need to be tweaked slightly if we wanted to extend our registration form to accept any number of a particular set of fields. There is some JavaScript available to help with such a situation (http://www.michaelpeacock.co.uk/blog/entry/add-another-item-with-php-and-jquery and http://www.michaelpeacock.co.uk/blog/entry/add-another-the-jquery-plugin should get you started if you want to try it).

For Dino Space, there are going to be certain profile fields we want, and some examples include:

- Dinosaur's name
- Dinosaur's breed
- Dinosaur's gender
- Dinosaur's date of birth

The registry extension works in a similar way to the core registration controller, except the data validation is more dynamic, based on how the additional profile fields are defined. For example, to create the four additional profile fields from above, we would define the following:

```php
private $registry;
private $extraFields = array();
private $errors = array();
private $submittedValues = array();
private $sanitizedValues = array();
private $errorLabels = array();

public function __construct( $registry )
{
    $this->registry = $registry;
    $this->extraFields['dino_name'] = array( 'friendlyname' =>
      'Pet Dinosaurs Name', 'table' => 'profile', 'field' =>
      'dino_name', 'type' => 'text', 'required' => false );
    $this->extraFields['dino_breed'] = array( 'friendlyname' =>
      'Pet Dinosaurs Breed', 'table' => 'profile', 'field' =>
      'dino_breed', 'type' => 'text', 'required' => false );
    $this->extraFields['dino_gender'] = array( 'friendlyname' =>
```

```
                'Pet Dnosaurs Gender', 'table' => 'profile', 'field' =>
                'dino_gender', 'type' => 'list', 'required' => false,
                'options' => array( 'male', 'female') );
        $this->extraFields['dino_dob'] = array( 'friendlyname' => 'Pet
            Dinosaurs Date of Birth', 'table' => 'profile', 'field' =>
            'dino_dob', 'type' => 'DOB', 'required' => false );
    }
```

Let's take a look at why we structure our `extraFields` like this. To do this, we need to look at how the extension validates the registration submission.

```
    public function checkRegistrationSubmission()
    {
```

We set a `$valid` variable (just like our `allClear` variable in the registration controller). If there are errors, we set this to `false`.

```
        $valid = true;
```

We now iterate through the fields to process them individually:

```
        foreach( $this->extraFields as $field => $data )
        {
```

Firstly, we check to see whether the field is required (from the required element of the data array). If it is, we check that the user has submitted a value. If they haven't, we store the necessary errors.

```
            if( ( ! isset( $_POST['register_' . $field] ) ||
              $_POST['register_' . $field] == '' )
              && $data['required'] = true )
            {
                $this->submittedValues[ $field ] = $_POST['register_' .
                    $field];
                $this->errorLabels['register_' . $field .'_label'] =
                    'error';
                $this->errors[] = 'Field ' . $data['friendlyname'] . '
                    cannot be blank';
                $valid = false;
            }
```

If the field isn't required, and hasn't been set, then we note that, and move on.

```
            elseif( $_POST['register_' . $field] == '' )
            {
                $this->submittedValues[ 'register_' . $field ] = '';
            }
            else
            {
```

If our field is set, we then validate it depending on the type of data we are expecting. By default, there are three options:

- Text—text inputs
- Int—integers
- List—list of predefined options

However, it has been designed to allow other types to be plugged in, for instance, dates. The type also dictates how the data should be sanitized.

```
if( $data['type'] == 'text' )
{
    $this->sanitizedValues[ 'register_' . $field ] = $this-
        >registry->getObject('db')->sanitizeData( $_
        POST['register_' . $field] );
    $this->submittedValues['register_' . $field] = $_
        POST['register_' . $field];
}
elseif( $data['type'] == 'int' )
{
    $this->sanitizedValues[ 'register_' . $field ] =
        intval( $_POST['register_' . $field] );
    $this->submittedValues['register_' . $field] = $_
        POST['register_' . $field];
}
elseif(  $data['type'] == 'list'  )
{
```

If the data type is a list, we simply check to see whether the value is in the array of options, if it isn't we have an error, if it is—everything is OK.

```
if( ! in_array( $_POST['register_' . $field],
    $data['options'] ) )
{
    $this->submittedValues[ $field ] = $_
        POST['register_' . $field];
    $this->errorLabels['register_' . $field .'_label'] =
        'error';
    $this->errors[] = 'Field ' . $data['friendlyname'] .
        ' was not valid';

    $valid = false;
}
else
{
    $this->sanitizedValues[ 'register_' . $field ] =
        intval( $_POST['register_' . $field] );
    $this->submittedValues['register_' . $field] = $_
        POST['register_' . $field];
```

```
            }
        }
        else
        {
```

Finally, for non-standard cases, we call a custom method, which we would create for each such type:

```
$method = 'validate_' . $data['type'];
if( $this->$method( $_POST['register_' . $field] ) ==
    true )
{
    $this->sanitizedValues[ 'register_' . $field ] =
        $this->registry->getObject('db')->sanitizeData(
        $_POST['register_' . $field] );
    $this->submittedValues['register_' . $field] = $_
        POST['register_' . $field];
}
else
{
    $this->sanitizedValues[ 'register_' . $field ] =
        $this->registry->getObject('db')->sanitizeData(
        $_POST['register_' . $field] );
    $this->submittedValues['register_' . $field] = $_
        POST['register_' . $field];
    $this->errors[] = 'Field ' . $data['friendlyname'] .
        ' was not valid';
    $valid = false;
}
    }
}
```

Once all the processing has been done, and sanitized data has been stored, we simply return whether there were errors or not:

```
if( $valid == true )
{
    return true;
}
else
{
    return false;
}
}
```

Processing the registration

Once we have processed all of the fields submitted and checked that they are all valid, we are then ready to create our user account and our profile. Creating the user is a simple case of inserting the serialized values into the users table. Then, we pass control to the extension so that it can process the profile fields.

```
/**
 * Process the users registration, and create the user and users
    profiles
 * @return int
 */
private function processRegistration()
{
  // insert
  $this->registry->getObject('db')->insertRecords( 'users',
    $this->sanitizedValues );
  // get ID
  $uid = $this->registry->getObject('db')->lastInsertID();
  // call extension to insert the profile
  $this->registrationExtention->processRegistration( $uid );
  // return the ID for the frameworks reference - autologin?
  return $uid;
}
```

Creating the profile

Within our extra fields array, we noted the table and field that the submitted value should be inserted into. This method goes through the array, and groups the values for each table, to ensure that only one insert is performed per additional table.

The advantage of this means if we added fields for another table (perhaps subscription information for paid user accounts), we can do this without needing to add more functionality to our extension.

```
/**
 * Create our user profile
 * @param int $uid the user ID
 * @return bool
 */
public function processRegistration( $uid )
{
  $tables = array();
  $tableData = array();
```

```
// group our profile fields by table, so we only need to do one
   insert per table
foreach( $this->extraFields as $field => $data )
{
   if( ! ( in_array( $data['table'], $tables ) ) )
   {
      $tables[] = $data['table'];
      $tableData[ $data['table'] ] = array( 'user_id' => $uid,
         $data['field'] => $this->sanitizedValues[ 'register_' .
         $field ]);
   }
   else
   {
      $tableData[ $data['table'] ] = array( 'user_id' => $uid,
         $data['field'] => $this->sanitizedValues[ 'register_' .
         $field ]);
   }
}
foreach( $tableData as $table => $data )
{
   $this->registry->getObject('db')->insertRecords( $table,
      $data );
}
return true;
}
```

Putting it all together: registration constructor

So, we have gone through our registration controller, and our registration controller extension to see how they process data to create our user account and user profile. We now just need to bring this all together in the constructor.

Firstly, we assign our registry object:

```
$this->registry = $registry;
```

Next, we include the extension file, and create the object:

```
require_once FRAMEWORK_PATH . 'controllers/authenticate/
   registrationcontrollerextention.php';
$this->registrationExtention = new
   Registrationcontrollerextention( $this->registry );
```

We then check to see if the user has tried to submit the registration form:

```
if( isset( $_POST['process_registration'] ) )
{
```

If they have submitted the form, we check the registration, to see if the values are valid:

```
if( $this->checkRegistration() == true )
{
```

If the form was completed properly, we can then process the registration and create the user account and the profile:

```
$userId = $this->processRegistration();
if( $this->activeValue == 1 )
{
```

If we have set all users to be active by default, we log the user in automatically:

```
$this->registry->getObject('authenticate')-
    >forceLogin( $this->submittedValues['register_
    user'], md5( $this->submittedValues['register_
    password'] ) );
}
$this->uiRegistrationProcessed();
}
else
{
```

If the registration attempt wasn't successful, we display the user interface, passing a parameter to indicate that errors need to be displayed.

```
$this->uiRegister( true );
}

}
```

Finally, if the user is just viewing the registration form, we simply show them that (courtesy of the uiRegister method).

```
else
{
    $this->uiRegister( false );
}
```

CAPTCHA

We don't want our social network to get clogged up with automated signups that aren't going to add anything to our site. We can use a **CAPTCHA** (Completely Automated Public Turing test to tell Computers and Human Apart) challenge to test that the sign up is a genuine person. A CAPTCHA challenge is often a series of words embedded in an image, many computer systems can't automatically pick up the text from this image, whereas a human can, helping to tell which signup is a human and which is an automated computer.

General CAPTCHA

Generally, CAPTCHA systems work by:

- Generating a random phrase or string.

- Storing this phrase in the user's session (so they can't see it, but we have a persistent copy as they move from the registration form, to process their registration. This is also useful as the image is generally generated by a separate HTTP request—so the session is needed to maintain the value).

- Displaying a slightly distorted version of the phrase on the registration form within an image.

- The user enters the text from the image into a text box.

- When they submit the registration form, we compare this value to the value of the appropriate session field—if they match, it passes.

reCAPTCHA

reCAPTCHA is a widely used CAPTCHA solution, we will look at implementing this in *Chapter 12, Deployment, Security, and Maintenance.*

Where do I sign up?

So we have all of this excellent sign up functionality, however, we need a template for our view! Below is code for our `views/default/templates/authenticate/register/main.tpl.php file`. This code contains HTML fields for all of the fields we have set in the registration controller and its extension:

```
<div id="main">

  <div id="rightside">
  </div>

  <div id="content">
  <h1>Join DINO SPACE!</h1>
```

If the user makes a mistake, we need to list any issues. To allow this, we have a template tag that is replaced with the errors list if there are errors. If there are no errors, the tag is removed:

```
{error}
<form action="authenticate/register" method="post">
```

The values for these fields are then set to what the user had typed in when they submitted the form, saving them the need to re-enter all of the data that was actually correct. We can also add a tag to change the style of the label to indicate a problem if we wish:

```
<label for="register_user">Username</label><br />
<input type="text" id="register_user" name="register_user"
value="{register_user}" /><br />

<label for="register_password">Password</label><br />
<input type="password" id="register_password" name="register_password"
value="" /><br />

<label for="register_password_confirm">Confirm password</label><br />
<input type="password" id="register_password_confirm" name="register_
password_confirm" value="" /><br />

<label for="register_email">Email</label><br />
<input type="text" id="register_email" name="register_email"
value="{register_email}" /><br />

<label for="register_dino_name">Name of dinosaur</label><br />
<input type="text" id="register_dino_name" name="register_dino_name"
value="{register_dino_name}" /><br />

<label for="register_dino_breed">Breed of dinosaur</label><br />
<input type="text" id="register_dino_breed" name="register_dino_breed"
value="{register_dino_breed}" /><br />

<label for="register_dino_gender">Gender of dinosaur</label><br />
<select id="register_dino_gender" name="register_dino_gender">
<option value="male">male</option>
<option value="female">female</option>
</select><br />

<label for="register_dino_dob">Dinosaurs Date of Birth (dd/mm/yy)</
label><br />
<input type="text" id="register_dino_dob" name="register_dino_dob"
value="{register_dino_dob}" /><br />

<label for="">Do you accept our terms and conditions?</label><br />
<input type="checkbox" id="register_terms" name="register_terms"
value="1" /> <br />
```

```
<input type="submit" id="process_registration" name="process_
  registration" value="Create an account" />
</form>

</div>

</div>
```

Now, assuming we have added authenticate as a controller in our controllers table in the database (so the framework knows to pass control to it), we can go to `http://ourwebsite/authenticate/register` to create an account, and we are presented with the following registration screen:

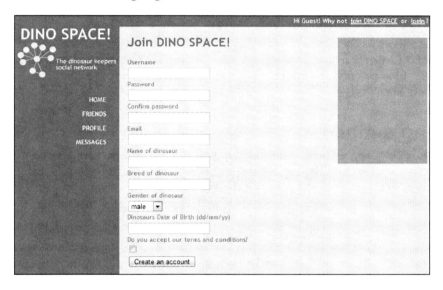

As well as this template, we need an error template, for any error messages to be inserted into, and a complete template, to thank the user for joining. These templates (`views/default/templates/authenticate/register/*.tpl.php`), as well as the header and footer, are included in the code accompanying this chapter.

E-mail verification

With CAPTCHA implemented, we know that our user is a human, however, we should still try and verify their e-mail address; there are a number of reasons for this, including:

- Preventing a user from signing up multiple times.

- Ensuring our records are up to date—particularly useful if a user forgets their password or e-mail address.

- If the user is troublesome, we have more ability to prevent repeat-sign ups (unless they have multiple e-mail addresses), and most ISP's have an abuse e-mail account we can contact to report such users.

- Adding value—when users build relationships through our site, or send messages to each other, they may want to receive e-mail notifications. If we don't have their valid e-mail address, then they won't get these, and they may lose interest in the site, when their own network is expanding without their knowledge.

Sending e-mails

As we are developing a social network, we will need to frequently send e-mails, not just for e-mail verification, but also for reminding users of their details, informing them of users who are connecting with them, and sending news updates. To make this easier, we should create a simple class to manage e-mail sending.

The code for this class is in the `mailout.class.php` file in the code that accompanies this chapter; however, let's have a look at some of the code. This class is based on the template manager class, in that it includes a template file, and replaces certain tags with the data that we supply. The main difference is we don't have a page object, and instead of being output to the browser, it is e-mailed to our user.

Another difference with our template handler is that once we have sent a series of templates to the browser, the handler has completed its job. With the e-mail object, we may wish to send more than one e-mail during a single execution of the script. To accommodate this, we use the `startFresh()` method. This method contains code that would be more suited to the constructor, but is called before each new e-mail we send, wiping the e-mail contents.

```
public function startFresh()
    {
        // not in constructor because object is reused, so this is done
          on each "new email"
        $this->lock = false;
```

```
        $this->error = 'Message not sent because: ';
        $this->message = '';
}
```

When sending an e-mail, we are more often than not, going to be sending it to a user of the site, or to the contact of a user. One concern with an e-mailing code, is sending automated spam. We can detect for this, by searching for text designed to create new headers (that is, setting new recipients, or recipients to be carbon-copied in on the e-mail).

```
/**
    * Sets the recipient
    * @param String the recipient
    * @return bool
    */
public function setTo( $to )
{
```

If the e-mail address contains header characters, it is rejected:

```
    if(eregi("\r",(urldecode($to))) || eregi("\n",(urldecode($to))))
    {

        // bad - header injections

        $this->lock();
        $this->error .= ' Receipient Email header injection attempt,
          probably caused by spam attempts';
        return false;


    }
```

If the e-mail address does not meet the standard format of an e-mail address, it is also rejected:

```
    elseif( ! eregi("^[_a-z0-9-]+(\.[_a-z0-9-]+)*@[a-z0-9-]+(\.[a-
    z0-9-]+)*(\.[a-z]{2,3})$", $to) )
    {
        // bad - invalid email

        $this->lock();
        $this->error .= ' Recipient Email address no valid';
        return false;

    }
```

Otherwise, we can send our e-mail:

```
else
{
   //good - let's do it!
   $this->to = $to;
   return true;

}

}
```

The content of the e-mail is built from a number of e-mail templates:

```
public function buildFromTemplates()
   {
      $bits = func_get_args();
      $content = "";
      foreach( $bits as $bit )
      {

         if( strpos( $bit, 'emailtemplates/' ) === false )
         {
            $bit = 'emailtemplates/' . $bit;
         }
         if( file_exists( $bit ) == true )
         {
            $content .= file_get_contents( $bit );
         }

      }
      $this->message =  $content;
   }
```

Template tags are replaced within the e-mail templates, in a similar way to the template manager:

```
public function replaceTags( $tags )
   {
      // go through them all
      if( sizeof($tags) > 0 )
      {
         foreach( $tags as $tag => $data )
         {
            // if the tag is an array, then we need to do more than
               a simple find and replace!
```

```
                   if( ! is_array( $data ) )
                   {
                       // replace the content
                       $newContent = str_replace( '{' . $tag . '}', $data,
                           $this->message );
                       // update the pages content
                       $this->message = $newContent;
                   }
               }
           }


       }
```

When it comes to sending the e-mail, we simply check that there are no "locks" caused by errors we have encountered, and then perform a simple `mail()` call to send the e-mail:

```
    /**
     * Sends the email using Send Mail
     * @return void
     */
    public function sendWithSendmail()
    {
       if($this->lock == true)
       {
          return false;
       }
       else
       {
           if( ! @mail($this->to, $this->subject, $this->message,
              $this->headers) )
           {
              $this->error .= ' problems sending via PHP\'s mail
                  function';
              return false;
           }
           else
           {
              return true;
           }
       }
    }
```

True or false is returned, so we know if our mail object was successful in its e-mail attempt, allowing us to either inform the user, or store a log of the error somewhere for the administrator, if we wish.

Room for improvement

As with everything, there is room for improvement in this code, for instance:

- The only mail delivery method it uses is PHP's mail() function
- Mails are sent instantly – if our system is sending lots of e-mails frequently, we may wish to integrate this with a queuing system
- Only plain text e-mails are sent (HTML e-mails can be sent using this, but this is a messy way to send HTML e-mails)

Sending the e-mail verification e-mail

With suitable functionality in our framework to send e-mails, how would we go about sending a verification e-mail to our new user?

1. Set the user to inactive.
2. Generate a random string, and assign it to the user. This is the verification key.
3. E-mail the user a link that includes their user ID and the verification key.
4. When they click on the link, we verify the verification key, and if appropriate, update their user account.

Authentication with our authentication object

With our user authentication object in place in our registry, we are now able to link into this to determine whether the current user is a logged in user, or not, and if they are we can also log them out.

Logging in

One of the first things our framework should do, once it has connected to the database, is perform authentication checks. This should do one of two things; it should either check the current user's session data to see if we potentially have a user who is already logged in. If this is the case, it should perform checks to see if they are a valid user, and build up the user object as appropriate. If this is not the case, it should check to see if certain form fields have been submitted (such as username and password); if they have been, it should check to see if these are valid, and if appropriate, authenticate the user:

```
$registry->getObject('authenticate')->checkForAuthentication();
```

This isn't part of the objects constructor, because we need to connect to the database (which is done after we instantiate the authentication object) first.

Are we logged in?

After calling our main authentication method within the authentication object, we now probably want to know whether our user is logged in or not. If they are not, we will give them an overview page about Dino Space, and why they should join, and give them access to the login page, the signup page, and some other generic pages of content, such as terms and conditions, contact us, privacy policy, and so on. If they are logged in, we will probably want to take them to their profile, from which they can check for recent activity and communicate with their contacts.

```
if( $registry->getObject('authenticate')->isLoggedIn() )
{
    //
}
else
{
    //
}
```

Logging out

When a user is done with the site for the time being, we want them to be able to log out to prevent anyone else who shares their computer from being able to log in as them. This problem is often illustrated by many student users of Facebook, who leave their account signed in and their computer switched on in shared accommodation, only to find their profiles have been vandalised.

Checking for a logout request can be handled by our authentication controller. This can simply check the URL to see if it contains a logout request, and if it does, it can logout the user, and redirect them to the homepage:

```
private function logout()
    {
        $this->registry->getObject('authenticate')->logout();
        $this->registry->getObject('template')-
            >addTemplateBit('userbar', 'userbar-guest.tpl.php');
        $this->registry->getObject('template')-
            >buildFromTemplates('header.tpl.php', 'login.tpl.php',
            'footer.tpl.php');
    }
```

Remember me

Our current implementation of an authentication system relies on SESSION data, which expires at the end of a user's session (either a specific time-limit set by the server, or when the user closes their browser, whichever occurs first). Many users want to be remembered when they log in to certain sites they use on a regular basis, to save the trouble of continually logging in every day, or even several times a day.

This can be achieved by combining sessions with cookies. However, as cookies last for longer periods of time and are stored on the user's computer (whereas sessions are stored on the server) cookie authentication will need to be more advanced. One option would be to store a random salted hash of the time the user logged in, within the cookie. If we simply relied on the user ID being stored in the cookie, it would be easy for users to create fake cookies, and thus take control of other users accounts.

Help! I've forgotten!

Some of our users will probably forget their login details, particularly if they haven't used our site for a while. If we don't have provisions for this, then we will lose users.

There are three types of reminder we should include:

- Username reminder
- Password reminder
- Resend e-mail verification message

Let's look at implementing these features in our authentication controller.

Username

If the user forgets his/her username, they simply supply their e-mail address, and we e-mail them a reminder:

```
private function forgotUsername()
{
    if( isset( $_POST['email'] ) && $_POST['email'] != '' )
    {
        $e = $this->registry->getObject('db')->sanitizeData( $_
            POST['email'] );
        $sql = "SELECT * FROM users WHERE email='{$e}'";
        $this->registry->getObject('db')->executeQuery( $sql );
        if( $this->registry->getObject('db')->numRows() == 1 )
        {
            $data = $this->registry->getObject('db')->getRows();
            // email the user
            $this->registry->getObject('mailout')->startFresh();
```

```
$this->registry->getObject('mailout')->setTo( $_
  POST['email'] );
$this->registry->getObject('mailout')->setSender( $this-
    >registry->getSetting('adminEmailAddress') );
$this->registry->getObject('mailout')->setFromName( $this-
    >registry->getSetting('cms_name') );
$this->registry->getObject('mailout')->setSubject(
  'Username details for ' .$this->registry-
  >getSetting('sitename') );
$this->registry->getObject('mailout')-
    >buildFromTemplates('authenticate/username.tpl.php');
$tags = $this->values;
$tags[ 'sitename' ] = $this->registry-
    >getSetting('sitename');
$tags['username'] = $data['username'];
$tags['siteurl'] = $this->registry->getSetting('site_
  url');
$this->registry->getObject('mailout')-
    >replaceTags( $tags );
$this->registry->getObject('mailout')-
    >setMethod('sendmail');
$this->registry->getObject('mailout')->send();

// tell them that we emailed them
$this->registry->errorPage('Username reminder sent',
  'We have sent you a reminder of your username, to the
    email address we have on file');

}
else
{
   // no user found
  $this->registry->getObject('template')-
    >buildFromTemplates( 'header.tpl.php', 'authenticate/
    username/main.tpl.php', 'footer.tpl.php');
  $this->registry->getObject('template')-
    >addTemplateBit('error_message', 'authenticate/username/
    error.tpl.php');
  }
}
else
{
  // form template
  $this->registry->getObject('template')->buildFromTemplates(
    'header.tpl.php', 'authenticate/username/main.tpl.php',
    'footer.tpl.php');
  $this->registry->getObject('template')->getPage()-
    >addTag('error_message', '');
  }
}
```

Password

If the user forgets his/her password, they enter their username, and we generate a password reset key, and e-mail them a link to reset the password:

```
private function forgotPassword()
{
    if( isset( $_POST['username'] ) && $_POST['username'] != '' )
    {
        $u = $this->registry->getObject('db')->sanitizeData( $_
            POST['username'] );
        $sql = "SELECT * FROM users WHERE username='{$u}'";
        $this->registry->getObject('db')->executeQuery( $sql );
        if( $this->registry->getObject('db')->numRows() == 1 )
        {
            $data = $this->registry->getObject('db')->getRows();
            // have they requested a new password recently?
            if( $data['reset_expires'] > date('Y-m-d h:i:s') )
            {
                // inform them
                $this->registry->errorPage('Error sending password
                    request', 'You have recently requested a password
                    reset link, and as such you must wait a short while
                    before requesting one again.  This is for security
                    reasons.');
            }
            else
            {
            // update their row
                $changes = array();
                $rk = $this->generateKey();
                $changes['reset_key'] = $rk;
                $changes['reset_expires'] = date( 'Y-m-d h:i:s',
                    time()+86400 );
                $this->registry->getObject('db')->updateRecords(
                    'users', $changes, 'ID=' . $data['ID'] );
                // email the user
                $this->registry->getObject('mailout')->startFresh();
                $this->registry->getObject('mailout')->setTo( $_
                    POST['email'] );
                $this->registry->getObject('mailout')->setSender(
                    $this->registry->getSetting('adminEmailAddress') );
                $this->registry->getObject('mailout')->setFromName(
                    $this->registry->getSetting('cms_name') );
                $this->registry->getObject('mailout')->setSubject(
                    'Password reset request for ' .$this->registry-
                    >getSetting('sitename') );
```

```
                    $this->registry->getObject('mailout')-
                       >buildFromTemplates('authenticate/password.tpl.php');
                    $tags = $this->values;
                    $tags[ 'sitename' ] = $this->registry-
                       >getSetting('sitename');
                    $tags['username'] = $data['username'];
                    $url = $this->registry->buildURL( 'authenticate',
                       'reset-password', $data['ID'], $rk );
                    $tags['url'] = $url;
                    $tags['siteurl'] = $this->registry->getSetting('site_
                       url');
                    $this->registry->getObject('mailout')->replaceTags(
                       $tags );
                    $this->registry->getObject('mailout')-
                       >setMethod('sendmail');
                    $this->registry->getObject('mailout')->send();

                    // tell them that we emailed them
                    $this->registry->errorPage('Password reset link sent',
                       'We have sent you a link which will allow you to
                       reset your account password');
                }

            }
            else
            {
                // no user found
                $this->registry->getObject('template')-
                   >buildFromTemplates( 'header.tpl.php', 'authenticate/
                   password/main.tpl.php', 'footer.tpl.php');
                $this->registry->getObject('template')-
                   >addTemplateBit('error_message', 'authenticate/password/
                   error.tpl.php');
            }
        }
        else
        {
            // form template
            $this->registry->getObject('template')->buildFromTemplates(
               'header.tpl.php', 'authenticate/password/main.tpl.php',
               'footer.tpl.php');
            $this->registry->getObject('template')->getPage()-
               >addTag('error_message', '');
        }
    }
```

The link is used to verify the user (as it is sent to their e-mail address) where they can reset the password.

Let them reset the password

The password is then reset by the user entering a new password, assuming their reset key is correct. Control is passed from the framework to our authentication controller, which calls the `resetPassword` method. This method takes two parameters, the user's ID and the reset key. This is used to perform a basic form of user authentication, to allow them to reset the password:

```
private function resetPassword( $user, $key )
  {
    $this->registry->getObject('template')->getPage()->addTag(
      'user', $user );
    $this->registry->getObject('template')->getPage()->addTag('key',
      $key );
    $sql = "SELECT * FROM users WHERE ID={$user} AND reset_
      key='{$key}'";
    $this->registry->getObject('db')->executeQuery( $sql );
    if( $this->registry->getObject('db')->numRows() == 1 )
    {
      $data = $this->registry->getObject('db')->getRows();
      if( $data['reset_expiry'] > date('Y-m-d h:i:s') )
      {
```

We can have a problem with either a user repeatedly requesting password reset links maliciously for another user, as when the user tried to reset their password a new key would be generated. Similarly, a user could use trial and error (brute force attacking) to try and guess a reset key and subsequently reset the user's password. To prevent these issues, only one key should be issued in a 24 hour period, and it should expire after this time. If the key they have supplied has expired, we need to tell them that.

```
        $this->registry->errorPage('Reset link expired', 'Password
          reset links are only valid for 24 hours.  This link is
          out of date and has expired.');

      }
      else
      {
```

If their key is valid, we then check to see whether they have completed the form and submitted a new password:

```
        if( isset( $_POST['password'] ) )
        {
```

If they have completed the form, we need to check that the password is at least seven characters long, and that it has been confirmed:

```
if( strlen( $_POST['password'] ) < 6 )
{
   $this->registry->errorPage( 'Password too short',
      'Sorry, your password was too short, passwords
      must be greater than 6 characters');
}
else
{
   if( $_POST['password'] != $_POST['password_confirm']
)

   {

      $this->registry->errorPage( 'Passwords do not
         match', 'Your password and password
         confirmation do not match, please try again.');
   }
   else
   {
```

We then hash the password, and update the user's database record:

```
// reset the password
$changes = array();
$changes['password_hash'] = md5( $_
   POST['passowrd'] );
$this->registry->getObject('db')->updateRecords(
   'users', $changes, 'ID=' . $user );
$this->registry->errorPage('Password reset',
   'Your password has been reset to the one you
   entered');


      }
   }
}
else
{
```

If the key is valid, and the user hasn't submitted the new password form, we show them the form:

```
// show the form
$this->registry->getObject('template')-
   >buildFromTemplates( 'header.tpl.php', 'authenticate/
   password/reset.tpl.php', 'footer.tpl.php');
```

```
                    }
                }
            }
        else
            {
```

Finally, if they key was invalid, we tell them that:

```
            $this->registry->errorPage('Invalid details', 'The password
                reset link was invalid');
        }
    }
```

I've lost my e-mail verification message

If we verify our users' e-mail addresses, we would also want to be able to resend this verification message, in case they delete the original. Why not try and implement this feature in our authentication controller?

Summary

In this chapter, we looked at allowing users to sign up to Dino Space, by developing registration logic to create a user account and their custom social profile. A user account on its own isn't enough—our users need to be able to log in to the user account, so that they can benefit from the site. To facilitate this we also created an authentication registry class.

Because e-mail sending is going to be a task we need to do frequently, as illustrated by the four use cases in this chapter, we also developed a simple e-mail sending class, to make it easy for us to generate and send e-mails as and when we need to.

Now that we can have users on our social network, and they can log in to access our social network, let's start developing some social features for it!

4
Friends and Relationships

We now have a social networking site, where the only feature is that users can sign up, log in, and log out. This is, of course, the first step to any such site, as we need users. Now that we have users, we need some way for them to be able to connect to one another. For this to be possible, we need to be able to see the users on the site, search the users on the site, and subsequently request to connect to them.

In this chapter, you will learn:

- How to allow users to invite their friends to the site
- How to automatically invite a user's contacts to befriend them on the site, by connecting to other websites
- How to list users on the site
- How to search for users on the site and display the resulting users
- How to allow users to connect with one another as friends or other types of relationship (for example, as colleagues)

Let's get started.

Inviting friends

Although users of Dino Space are going to sign up and connect with other users on the site, to help them build up their profile on the site more quickly and to help us increase our user base, we can allow our users to invite friends and contacts who they know from outside of the social network to join and connect with them. At the same time, we can also see if these people have already signed up to the site, and inform the user of this.

There are two main ways we can do this:

- Asking our users to enter a friend's name and e-mail address
- Asking our users to enter their details for their webmail, connecting to their address book, and obtaining a list of their contacts

Once we have a name and an e-mail address we can either:

- Send the user an e-mail inviting them to join Dino Space to connect with their friend
- Inform the user that someone with that e-mail address has already signed up and suggest they connect with them directly, or automatically connect them (this is another reason e-mail verification from Chapter 3 is useful, otherwise it could be any user with our friends e-mail address, and not actually our friend)

A note on privacy

When a user gives us details of a friend who isn't on their site, their credentials or access to their online contacts, or a list of their contacts, we shouldn't keep a copy of this without their explicit permission. A suitable privacy policy should be clear on the website, indicating what happens with any data they enter into the website.

Manually inviting friends

If John thinks his friend Bill, who keeps a pet pterodactyl, would benefit from using Dino Space, he may want to recommend the site to him. To allow users to invite other users we need to:

1. Request John to enter Bill's name and e-mail address.

2. Check to see if Bill's e-mail address exists in the website (that is, is Bill already a member).

3. If Bill is already a member, we suggest that John connect with him and show him Bill's profile.

4. If Bill hasn't already joined Dino Space, we want to validate this data and display a template message to John showing the invitation message, which he can edit and personalise.

5. We allow John to edit the message.

6. Once John clicks on Send, we e-mail the invitation to Bill dynamically inserting John's details so Bill knows who it was that invited him.

Invitation controller

To manually invite friends, we need an invitation controller to take and process the user's requests. This controller would then present the user with an invitation form, for the user to enter their friend's details. On submitting the form, the controller will check to see if the friend is already a member (by looking up the friend's e-mail address in the user's table). If the friend isn't a member, the personalized invitation message will have the friend's details inserted into it, and will then be e-mailed to the friend.

If you do implement this feature, you will also need a number of template files to make up the view, and an e-mail template for sending the invitation to the friend.

Automatically inviting friends

Most social networking websites offer the user the chance to enter their details for their webmail login, to have the site automatically invite their contacts to use the site. In the past, this would be done by scripts that would connect to the various websites using libraries such as cURL, pretending to be a user, to obtain the contacts list. This technique isn't ideal, as the code obviously needs to be updated each time the site changes how it works.

Thankfully, most e-mail providers realise this is a useful feature, and so they have provided APIs that developers can interact with to obtain a list of contacts to e-mail. Of course, APIs change, but changes are generally announced in advance, and there is normally a wealth of resources for developers.

Google Friend Connect

Google has a service that aims to allow users to invite their friends from a number of social networking sites (currently Orkut and Plaxo) as well as contacts from Google Talk and friends with a known e-mail address.

This service also provides a number of other "gadgets" that can add social functionality to your site, including commenting and rating content, as well as providing some interesting reporting tools.

More information on this is available on the Google Friend Connect website: `http://www.google.com/friendconnect`.

Windows Live contacts

Microsoft has developer documentation and a RESTful Contacts API for Windows Live contacts that gives developers access to a user's contacts from Hotmail, Messenger, and Mobile contacts.

More information is available on their developer website: `http://dev.live.com/contacts/`.

Yahoo!

Yahoo! has a Contacts API that can be used to look up a user's address book contacts. More information is available from the Yahoo! Developer Network: `http://developer.yahoo.com/social/rest_api_guide/contact_api.html`.

Gmail contacts

Gmail has a Data API for accessing contacts from other applications. More information on this is available at: `http://code.google.com/apis/contacts/`.

Automatically connecting with friends

Don't forget, if the e-mail address already exists in the database, we wouldn't want to send them an e-mail inviting them to join. Instead, we would either want to automatically create a relationship between the two users (e-mailing the recipient friend that they have a new pending friend request), or once the invitations had been sent, we would list all of the contacts from their address book(s) that already exist on the site, allowing them to view their profiles and connect with them if they wish.

Members

Once our site has a few members, we need to be able to view and search for members, so that we can connect and communicate with them. Let's look at creating a member list and basic member search.

We will do this by creating a model and a controller for members. The model should be a class `Members`, and saved as `members.php` in the `models` folder, and the controller should be a class `Memberscontroller` saved as `controller.php` in the `controllers/members` folder.

Listing users

User lists have a limitation with large social networks—they end up being large lists of users that are irrelevant to the user viewing the list. This can be overcome by listing a subset of users; for instance, those in a particular group, contact sphere, or network. For example, when Facebook started, users joined up to two networks, which was generally their university, school, workplace, or city. This could be used to segregate groups of users when listing them; obviously we wouldn't want to segregate users from each other, but this could make lists more meaningful.

At this stage we don't have this concern; we can simply provide a paginated list of our users.

Pagination

In order for us to display a nice paginated list, we need some way to easily paginate through results of a query. To save this from getting repetitive, we could encapsulate the functionality within a class, and use this each time we need a paginated list.

Because this isn't really a core class, and we may need to create more than one during an execution of the framework, we shouldn't have this as a registry object. Instead, we should have this in a `libraries` folder. Generally, I prefer to keep self-contained libraries in a `libraries` folder, which require no framework interaction; however, I think this is a suitable exception.

Let's look through the code for a suitable `/lib/pagination/pagination.class.php` file:

```php
<?php
/**
 * Pagination class
 * Making pagination of records easy(ier)
 */
class Pagination {
```

We should define a number of properties for the object, including:

- The query we wish to paginate:

```php
/**
 * The query we will be paginating
 */
private $query = "";
```

- The query that we actually execute to give us the paginated results (as we will need to dynamically add limits to the initial query):

```
/**
 * The processed query which will be executed / has been
   executed
 */
private $executedQuery = "";
```

- A limit to define how many results should be displayed on a page (default 25):

```
/**
 * The maximum number of results to display per page
 */
private $limit = 25;
```

- An offset that indicates which page of results we are on, and which results should be returned:

```
/**
 * The results offset - i.e. page we are on (-1)
 */
private $offset = 0;
```

- The method we wish to generate the pagination data with:

```
/**
 * The method of pagination
 */
private $method = 'query';
```

- The cache reference for the results of the query (if we opted to cache the results):

```
/**
 * The cache ID if we paginate by caching results
 */
private $cache;
```

- The results of the query (if we didn't opt to cache the results):

```
/**
 * The results set if we paginate by executing directly
 */
private $results;
```

- The number of rows there are in the original query (used within the class to calculate page numbers):

```
/**
 * The number of rows there were in the query passed
 */
private $numRows;
```

- The number of rows on the current page. Although we limit the results, on the last page we may actually have less results than this:

```
/**
 * The number of rows on the current page (main use if on last
   page, may not have as many as limit on the page)
 */
private $numRowsPage;
```

- The number of pages there are:

```
/**
 * Number of pages of results there are
 */
private $numPages;
```

- If the current page is the first page:

```
/**
 * Is this the first page of results?
 */
private $isFirst;
```

- If the current page is the last page:

```
/**
 * Is this the last page of results?
 */
private $isLast;
```

- The current page the user is on:

```
/**
 * The current page we are on
 */
private $currentPage;
```

We construct our object by passing the registry and assigning it to a variable:

```
/**
 * Our constructor
 * @param Object registry
 * @return void
 */
 function __construct( Registry $registry)
 {
   $this->registry = $registry;
 }
```

We also need a number of setter methods to set some of the variables, including:

- Setting the query:

```
/**
 * Set the query to be paginated
 * @param String $sql the query
 * @return void
 */
public function setQuery( $sql )
{
  $this->query = $sql;
}
```

- Setting the limit of how many results are to be displayed:

```
/**
 * Set the limit of how many results should be displayed per
   page
 * @param int $limit the limit
 * @return void
 */
public function setLimit( $limit )
{
  $this->limit = $limit;
}
```

- Setting the offset:

```
/**
 * Set the offset - i.e. if offset is 1, then we show the next
   page of results
 * @param int $offset the offset
 * @return void
 */
public function setOffset( $offset )
{
  $this->offset = $offset;
}
```

- Setting the method of pagination we wish to use:

```
/**
 * Set the method we want to use to paginate
 * @param String $method [cache|do]
 * @return void
 */
public function setMethod( $method )
{
  $this->method = $method;
}
```

With our data set, we need a method to call to perform the pagination, and generate the results:

```
/**
 * Process the query, and set the paginated properties
 * @return bool
 */
public function generatePagination()
{
  $temp_query = $this->query;
```

The first thing this method does is performs the query we passed it, to get the number of results. This is used later to determine which page we are on, and how many pages there on, by combining it with the limit:

```
// how many results?
$this->registry->getObject('db')->executeQuery( $temp_query );
$this->numRows = $this->registry->getObject('db')->numRows();
```

We then add to the query a limit that is based off the offset, and the limit of how many results we wish to display. If the limit is 25, and the offset is 1, this would generate results 26 – 50:

```
// limit!
$limit = " LIMIT ";
$limit .= ( $this->offset * $this->limit ) . ", " .
  $this->limit;
$temp_query = $temp_query . $limit;
$this->executedQuery = $temp_query;
```

Depending on the method of pagination, we either cache the query or execute it:

```
if( $this->method == 'cache' )
{
  $this->cache = $this->registry->getObject('db')->
    cacheQuery( $temp_query );
}
elseif( $this->method == 'do' )
{
  $this->registry->getObject('db')->
    executeQuery( $temp_query );
  $this->results = $this->registry->getObject('db')->getRows();
}
```

The final work for this method is to calculate the number of pages, the current page, and if we are on the first and/or last page of results:

```
  // be nice...do some calculations - so controllers don't have
    to!

// num pages
$this->numPages = ceil($this->numRows / $this->limit);

// is first
$this->isFirst = ( $this->offset == 0 ) ? true : false;

// is last

$this->isLast = ( ( $this->offset + 1 ) == $this->numPages ) ?
  true : false;

// current page
$this->currentPage = ( $this->numPages == 0 ) ? 0 : $this->offset
  +1;
$this->numRowsPage = $this->registry->getObject('db')->numRows();
if( $this->numRowsPage == 0 )
{
  return false;
}
else
{
  return true;
}

}
```

Finally we require some getter methods, to return the values of some of the objects properties:

```php
/**
 * Get the cached results
 * @return int
 */
public function getCache()
{
  return $this->cache;
}

/**
 * Get the result set
 * @return array
 */
public function getResults()
{
  return $this->results;
}

/**
 * Get the number of pages of results there are
 * @return int
 */
public function getNumPages()
{
  return $this->numPages;
}

/**
 * Is this page the first page of results?
 * @return bool
 */
public function isFirst()
{
  return $this->isFirst;
}

/**
 * Is this page the last page of results?
 * @return bool
 */
```

```php
      public function isLast()
      {
        return $this->isLast;
      }


      /**
       * Get the current page within the paginated results we are
          viewing
       * @return int
       */
      public function getCurrentPage()
      {
        return $this->currentPage;
      }
  }
  ?>
```

Now we have a simple class, which we can include, instantiate, and use when we need to paginate the results of a query.

Paginated members

Within our members model we need a method to generate the paginated list of members. This simply involves including our pagination class, creating a pagination object, setting some variables through the appropriate setter methods, calling the generatePagination method, and returning the pagination object to the controller (which calls the listMembers method).

The query to paginate is simply a list of members, a join of the users table, and the profile table. The offset is detected by the controller and passed to the listMembers method, which in turn passes this to the pagination object:

```php
  /**
     * Generate paginated members list
     * @param int $offset the offset
     * @return Object pagination object
     */
    public function listMembers( $offset=0 )
    {
      require_once( FRAMEWORK_PATH .
        'lib/pagination/pagination.class.php');
      $paginatedMembers = new Pagination( $this->registry );
      $paginatedMembers->setLimit( 25 );
      $paginatedMembers->setOffset( $offset );
      $query = "SELECT u.ID, u.username, p.name, p.dino_name,
```

```
        p.dino_gender, p.dino_breed FROM users u, profile p WHERE
        p.user_id=u.ID AND u.active=1 AND u.banned=0 AND u.deleted=0";
    $paginatedMembers->setQuery( $query );
    $paginatedMembers->setMethod( 'cache' );
    $paginatedMembers->generatePagination();
    return $paginatedMembers;


}
```

Our controller needs to detect that the user is viewing a list of members, take the offset, and pass this to the model, receiving a pagination object in return. With the pagination object it can then determine if it should display the members' list view or a view indicating that there are no members, or no members with the offset specified.

If there are members, it can build the pagination links with data from the pagination object, and take the results database cache and assign it to a template variable, which displays the list in the page.

```
private function listMembers( $offset )
  {
    require_once( FRAMEWORK_PATH . 'models/members.php');
    $members = new Members( $this->registry );
    $pagination = $members->listMembers( $offset );
    if( $pagination->getNumRowsPage() == 0 )
    {
      $this->registry->getObject('template')->
       buildFromTemplates('header.tpl.php', 'members/invalid.tpl.php'
       , 'footer.tpl.php');
    }
    else
    {
      $this->registry->getObject('template')
        ->buildFromTemplates('header.tpl.php', 'members/list.tpl.php'
       , 'footer.tpl.php');
      $this->registry->getObject('template')->getPage()->
        addTag( 'members', array( 'SQL', $pagination->getCache() ) );

      $this->registry->getObject('template')->getPage()->
        addTag( 'page_number', $pagination->getCurrentPage() );
      $this->registry->getObject('template')->getPage()->
        addTag( 'num_pages', $pagination->getNumPages() );
      if( $pagination->isFirst() )
      {
        $this->registry->getObject('template')->getPage()->
          addTag( 'first', '' );
        $this->registry->getObject('template')->getPage()->
```

```
        addTag( 'previous', '' );
      }
      else
      {
        $this->registry->getObject('template')->getPage()->
         addTag( 'first', "<a href='members/list/'>First page</a>" );
        $this->registry->getObject('template')->getPage()->
          addTag( 'previous', "<a href='members/list/" . (
          $pagination->getCurrentPage() - 2 ) . "'>Previous page</a>"
           );
      }
      if( $pagination->isLast() )
      {
        $this->registry->getObject('template')->getPage()->
          addTag( 'next', '' );
        $this->registry->getObject('template')->getPage()->
          addTag( 'last', '' );
      }
      else
      {
        $this->registry->getObject('template')->getPage()->
          addTag( 'first', "<a href='members/list/" .
          $pagination->getCurrentPage() . "'>Next page</a>" );
        $this->registry->getObject('template')->getPage()->
          addTag( 'previous', "<a href='members/list/" . (
          $pagination->getNumPages() - 1 ) . "'>Last page</a>" );
      }
    }
  }
}
```

To actually display the results of the lookup to the user, we need a template to form our members' list view. This is essentially a copy of the main template file, with a template loop for the members' information. This is saved in the `views/default/templates/members/list.tpl.php` file:

```
<div id="main">

  <div id="rightside">
  </div>

  <div id="content">
    <h1>DINO SPACE! Members List</h1>
    <!-- START members -->
    <p><strong>{name}</strong></p>
    <p>Keeper of <strong>{dino_name}</strong> a
      <strong>{dino_gender} {dino_breed}</strong></p>
```

```
          <hr />
          <!-- END members -->
          <p>Viewing page {page_number} of {num_pages}</p>
          <p>{first} {previous} {next} {last}</p>
      </div>

  </div>
```

This then displays our users list, which currently only contains me, as shown below!:

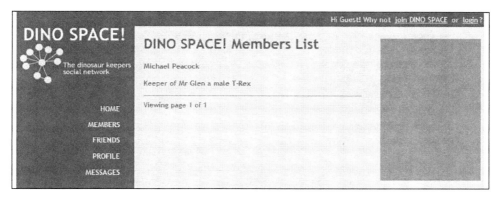

Paginated users by letter

As the site grows, but before we have such a large user base we need to consider listing more relevant users, we are going to end up with a paginated list, which isn't particularly easy to navigate. For example, if we have 20 users listed on each page and 100 pages of results, if our user wants to quickly jump to users with a surname beginning with P, it may take them several attempts. To make this easier, we can also provide filtering by alphabetical character, so the user can click on P and be taken to a list of users with surnames beginning with P. These lists may also be long, so they too should be paginated.

The required model method to do this takes an additional parameter, which is the letter the surname should start with. This is sanitized and then passed to the query—the query works slightly differently by searching for spaces in the user's name, then taking the word before the final space and comparing the first letter of this word to the letter passed:

```
/**
    * Generated paginated members list by surname
    * @param String $letter
    * @param int $offset the offset
    * @return Object pagination object
```

```
    */
    public function listMembersByLetter( $letter='A', $offset=0 )
    {
      $alpha = strtoupper( $this->registry->getObject('db')->
        sanitizeData( $letter ) );
      require_once( FRAMEWORK_PATH .
        'lib/pagination/pagination.class.php');
      $paginatedMembers = new Pagination( $this->registry );
      $paginatedMembers->setLimit( 25 );
      $paginatedMembers->setOffset( $offset );
      $query = "SELECT u.ID, u.username, p.name, p.dino_name,
        p.dino_gender, p.dino_breed FROM users u, profile p WHERE
        p.user_id=u.ID AND u.active=1 AND u.banned=0 AND u.deleted=0
        AND SUBSTRING_INDEX(p.name,' ', -1)LIKE'".$alpha."%' ORDER BY
        SUBSTRING_INDEX(p.name,' ', -1) ASC";
      $paginatedMembers->setQuery( $query );
      $paginatedMembers->setMethod( 'cache' );
      $paginatedMembers->generatePagination();
      return $paginatedMembers;
    }
```

Let's take a look at how this code fits together in our controller. The only real difference is the method we call in our model:

```
    private function listMembersAlpha( $alpha='A', $offset=0 )
    {
```

Require and create our members model:

```
      require_once( FRAMEWORK_PATH . 'models/members.php');
      $members = new Members( $this->registry );
```

Call the `listMembersByLetter` method to get our pagination object:

```
      $pagination = $members->listMembersByLetter( $alpha, $offset );
      if( $pagination->getNumRowsPage() == 0 )
      {
```

If there are no members, show that view:

```
        $this->registry->getObject('template')->
         buildFromTemplates('header.tpl.php', 'members/invalid.tpl.php'
          , 'footer.tpl.php');
      }
      else
      {
```

If there are members, show that view, and insert the appropriate data into the view:

```
$this->registry->getObject('template')->
  buildFromTemplates('header.tpl.php', 'members/list.tpl.php',
  'footer.tpl.php');
$this->registry->getObject('template')->getPage()->
  addTag( 'members', array( 'SQL', $pagination->getCache() ) );
$this->registry->getObject('template')->getPage()->
  addTag( 'letter', " - Letter: " . $alpha );

$this->registry->getObject('template')->getPage()->
  addTag( 'page_number', $pagination->getCurrentPage() );
$this->registry->getObject('template')->getPage()->
  addTag( 'num_pages', $pagination->getNumPages() );
if( $pagination->isFirst() )
{
  $this->registry->getObject('template')->getPage()->
    addTag( 'first', '');
  $this->registry->getObject('template')->getPage()->
    addTag( 'previous', '' );
}
else
{
  $this->registry->getObject('template')->getPage()->
    addTag( 'first', "<a href='members/alpha/".$alpha."/'>First
    page</a>" );
  $this->registry->getObject('template')->getPage()->
    addTag( 'previous', "<a href='members/alpha/".$alpha."/" .
    ( $pagination->getCurrentPage() - 2 ) . "'>Previous
    page</a>" );
}
if( $pagination->isLast() )
{
  $this->registry->getObject('template')->getPage()->
    addTag( 'next', '' );
  $this->registry->getObject('template')->getPage()->
    addTag( 'last', '' );
}
else
{
  $this->registry->getObject('template')->getPage()->
    addTag( 'first', "<a href='members/alpha/".$alpha."/" .
    $pagination->getCurrentPage() . "'>Next page</a>" );
  $this->registry->getObject('template')->getPage()->
    addTag( 'previous', "<a href='members/alpha/".$alpha."/" .
    ( $pagination->getNumPages() - 1 ) . "'>Last page</a>" );
}
}
}
```

We need to slightly update our members' list template; it needs a template variable to display the currently active letter, and the letters A – Z as links to filter down the list:

```
<div id="main">

  <div id="rightside">
  </div>

  <div id="content">
    <h1>DINO SPACE! Members List {letter}</h1>
    <!-- START members -->
    <p><strong>{name}</strong></p>
    <p>Keeper of <strong>{dino_name}</strong> a
      <strong>{dino_gender} {dino_breed}</strong></p>
    <hr />
    <!-- END members -->
    <p>Viewing page {page_number} of {num_pages}</p>
    <p>{first} {previous} {next} {last}</p>
    <p>
      <a href="members/alpha/A/">A</a>
      <a href="members/alpha/B/">B</a>
      <a href="members/alpha/C/">C</a>
      <a href="members/alpha/D/">D</a>
      <a href="members/alpha/E/">E</a>
      <a href="members/alpha/F/">F</a>
      <a href="members/alpha/G/">G</a>
      <a href="members/alpha/H/">H</a>
      <a href="members/alpha/I/">I</a>
      <a href="members/alpha/J/">J</a>
      <a href="members/alpha/K/">K</a>
      <a href="members/alpha/L/">L</a>
      <a href="members/alpha/M/">M</a>
      <a href="members/alpha/N/">N</a>
      <a href="members/alpha/O/">O</a>
      <a href="members/alpha/P/">P</a>
      <a href="members/alpha/Q/">Q</a>
      <a href="members/alpha/R/">R</a>
      <a href="members/alpha/S/">S</a>
      <a href="members/alpha/T/">T</a>
      <a href="members/alpha/U/">U</a>
      <a href="members/alpha/V/">V</a>
      <a href="members/alpha/W/">W</a>
      <a href="members/alpha/X/">X</a>
```

```
        <a href="members/alpha/Y/">Y</a>
        <a href="members/alpha/Z/">Z</a>
    </p>
</div>

</div>
```

Now if we go to `http://ourwebsite/members/` we should see the following:

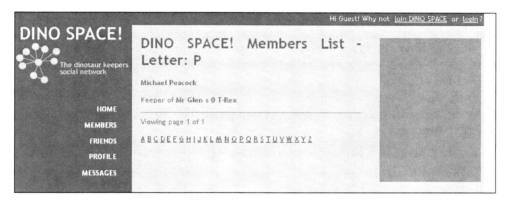

Searching for users

The user lists in themselves are primarily useful if a user spots someone they know of, or if the results display some information about them that the user can relate to, for example, the breed of their dinosaur, which may make them think "they also have a T-Rex, I'll connect with them!".

We should also have a search feature, so that our users can search for other users:

```php
/**
 * Search for members based on their name
 * @param String $filter name
 * @param int $offset the offset
 * @return Object pagination object
 */
public function filterMembersByName( $filter='', $offset=0 )
{
  $filter = ( $this->registry->getObject('db')->
    sanitizeData( urldecode( $filter ) ) );
  require_once( FRAMEWORK_PATH .
    'lib/pagination/pagination.class.php');
  $paginatedMembers = new Pagination( $this->registry );
  $paginatedMembers->setLimit( 25 );
```

```
    $paginatedMembers->setOffset( $offset );
    $query = "SELECT u.ID, u.username, p.name, p.dino_name,
      p.dino_gender, p.dino_breed FROM users u, profiles p WHERE
      p.user_id=u.ID AND u.active=1 AND u.banned=0 AND u.deleted=0
      AND p.name LIKE'%".$filter."%' ORDER BY p.name ASC";
    $paginatedMembers->setQuery( $query );
    $paginatedMembers->setMethod( 'cache' );
    $paginatedMembers->generatePagination();
    return $paginatedMembers;
}
```

Our controller now needs a method to process the search request. One important thing to note is that if we have performed a search, we can paginate because the search field is encoded with urlencode and passed in the URL, whereas when we first search, the name is in the name POST field. We need to detect which is which, and process accordingly. We can use an extra parameter in the method to indicate where the name data is:

```
private function searchMembers( $search=true, $name='', $offset=0 )
    {
    require_once( FRAMEWORK_PATH . 'models/members.php');
    $members = new Members( $this->registry );

    if( $search == true )
    {
```

If we are searching, take the name from the POST data:

```
        // we are performing the search
        $pagination = $members->filterMembersByName( urlencode(
          $_POST['name'] ), $offset );
        $name = urlencode( $_POST['name']  );
    }
    else
    {
```

If we are not searching, take the name from the URL (passed to this method directly):

```
        // we are paginating search results
        $pagination = $members->filterMembersByName( $name, $offset );
    }
    if( $pagination->getNumRowsPage() == 0 )
    {
      $this->registry->getObject('template')->
        buildFromTemplates('header.tpl.php', 'members/invalid.tpl.php'
          , 'footer.tpl.php');
    }
```

```
else
{
  $this->registry->getObject('template')->
    buildFromTemplates('header.tpl.php', 'members/search.tpl.php'
    , 'footer.tpl.php');
  $this->registry->getObject('template')->getPage()->
    addTag( 'members', array( 'SQL', $pagination->getCache() ) );
  $this->registry->getObject('template')->getPage()->
    addTag( 'public_name', urldecode( $name ) );
  $this->registry->getObject('template')->getPage()->
    addTag( 'encoded_name', $name );

  $this->registry->getObject('template')->getPage()->
    addTag( 'page_number', $pagination->getCurrentPage() );
  $this->registry->getObject('template')->getPage()->
    addTag( 'num_pages', $pagination->getNumPages() );
```

Our pagination links require a reference to the name we are searching for:

```
if( $pagination->isFirst() )
{
  $this->registry->getObject('template')->getPage()->
    addTag( 'first', '');
  $this->registry->getObject('template')->getPage()->
    addTag( 'previous', '' );
}
else
{
  $this->registry->getObject('template')->getPage()->
    addTag( 'first', "<a href='members/search-results/".
    $name."/'>First page</a>" );
  $this->registry->getObject('template')->getPage()->
    addTag( 'previous', "<a href='members/search-results/".
    $name."/" . ( $pagination->getCurrentPage() - 2 ) .
     "'>Previous page</a>" );
}
if( $pagination->isLast() )
{
  $this->registry->getObject('template')->getPage()->
    addTag( 'next', '' );
  $this->registry->getObject('template')->getPage()->
    addTag( 'last', '' );
}
else
{
  $this->registry->getObject('template')->getPage()->
    addTag( 'first', "<a href='members/search-results/".
```

```
    $name."/" .        $pagination->getCurrentPage() .
     "'>Next page</a>" );
   $this->registry->getObject('template')->getPage()->
     addTag( 'previous', "<a href='members/search-results/"
     .$name.        "/" . ( $pagination->getNumPages() - 1 ) .
     "'>Last page</a>" );
   }
  }
}
```

In our controllers constructor, we need to perform our detection (if a search is being performed or not) and pass a suitable $search parameter to the searchMembers method:

```
case 'search':
  $this->searchMembers( true, '', 0 );
  break;
case 'search-results':
  $this->searchMembers( false, $urlBits[2] , intval( isset(
    $urlBits[3] ) ? $urlBits[3] : 0 )  );
  break;
```

We also need a search box in our main members' list page, and a new template showing the results of the search:

```
<form action="members/search" method="post">
  <h2>Search for a member</h2>
  <label for="name">Their name</label><br />
  <input type="text" id="name" name="name" value="" /><br />
  <input type="submit" id="search" name="search" value="Search" />
</form>
```

We now have a fully working search feature, as shown below:

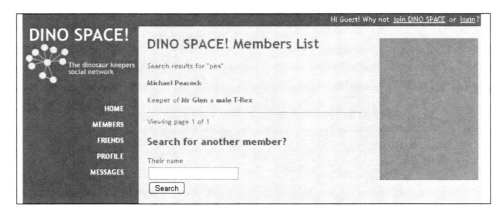

Custom relationships

Before we can connect to a user as a friend, we need to define the types of relationship our social network will support. Within Dino Space, we should have relationships for:

- Friends: For users who are friends with one another
- Colleagues: For users who are colleagues with one another
- Jogging buddies: For users who take their dinosaurs to the same morning jogging group

We may, of course, wish to extend this as the site grows and changes as time goes on.

To facilitate these relationships we are going to need two database tables, one to maintain a list of types of relationships, and one to maintain a list of relationships between users.

Relationship types

To represent the relationship types in the database, we could use the following database structure, for a `relationship_types` table:

Field	Type	Description
ID	Integer, Auto Increment, Primary Key	A unique ID for the relationship type
Name	Varchar	The name of the relationship type, for example, friend
Plural_name	Varchar	Plural version of the relationship type, for example, friends
Active	Boolean	If this relationship type is active, and should users be able to form such relationships?
Mutual	Boolean	Does this relationship require it to be a mutual connection, or can users connect without the permission of the other?

Relationships

Our relationships table needs to relate two users together, as well as record the type of relationship. Since some relationships require mutual consent, we need to indicate if the non-requesting user accepted the request to connect. The following is a suitable structure for our `relationships` table:

Field	Type	Description
ID	Integer, Primary Key, Auto Increment	A unique ID for the relationship between the two users
Type	ID	The type of relationship (a reference to the `relationship_types` table)
Usera	Integer	The user who initiated the relationship, a relation to the users table
Userb	Integer	The user who usera initiated a relationship with, a relation to the users table
Accepted	Boolean	Indicates if this is a mutual relationship (which is only used if the relationship type is a mutual relationship)

Adding friends

Our users can see other users on the site, either by searching for them or viewing a list of users; from here we can add a link to enable the user to form a relationship. We have a suitable database structure to facilitate this, but we now need functionality to connect our users together.

Forming a relationship

Let's walk through what the process should be for our users to form relationships with each other:

1. View the listing of the user they wish to connect with.
2. Click on a link, or select a relationship type from a list and click on **Submit**.
3. Check for pre-existing relationships.
4. Check if the relationship type selected is active.
5. Create the relationship in the database.

6. If the relationship type is mutual, e-mail the other user an approval request message asking them to confirm the relationship.

7. If the relationship type isn't mutual, e-mail the other user a message informing them that someone has connected with them.

We already have step one set up—the list of members. For step two, we either need a link on the user's name or a list of relationship types (which are links or part of a form submission). Since we have a number of relationship types, let's list the types of relationships in a drop-down list next to each member as part of a form the user can submit to create a relationship of that type.

We should create a relationships model for listing relationships, and while we don't need to do this yet, we could use it to display lists of relationship types too.

A simple method in the model that we can call from the controller to give us a list of relationship types will suffice. The method below can return a database cache of the results provided we instruct it to with the $cache parameter.

```
public function getTypes( $cache=false )
  {
    $sql = "SELECT ID as type_id, name as type_name, plural_name as
      type_plural_name, mutual as type_mutual FROM relationship_types
       WHERE active=1";
    if( $cache == true )
    {
      $cache = $this->registry->getObject('db')->cacheQuery( $sql );
      return $cache;
    }
    else
    {
      $types = array();
      while( $row = $this->registry->getObject('db')->getRows() )
      {
        $types[] = $row;
      }
      return $types;
    }
  }
```

With a list of types at our disposal, we now need to get them and send them to the template, but only if we are logged in. This should be a new method in our members controller, which is called after the paginated list is generated (to prevent it being called when there are no results, and to ensure the code isn't duplicated in the different listing methods in the controller).

```
private function formRelationships()
  {
    if( $this->registry->getObject('authenticate')->isLoggedIn() ==
      true )
    {
      require_once( FRAMEWORK_PATH . 'models/relationships.php');
      $relationships = new Relationships( $this->registry );
      $types = $relationships->getTypes( true );
```

If the user is logged in, then a template bit containing a form is placed next to each member listing, and within there a list of relationship types is dynamically inserted.

```
      $this->registry->getObject('template')->addTemplateBit(
        'form_relationship', 'members/form_relationship.tpl.php');
      $this->registry->getObject('template')->getPage()->addPPTag(
        'relationship_types', array( 'SQL', $types ) );
    }
    else
    {
```

If the user isn't logged in, then we don't want to show them a form, so we set the tag to either nothing, or a placeholder comment.

```
      $this->registry->getObject('template')->getPage()->addTag(
        'form_relationship', '<!-- relationship types dropdown -->'
        );
    }
  }
```

We now need to change our member listing template to have a {form_relationship} tag within the members list loop.

```
<!-- START members -->
  <p><strong>{name}</strong></p>
  <p>Keeper of <strong>{dino_name}</strong> a <strong>{dino_gender}
    {dino_breed}</strong></p>
  {form_relationship}
  <hr />
<!-- END members -->
```

Finally, we need a template that is inserted into the template variable when the user is logged in (`views/default/templates/members/form_relationship.tpl.php`). This has a template loop within it, into which the relationship types are inserted.

```
<form action="relationship/create/{ID}" method="post">
<select name="relationship_type">
<!-- START relationship_types -->
<option value="{type_id}">{type_name}</option>
<!-- END relationship_types -->
</select>
<input type="submit" name="create" value="Connect with {name}" />
</form>
```

Now if we are logged in and take a look at our members list, we see a form next to each member allowing us to connect with them.

This is a good start, but of course if we or a user clicks on the button, nothing is going to happen. We now need to create the relationship. To do this we are going to need a relationship model and a relationship controller.

Relationship model

This needs to encapsulate the data from the relationships table for a specific relationship, as well as delete, approve, and update existing relationships, and create new relationships.

```
<?php
class Relationship{
```

As usual, we start with a number of class variables for the data the model represents to be stored in, and one for our registry too.

```
private $registry;
private $usera;
private $userb;
private $approved;
private $id = 0;
private $type;
```

Our constructor needs to create a new relationship for us, if no ID is passed; otherwise, it needs to look up an existing relationship in the database. If an ID is passed, it simply queries the database and populates the class variables accordingly.

```
/**
 * Relationship constructor
 * @param Registry $registry the registry
 * @param int $id the relationship ID
 * @param int $usera the id of user a
 * @param int $userb the id of user b
 * @param bool $approved if the relationship is approved
 * @param int $type the ID of the relationship type
 * @return void
 */
public function __construct( Registry $registry, $id=0, $usera,
  $userb, $approved=0, $type=0 )
{
  $this->registry = $registry;
  // if no ID is passed, then we want to create a new relationship
  if( $id == 0 )
  {
    $this->createRelationship( $usera, $userb, $approved, $type );
  }
  else
  {
    // if an ID is passed, populate based off that
    $sql = "SELECT * FROM relationships WHERE ID=" . $id;
    $this->registry->getObject('db')->executeQuery( $sql );
    if( $this->registry->getObject('db')->numRows() == 1 )
    {
      $data = $this->registry->getObject('db')->getRows();
      $this->populate( $data['ID'], $data['usera'], $data['userb'],
        $data['type'], $data['approved'] );
    }
  }
}
```

When creating a new relationship, there are a number of checks that must be done first:

- It must check to ensure there isn't a pre-existing relationship; if there is, we can't create a new one!

- If one doesn't exist, then it must check the type of relationship:
  - If the relationship type is "mutual", then we set the approved field to 1, to indicate that the recipient friend must approve the relationship
  - The relationship is then created in the database

```
/**
 * Create a new relationship where one currently doesn't exist,
   if one does exist, populate from that
 */
public function createRelationship( $usera, $userb, $approved=0,
  $type=0 )
{
  // check for pre-existing relationship
  $sql = "SELECT * FROM relationships WHERE (usera={$usera} AND
    userb={$userb}) OR (usera={$userb} AND userb={$userc})";
  $this->registry->getObject('db')->executeQuery( $sql );
  if( $this->registry->getObject('db')->numRows() == 1 )
  {
    // one exists: populate
    $data = $this->registry->getObject('db')->getRows();
   $this->populate( $data['ID'], $data['usera'], $data['userb'],
      $data['type'], $data['approved'] );
  }
  else
  {
    // one doesnt exist
    if( $type != 0 )
    {
      // check type for mutual
    $sql = "SELECT * FROM relationship_types WHERE ID=" . $type;
      $this->registry->getObject('db')->executeQuery( $sql );
      if( $this->registry->getObject('db')->numRows() == 1 )
      {
        $data = $this->registry->getObject('db')->getRows();
        // auto approve non-mutual relationships
        if( $data['mutual'] == 0 )
```

```
            {
                $approved = 1;
            }
        }
    }
    // create the relationsip
    $insert = array();
    $insert['usera'] = $usera;
    $insert['userb'] = $userb;
    $insert['type'] = $type;
    $insert['approved'] = $approved;
    $this->registry->getObject('db')->insertRecords(
        'relationships', $insert );
    $this->id = $this->registry->getObject('db')->lastInsertID();
        }
    }
}
```

The model also requires a setter method to update the approved status of the relationship.

```
/**
 * Approve relationship
 * @return void
 */
public function approveRelationship()
{
    $this->approved = true;
}
```

A delete method is also useful to delete the relationship.

```
/**
 * Delete relationship
 * @return void
 */
public function delete()
{
    $this->registry->getObject('db')->deleteRecords( 'relationships',
        'ID=' . $this->id, 1 );
    $this->id = 0;
}
```

We have our standard save method that either creates a new record or updates an existing one depending on whether the relationship is being created or saved.

```
/**
 * Save relationship
 * @return void
 */
public function save()
{
  $changes = array();
  $changes['usera'] = $this->usera;
  $changes['userb'] = $this->userb;
  $changes['type'] = $this->type;
  $changes['accepted'] = $this->accepted;
  $this->registry->getObject('db')->updateRecords( 'relationships',
    $changes, "ID=" . $this->id );
}

/**
 * Populate relationship object
 * @param int $id the user id
 * @param int $usera user a
 * @param int $userb user b
 * @param int $type the type
 * @param bool $approved
 * @return void
 */
private function populate( $id, $usera, $userb, $type, $approved )
{
  $this->id = $id;
  $this->type = $type;
  $this->usera = $usera;
  $this->userb = $userb;
  $this->approved = $approved;
}
}
?>
```

Relationship controller

With a relationship model in place to make creating, updating, and deleting relationships easy, we need a controller to process the user's request to create, approve, or reject a relationship.

```
private function createRelationship( $userb )
  {
    if( $this->registry->getObject('authenticate')->isLoggedIn() )
    {
```

If we are logged in, then we take our user ID, the ID of the user we wish to connect with, and the relationship type, and create our relationship.

```
$usera = $this->registry->getObject('authenticate')->
  getUser()->getUserID();
$type = intval( $_POST['relationship_type'] );
require_once( FRAMEWORK_PATH . 'models/relationship.php');
$relationship = new Relationship( $this->registry, 0, $usera,
  $userb, $type, 0 );
if( $relationship->isApproved() )
{
```

If the relationship is automatically approved, we can e-mail the user to tell them they have a new connection, and then display a message to the logged in user.

```
    // email the user, tell them they have a new connection
    /**
     * Can you remember how the email sending object works?
     */
    $this->registry->errorPage('Relationship created', 'Thank
     you for connecting!');
}
else
{
```

If the relationship isn't automatically approved, we can e-mail the user to tell them they have a new pending connection, and display a message to the logged in user.

```
    // email the user, tell them they have a new pending
      connection
    /**
     * Can you remember how the email sending object works?
     */
    $this->registry->errorPage('Request sent', 'Thanks for
      requesting to connect!');
  }
}
else
{
```

If the user isn't logged in, we display an error message.

```
$this->registry->errorPage('Please login', 'Only logged in
  members can connect on this site');
// display an error
}
}
```

Now if we click on the **Connect with** button on the relationship form, our relationship is created and we are shown a confirmation message. This could be expanded in the future to use AJAX to display the notification on the previous page, without causing the page to reload.

Mutual relationships—accepting or rejecting a request

If a relationship type is mutual, we need users to be able to see, accept, and reject these requests.

- View list of requests
- Accept: Update the database record
- Reject: Remove the database record

Pending requests

Pending requests can be found by querying the database for relationships where the `userb` column is the current logged in user, and the relationship isn't approved. This query should be in our relationships model.

New model method

Our model method should take parameters for `usera`, `userb`, and `approved`, and if either of the user parameters are set, filter based on those users, returning a cached query.

```
public function getRelationships( $usera, $userb, $approved=0 )
  {
    $sql = "SELECT t.name as type_name, t.plural_name as
```

```
        type_plural_name, uap.name as usera_name, ubp.name as
        userb_name FROM relationships r, relationship_types t,
        profile uap, profile ubp WHERE t.ID=r.type AND
        uap.user_id=r.usera AND ubp.user_id=r.userb AND
        r.accepted={$approved}";
    if( $usera != 0 )
    {
      $sql .= " AND r.usera={$usera} ";
    }
    if( $userb != 0 )
    {
      $sql .= " AND r.userb={$userb} ";
    }
    $cache = $this->registry->getObject('db')->cacheQuery( $sql );
    return $cache;
  }
```

New controller method

The controller needs to check if the user is logged in, include our relationships model, get the pending requests, and display them to the user in the view.

```
    private function pendingRelationships()
    {
      if( $this->registry->getObject('authenticate')->isLoggedIn() )
      {
        require_once( FRAMEWORK_PATH . 'models/relationships.php');
        $relationships = new Relationships( $this->registry );
        $pending = $relationships->getRelationships( 0,
          $this->registry->getObject('authenticate')->
          getUser()->getUserID(), 0 );
        $this->registry->getObject('template')->buildFromTemplates(
          'header.tpl.php', 'friends/pending.tpl.php',
          'footer.tpl.php');
        $this->registry->getObject('template')->getPage()
          ->addTag('pending', array( 'SQL', $pending ) );
      }
      else
      {
        $this->registry->errorPage( 'Please login', 'Please login to
          manage pending connections');
      }
    }
```

The result

Now if we navigate to http://oursite/relationships/pending, we see a list of pending requests!

Pending connections

Michael Peacock wants to be **Jogging buddies** with you.

Approve or Reject this request.

Accepting a pending request

We simply check that we are logged in, that we are permitted to accept the request, then we call the accept method, and save the relationship. This is within the relationship model.

```
private function approveRelationship( $r )
  {
    if( $this->registry->getObject('authenticate')->isLoggedIn() )
    {
      require_once( FRAMEWORK_PATH . 'models/relationship.php');
      $relationship = new Relationship( $this->registry, $r, 0,
        0, 0, 0 );
      if( $relationship->getUserB() == $this->registry->getObject(
        'authenticate')->getUser()->getUserID() )
      {
        // we can approve this!
        $relationship->approveRelationship();
        $relationship->save();
        $this->registry->errorPage( 'Relationship approved', 'Thank
          you for approving the relationship');
      }
      else
      {
        $this->registry->errorPage('Invalid request', 'You are not
          authorized to approve that request');
      }
    }
    else
    {
      $this->registry->errorPage('Please login', 'Please login to
        approve this connection');
    }
  }
```

Rejecting a pending request

To do this we need to check if we are logged in, check if we can reject the request, and delete the relationship record. This is within the relationship model.

```
private function rejectRelationship( $r )
  {
    if( $this->registry->getObject('authenticate')->isLoggedIn() )
    {
      require_once( FRAMEWORK_PATH . 'models/relationship.php');
      $relationship = new Relationship( $this->registry, $r, 0, 0,
        0, 0 );
      if( $relationship->getUserB() == $this->registry->getObject(
        'authenticate')->getUser()->getUserID() )
      {
        // we can reject this!
        $relationship->delete();
        $this->registry->errorPage( 'Relationship rejected', 'Thank
          you for rejecting the relationship');
      }
      else
      {
        $this->registry->errorPage('Invalid request', 'You are not
          authorized to reject that request');
      }
    }
    else
    {
      $this->registry->errorPage('Please login', 'Please login to
        reject this connection');
    }
  }
```

Listing friends

So far thanks to this chapter we already have lists of users and the functionality for our users to build relationships. Now we need to combine these to build a friends list for our users. This would either be a user viewing their own friends, or viewing the friends of another user.

Our friends

To view our own friends, we would visit http://oursite/relationships. This would call our relationship controller's default method, which needs to get our friends and display them on the page.

In our model, we need a query that looks up all relationships where we are either `usera` or `userb`, and depending on which we are, looks up the details of our connection from the other user field. This is done with a simple IF statement within the query.

```
public function getByUser( $user )
  {
    $sql = "SELECT t.plural_name, p.name as users_name, u.ID FROM
      users u, profile p, relationships r, relationship_types t
       WHERE t.ID=r.type AND r.accepted=1 AND (r.usera={$user}
       OR r.userb={$user}) AND IF( r.usera={$user},u.ID=
      r.userb,u.ID=r.usera) AND p.user_id=u.ID";
    $cache = $this->registry->getObject('db')->cacheQuery( $sql );
    return $cache;
  }
```

Our controller simply needs to check we are logged in, call this method, and generate the view.

```
private function myRelationships()
  {
    if( $this->registry->getObject('authenticate')->isLoggedIn() )
    {
      require_once( FRAMEWORK_PATH . 'models/relationships.php');
      $relationships = new Relationships( $this->registry );
      $relationships = $relationships->getByUser( $this->registry
        ->getObject('authenticate')->getUser()->getUserID() );
      $this->registry->getObject('template')->buildFromTemplates(
        'header.tpl.php', 'friends/mine.tpl.php', 'footer.tpl.php');
      $this->registry->getObject('template')->getPage()->addTag(
        'connections', array( 'SQL', $relationships ) );
    }
    else
    {
      $this->registry->errorPage('Please login', 'You need to be a
        logged in user to see your friends');
    }
  }
```

Finally, we need a suitable `friends/mine.tpl.php` template to generate our view. This needs to contain a loop for the connections.

```
<div id="main">
  <div id="rightside">
  </div>
  <div id="content">
```

```
<h1>Your connections</h1>
<p>You are...</p>
<ul>
<!-- START connections -->
<li>{plural_name} with {users_name}</li>
<!-- END connections -->
</ul>
</div>
</div>
```

Now if we visit the URL mentioned earlier in this section, we get our list of connections.

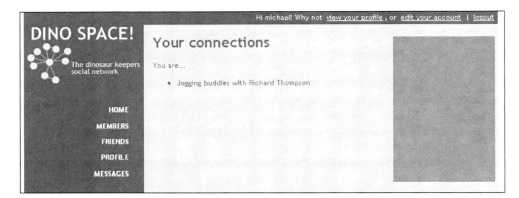

Pagination
This list isn't paginated. Don't forget to use the pagination object to break up big lists.

Their friends

The principles we have used to generate our list of friends can be used to create a friends list for other users, so that once users have viewable profiles, we can click to see their friends list.

Mutual friends

We may have friends in common with some of the users on the site. We should show this as it will help enforce the "network" aspect of our social network, and if the two users aren't connected already, a number of friends in common may encourage them to connect.

Within our friends model, we would want to set if we are viewing our own friends, or friends of another user. If we opted to list the friends of another user, then the model should build a different query to list friends, and mark any which are in common between the two users.

Friends in your profile

Like most social networking sites, we will want to show a selection of a user's connections within their profile. We will discuss this in *Chapter 5, Profiles and Statuses*, as to do this, we need to have a profile controller and a profile model, which we will create in Chapter 5.

Summary

In this chapter, we have looked at allowing our users to invite friends and contacts to participate in the site and connect with them. If their friends are already members of the site, we inform them of this so that they can connect, instead of sending an unnecessary e-mail to the user. We also looked at listing and performing basic searches in our user list, so that users can see other users, to enable them to connect with one another. To facilitate their connections, we set up a number of types of connection, and enabled users to connect to one another, forming online relationships.

Now that we have users on our site who can connect to one another, we should move onto the user profile and status updates, so that users can see more about each other, and see what it is that they are up to.

.

5
Profiles and Statuses

With users able to join Dino Space, and befriend one another, we can now look at displaying detailed information on our users so that they can find out about each other, and be encouraged to befriend each other through the site. Once we have the profiles in place, we can then allow our users to update their own status to inform their friends what they are doing, and allow their friends to post messages and comments onto their profiles.

In this chapter, you will learn:

- How to create a customizable profile for our users
- How to display a random sample of a user's friends on all aspects of the profile
- How to display the user's name and profile picture on all aspects of their profile
- How to allow users to update their status as well as:
  - Allowing others to comment on statuses
  - Allowing others to indicate whether they like or dislike a status

User profiles

When our users signed up to the site, they provided some profile information that they wanted to form a part of their user profile. Obviously, not all of this information is intended for their profile, such as their password, e-mail address, and perhaps their date of birth depending on the privacy policy of the site. All of the information related to their pet dinosaur, however, would be for their profile.

Extendable profile

If we look at most social networking websites, their user profiles are generally multi-purpose; they show a stream of status updates, often with comments and additional features too; they show general information about the user, and they often show photographs of, or taken by, the user. As the social network grows, the profiles generally do more and more, often with sections displaying information from third-party applications.

With this in mind, we need to build an extendable profile system, which allows us to easily add-in new features as and when they are developed, and keeps the code for features we are going to develop, such as profile information, photographs, and user updates, separate.

Profile controller

The easiest way for us to separate the aspects of the profile, is through the profile controller. The controller should act in a way similar to our main `index.php` file, passing control to additional controllers such as a profile information controller, or a profile statuses controller. This also means we can simply slot in new child controllers to the profile controller in the future, bringing new features to the profile.

Below we have the code for the `controllers/profile/controller.php` file, which as you can see, depending on the user's request, delegates control to either the profile information controller or the profile statuses controller. A switch statement is used to process the first part of the user's request, to work out what aspect of the profile they are trying to view. The function which is then called includes the controller file and instantiates the controller object.

```php
<?php

/**
 * Profile controller
 * Delegates control to profile controllers to seperate the distinct
     profile features
 */
class Profilecontroller {
```

The constructor calls an appropriate delegator method depending on the structure of the URL.

```php
    /**
     * Constructor
     * @param Object $registry the registry
```

```
 * @param bool $directCall - are we directly accessing this
   controller?
 */
public function __construct( $registry, $directCall=true )
{
   $this->registry = $registry;

   $urlBits = $this->registry->getObject('url')->getURLBits();
     switch( $urlBits[1] )
   {
      case 'view':
         $this->staticContentDelegator( intval( $urlBits[2] ) );
         break;
      case 'statuses':
         $this->statusesDelegator( intval( $urlBits[2] ) );
         break;
      default:
         $this->profileError();
         break;
   }
}
```

The delegator methods simply require the appropriate sub-controller, and instantiate it, passing control to it.

```
/**
 * Delegate control to the static content profile controller
 * @param int $user the user whose profile we are viewing
 * @return void
 */
private function staticContentDelegator( $user )
{
   require_once( FRAMEWORK_PATH . 'controllers/profile/
     profileinformationcontroller.php' );
   $sc = new Profileinformationcontroller( $this->registry, true,
     $user );
}

/**
 * Delegate control to the statuses profile controller
 * @param int $user the user whose profile we are viewing
 * @return void
 */
private function statusesDelegator( $user )
{
```

```
        require_once( FRAMEWORK_PATH . 'controllers/profile/
           profilestatusescontroller.php' );
        $sc = new Profilestatusescontroller( $this->registry, true,
           $user );
    }
```

If the user tried to access a sub-controller that doesn't exist, we would display an error.

```
    /**
     * Display an error - you cannot access profiles simply by visiting
        /profile/ !
     * @return void
     */
    private function profileError()
    {
        $this->registry->errorPage( 'Sorry, an error has occured',
           'The link you followed was invalid, please try again');
    }


}

?>
```

Core shared information

Although the user's profile is going to be broken down into different areas, which are accessed through different links showing different pages, there will be some information that should be common throughout all of these aspects, such as:

- The name of the user whose profile we are viewing
- Their photograph
- A sample of their friends

This core shared information is something we can generate from within the profile controller, which is called regardless of which sub controller control is subsequently delegated to. This information can be generated and sent to the template handler ready for when the page is outputted to the user's browser.

Name, ID, and photograph

To get the name, ID, and photograph of a user, we are going to require a profile model to access and manage the data from a user's profile. We are also going to need to add a new field to our profile table, one for a user's profile picture (as we didn't consider that when the user signed up to Dino Space). While we are creating this model, we should also create a field in the database for the users' biography information, for them to tell everyone about themselves.

Profile model

We need to create a profile model (`models/profile.php`), which we will need to do the following things:

- Populate its fields based on a user's profile in the database
- Update its fields based on changes to a user's profile
- Update the corresponding database record for the profile, provided the user updating the profile is either an administrator or the user themselves
- Generate template tags for the data within
- Return certain information on demand — for us, we want to get the user's name and the user's photograph

The code for such a model is as follows:

```php
<?php

/**
 * Profile model
 */
class Profile{

    /**
     * The registry
     */
    private $registry;

    /**
     * Profile ID
     */
    private $id;

    /**
     * Fields which can be saved by the save() method
     */
    private $savable_profile_fields = array( 'name', 'dino_name',
        'dino_dob', 'dino_breed', 'dino_gender', 'photo', 'bio'  );

    /**
     * Users ID
     */
    private $user_id;

    /**
```

```
    * Users name
    */
   private $name;

   /**
    * Dinosaurs name
    */
   private $dino_name;

   /**
    * Dinosaurs Date of Birth
    */
   private $dino_dob;

   /**
    * Dinosaurs breed
    */
   private $dino_breed;

   /**
    * Dinosaurs gender
    */
   private $dino_gender;

 /**
    * Users bio
    */
   private $bio;


   /**
    * Users photograph
    */
   private $photo;
```

Upon construction, if an ID has been passed, the database should be queried, and the fields of the object populated with the result from the query.

```
   /**
    * Profile constructor
    * @param Registry $registry the registry
    * @param int $id the profile ID
    * @return void
    */
   public function __construct( Registry $registry, $id=0 )
   {
       $this->registry = $registry;
```

```
        if( $id != 0 )
        {
            $this->id = $id;
            // if an ID is passed, populate based off that
            $sql = "SELECT * FROM profile WHERE user_id=" . $this->id;
            $this->registry->getObject('db')->executeQuery( $sql );
            if( $this->registry->getObject('db')->numRows() == 1 )
            {
                $data = $this->registry->getObject('db')->getRows();
                // populate our fields
                foreach( $data as $key => $value )
                {
                    $this->$key = $value;
                }
            }

        }
    }
```

As usual, we have a number of setter methods:

```
    /**
     * Sets the users name
     * @param String $name
     * @return void
     */
    public function setName( $name )
    {
        $this->name = $name;
    }

    /**
     * Sets the dinosaurs name
     * @param String $name the name
     * @return void
     */
    public function setDinoName( $name )
    {
        $this->dino_name = $name;
    }

    /**
     * Sets the users bio
     * @param String $bio the bio
     * @return void
```

```
   */
public function setBio( $bio )
{
    $this->bio = $bio;
}
```

The dinosaur date of birth setter method also accepts a formatted parameter, which indicates that the date being passed has already been formatted appropriately, or that it hasn't and additional processing is necessary.

```
/**
 * Set the dinosaurs data of birth
 * @param String $dob the date of birth
 * @param boolean $formatted - indicates if the controller has
     formatted the dob, or if we need to do it here
 */
public function setDinoDOB( $dob, $formatted=true )
{
    if( $formatted == true )
    {
        $this->dino_dob = $dob;
    }
    else
    {
        $temp = explode('/', $dob );
        $this->dob = $temp[2].'-'.$temp[1].'-'.$temp[0];
    }
}

/**
 * Sets the breed of the users dinosaur
 * @param String $breed
 * return void
 */
public function setDinoBreed( $breed )
{
    $this->dino_breed = $breed;
}

/**
 * Set the gender of the users dinosaur
 * @param String $gender the gender
 * @param boolean $checked - indicates if the controller has
     validated the gender, or if we need to do it
 * @return void
```

```
    */
    public function setDinoGender( $gender, $checked=true )
    {
        if( $checked == true )
        {
            $this->dino_gender = $gender;
        }
        else
        {
            $genders = array();
            if( in_array( $gender, $genders ) )
            {
                $this->dino_gender = $gender;
            }
        }
    }


    /**
     * Sets the users profile picture
     * @param String photo name
     * @return void
     */
    public function setPhoto( $photo )
    {
        $this->photo = $photo;
    }
```

If the user or administrator saves the profile, we take each of the values from the savable profile fields, add them to an update array, and then pass this to the database object's updateRecords method to save the profile, provided that the user is either the administrator or changing their own profile.

```
    /**
     * Save the user profile
     * @return bool
     */
    public function save()
    {
        // handle the updating of a profile
        if( $registry->getObject('authenticate')->isLoggedIn() &&
            ( $registry->getObject('authenticate')->getUser()-
            >getUserID() ==   $this->id || $registry-
            >getObject('authenticate')->getUser()->isAdmin() == true  ) )
        {
            // we are either the user whose profile this is, or we are
                the administrator
```

```
$changes = array();
foreach( $this->saveable_profile_fields as $field )
{
    $changes[ $field ] = $this->$field;
}
$this->registry->getObject('db')->updateRecords( 'profile',
  $changes, 'user_id=' . $this->id );
if( $this->registry->getObject('db')->affectedRows() == 1 )
{
    return true;
}
else
{
    return false;
}
}
else
{
    return false;
}
}
```

Next, we have a method to convert the data from the model into template tags to make it easy to populate the view:

```
/**
 * Convert the users profile data to template tags
 * @param String $prefix prefix for the template tags
 * @return void
 */
public function toTags( $prefix='' )
{
    foreach( $this as $field => $data )
    {
        if( ! is_object( $data ) && ! is_array( $data ) )
        {
            $this->registry->getObject('template')->getPage()-
                >addTag( $prefix.$field, $data );
        }
    }
}
```

Finally, we have a number of getter methods to retrieve data from the model:

```
/**
 * Get the users name
 * @return String
 */
public function getName()
{
    return $this->name;
}

/**
 * Get the users photograph
 * @return String
 */
public function getPhoto()
{
    return $this->photo;
}

/**
 * Get the users ID
 * @return int
 */
public function getID()
{
    return $this->user_id;
}

}

?>
```

Sample of friends

Our relationships model (`models/relationships.php`) contains a method to return a cached query of a user's friends and contacts. We can extend this method to, if we request, return a random sample of these friends. We can do this by adding two additional parameters to the method, one to indicate if the results should be random, and another to limit the result set, and by checking the values of these parameters and modifying the query appropriately, as highlighted in the code below:

```
/**
 * Get relationships by user
 * @param int $user the user whose relationships we wish to list
 * @param boolean $obr should we randomly order the results?
 * @param int $limit should we limit the results? ( 0 means no, > 0
   means limit to $limit )
 * @return int the query cache ID
```

```
    */
    public function getByUser( $user, $obr=false, $limit=0 )
    {
        // the standard get by user query
        $sql = "SELECT t.plural_name, p.name as users_name, u.ID FROM users
            u, profile p, relationships r, relationship_types t WHERE t.ID=r.
            type AND r.accepted=1 AND (r.usera={$user} OR r.userb={$user})
            AND IF( r.usera={$user},u.ID=r.userb,u.ID=r.usera)
            AND p.user_id=u.ID";
        // if we are ordering by random
        if( $obr == true )
        {
            $sql .= " ORDER BY RAND() ";
        }
        // if we are limiting
        if( $limit != 0 )
        {
            $sql .= " LIMIT " . $limit;
        }
        // cache and return
        $cache = $this->registry->getObject('db')->cacheQuery( $sql );
        return $cache;
    }
```

Currently, this query will give us a list of friend's names and the type of relationship the user has with them. We may wish to extend this in the future to pull in profile pictures and other information to make the sample of friends more interesting to the user viewing the profile.

Pulling the core shared information together

By using the relationships model and the profile model, we can get the core shared information we need. We now need a method in our profile controller (`controllers/profile/controller.php`) to get the data, and assign it to appropriate template variables.

```
    /**
     * Set common template tags for all profile aspects
     * @param int $user the user id
     * @return void
     */
    private function commonTemplateTags( $user )
    {
        // get a random sample of 6 friends.
        require_once( FRAMEWORK_PATH . 'models/relationships.php' );
        $relationships = new Relationships( $this->registry );
```

```
$cache = $relationships->getByUser( $user, true, 6 );
$this->registry->getObject('template')->getPage()->addTag(
   'profile_friends_sample', array( 'SQL', $cache ) );

// get the name and photo of the user
require_once( FRAMEWORK_PATH . 'models/profile.php' );
$profile = new Profile( $this->registry, $user );
$name = $profile->getName();
$uid = $profile->getID();
$photo = $profile->getPhoto();
$this->registry->getObject('template')->getPage()->addTag(
   'profile_name', $name );
$this->registry->getObject('template')->getPage()->addTag(
   'profile_photo', $photo );
$this->registry->getObject('template')->getPage()->addTag( 'profile_
user_id', $uid );
// clear the profile
$profile = "";
}
```

This method should be called before we pass control to the various other controllers.

Static profile

Let us now look at providing functionality for the user's "static profile", that is, the information about them, interests, hobbies, facts, and other information that is unlikely to change on a regular basis.

Our profile model that we created earlier in the chapter should make accessing and displaying profile information much easier.

Viewing the profile

What do we need to do to facilitate viewing a user's profile:

- We need to put a profile link in the members list, and the member's search results pages, so users can actually get to these profiles!

- We need to create a profile information controller, which:
    ° Gets profile data from the profile model, and sends it to the template engine

- We need to create a template, which includes provisions for both profile information, and the common profile information

Profile link

The link to view a user's profile will simply be: `profile/view/userid,`. This enacts the profile controller, which in turn passes control to the profile information controller. We need to add this link to the following templates we already have:

- `Views/default/templates/members/list.tpl.php`
- `Views/default/templates/members/search.tpl.php`

The link is shown below:

```
<h1>DINO SPACE! Members List {letter}</h1>
<!-- START members -->
<p><strong><a href="profile/view/{ID}">{name}</a></strong></p>
<p>Keeper of <strong>{dino_name}</strong> a <strong>{dino_gender}
{dino_breed}</strong></p>
{form_relationship}
<hr />
<!-- END members -->
```

Controller

The profile information controller (`controllers/profile/profileinformationcontroller.php`) needs to communicate with the model, to get the data for the profile, and have the data assigned to template variables. We already have a method in the controller to do this, so it should be a fairly trivial task: include the model, and call the `toTags` method to push the profile information to template tags, as highlighted in the code below:

```php
<?php

/**
 * Profile information controller
 */
class Profileinformationcontroller {

    /**
     * Constructor
     * @param Registry $registry
     * @param int $user the user id
     * @return void
     */
    public function __construct( $registry, $user )
    {
        $this->registry = $registry;
        $this->viewProfile( $user );
```

```
    }

    /**
     * View a users profile information
     * @param int $user the user id
     * @return void
     */
    private function viewProfile( $user )
    {
        // load the template
        $this->registry->getObject('template')->buildFromTemplates(
            'header.tpl.php', 'profile/information/view.tpl.php', 'footer.
            tpl.php' );
        // get all the profile information, and send it to the template
        require_once( FRAMEWORK_PATH . 'models/profile.php' );
        $profile = new Profile( $this->registry, $user );
        $profile->toTags( 'p_' );
    }

}

?>
```

Template

The template for this aspect of the profile is shown below (`views/default/
templates/profile/information/view.tpl.php`); the highlighted aspects
show the common template information shared by all aspects of the profile
(including aspects we may add in the future).

```
<div id="main">

<div id="rightside">
    <div style="text-align:center; padding-top: 5px;">
        <img src="uploads/profile/{profile_photo}" />
    </div>
    <div style="padding: 5px;">
        <h2>Friends</h2>
        <ul>
            <!-- START profile_friends_sample -->
            <li><a href="profile/view/{ID}">{users_name}</a></li>
            <!-- END profile_friends_sample -->
            <li><a href="relationships/all/{profile_user_id}">View all</
                a></li>
            <li><a href="relationships/mutual/{profile_user_id}">View
                mutual friends</a></li>
```

```
        </ul>
      <h2>Rest of my profile</h2>
        <ul>
            <li><a href="profile/statuses/{ID}">Status updates</a></li>
        </ul>
      </div>
   </div>

   <div id="content"><h1>{profile_name}</h1>
      <p>{p_bio}</p>
      <h2>My Dinosaur</h2>
      <table>
         <tr>
            <th>Name</th>
            <td>{p_dino_name}</td>
         </tr>
         <tr>
            <th>DOB</th>
            <td>{p_dino_dob}</td>
         </tr>
         <tr>
            <th>Breed</th>
            <td>{p_dino_breed}</td>
         </tr>
         <tr>
            <th>Gender</th>
            <td>{p_dino_gender}</td>
         </tr>

      </table>
   </div>
   </div>
```

In action

If we now visit a user's profile (`http://localhost/folder-containing-socialnetwork/profile/view/1`), we see the user's profile on the screen as shown in the following screenshot:

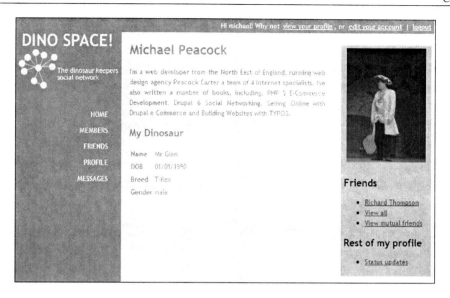

Relationships—some improvements

At present, our relationships controller is only set to either list our relationships with other users, or pending relationship requests. It isn't set up to show all of the contacts of a user, or all of the mutual contacts we have in common with a user. Let's extend our relationships controller to facilitate these; after all, we have placed a link to them on our profile pages.

All contacts

To get a list of all the contacts of a user, we simply require the relationships model, and call the `getRelationships` method, passing the user whose profile we were viewing:

```
/**
 * View all users connections
 * @param int $user
 * @return void
 */
private function viewAll( $user )
{
    if( $this->registry->getObject('authenticate')->isLoggedIn() )
    {
        require_once( FRAMEWORK_PATH . 'models/relationships.php');
        $relationships = new Relationships( $this->registry );
        $all = $relationships->getByUser( $user, false, 0 );
        $this->registry->getObject('template')-
```

```
            >buildFromTemplates('header.tpl.php', 'friends/all.tpl.php',
            'footer.tpl.php');
            $this->registry->getObject('template')->getPage()->addTag('all',
               array( 'SQL', $all ) );
            require_once( FRAMEWORK_PATH . 'models/profile.php');
            $p = new Profile( $this->registry, $user );
            $name = $p->getName();
            $this->registry->getObject('template')->getPage()->addTag(
               'connecting_name', $name );

        }
        else
        {
            $this->registry->errorPage( 'Please login', 'Please login to
               view a users connections');
        }
    }
}
```

Template

We need a template file called `views/default/templates/friends/all.tpl.php` to act as the template for viewing all of a user's friends.

```
    <div id="main">

       <div id="rightside">
       </div>

       <div id="content">
          <h1>Connections of {connecting_name}</h1>
          <ul>
          <!-- START all -->
          <li>{plural_name} with {users_name}</p>
          <!-- END all -->
          </ul>
       </div>

    </div>
```

In action

Now, if we click the view all contacts link on a user's profile, we are shown a list of all of their contacts as shown in the following screenshot:

Editing the profile

Again, our model will make things much easier for us here, as it allows us to get all of the information from the profile (to populate the edit form fields) and includes provisions for saving changes to a profile. It won't, however, deal with a user requesting to change their password or update their e-mail address; we will discuss that separately.

Controller additions

Our controller needs to have a new method added to display an edit page, and process the form submission when a user edits their profile. This will then interact with the model, calling the save method to save the profile changes in the database.

Uploading a photograph—an image handler

As we are going to be uploading and scaling a user's photograph to act as their profile picture, we should consider developing an image handler class, which can process uploads, save images, and deal with resizing, keeping all of our image related code in a single place.

Following is the code for such a file (`lib/images/imagemanager.class.php`). Some important aspects are highlighted and discussed within.

```php
<?php

/**
 * Image manager class
 * @author Michael Peacock
 */
class Imagemanager
{
    private $type = '';
```

We define extensions and file types that we wish to allow users to upload.

```php
private $uploadExtentions = array( 'png', 'jpg', 'jpeg', 'gif' );
private $uploadTypes = array( 'image/gif', 'image/jpg', 'image/
 jpeg', 'image/pjpeg', 'image/png' );
private $image;
private $name;

public function __construct(){}
```

If we load the image from the file system, we need to know the type of image it is, so we can use the correct `imagecreate` function, we can get the type of image from the `getimagesize` function. . This requires the GD image library to be enabled with PHP.

```php
/**
 * Load image from local file system
 * @param String $filepath
 * @return void
 */
public function loadFromFile( $filepath )
{
    $info = getimagesize( $filepath );
    $this->type = $info[2];
    if( $this->type == IMAGETYPE_JPEG )
    {
        $this->image = imagecreatefromjpeg($filepath);
    }
     elseif( $this->type == IMAGETYPE_GIF )
     {
        $this->image = imagecreatefromgif($filepath);
     }
     elseif( $this->type == IMAGETYPE_PNG )
     {
        $this->image = imagecreatefrompng($filepath);
     }
}
```

This class can also wrap the `imagesx` and `imagesy` functions to provide a nice way to get the width and height of the image.

```php
/**
 * Get the image width
 * @return int
 */
public function getWidth()
```

```
{
    return imagesx($this->image);
}

/**
 * Get the height of the image
 * @return int
 */
public function getHeight()
{
    return imagesy($this->image);
}
```

Using `imagecopyresampled`, we can resize the image.

 Imagecopyresampled allows us to resize the image without distorting the image, whereas `imagecopyresized` does result in some distortion.

```
/**
 * Resize the image
 * @param int $x width
 * @param int $y height
 * @return void
 */
public function resize( $x, $y )
{
    $new = imagecreatetruecolor($x, $y);
    imagecopyresampled($new, $this->image, 0, 0, 0, 0, $x, $y,
        $this->getWidth(), $this->getHeight());
        $this->image = $new;
}
```

In most cases, we, or the user, won't know the exact dimensions to resize an image to. To get around this, we can resize one dimension based on a set amount (for example , a thumbnail width) and scale the other dimension to match.

```
/**
 * Resize the image, scaling the width, based on a new height
 * @param int $height
 * @return void
 */
public function resizeScaleWidth( $height )
```

```
    {
        $width = $this->getWidth() * ( $height / $this->getHeight() );
        $this->resize( $width, $height );
    }

    /**
     * Resize the image, scaling the height, based on a new width
     * @param int $width
     * @return void
     */
    public function resizeScaleHeight( $width )
    {
        $height = $this->getHeight() * ( $width / $this->getWidth() );
        $this->resize( $width, $height );
    }
```

Similar to the two methods above, we can also scale both dimensions
by a percentage.

```
    /**
     * Scale an image
     * @param int $percentage
     * @return void
     */
    public function scale( $percentage )
    {
        $width = $this->getWidth() * $percentage / 100;
        $height = $this->getheight() * $percentage / 100;
        $this->resize( $width, $height );
    }
```

The display method can be used to display the image in the user's browser.

```
    /**
     * Display the image to the browser - called before output is sent,
     *   exit() should be called straight after.
     * @return void
     */
    public function display()
    {
        $type = '';
        if( $this->type == IMAGETYPE_JPEG )
        {
            $type = 'image/jpeg';
        }
        elseif( $this->type == IMAGETYPE_GIF )
```

```
    {
        $type = 'image/gif';
    }
    elseif( $this->type == IMAGETYPE_PNG )
    {
        $type = 'image/png';
    }

    header('Content-Type: ' . $type );

    if( $this->type == IMAGETYPE_JPEG )
    {
        imagejpeg( $this->image );
    }
    elseif( $this->type == IMAGETYPE_GIF )
    {
        imagegif( $this->image );
    }
    elseif( $this->type == IMAGETYPE_PNG )
    {
        imagepng( $this->image );
    }

}
```

The most useful aspect for our current requirements is this loadFromPost method; the postfield is passed so the method can check to see if a file has been uploaded, checks the type of file, and then uploads it to the moveto location.

```
/**
 * Load image from postdata
 * @param String $postfield the field the image was uploaded via
 * @param String $moveto the location for the upload
 * @param String $name_prefix a prefix for the filename
 * @return boolean
 */
public function loadFromPost( $postfield, $moveto, $name_prefix=''
)
{
    if( is_uploaded_file( $_FILES[ $postfield ]['tmp_name'] ) )
    {
        $i = strrpos( $_FILES[ $postfield ]['name'], '.');
        if (! $i )
        {
            //'no extention';
```

```
                            return false;
            }
             else
             {
                    $l = strlen(  $_FILES[ $postfield ]['name'] ) - $i;
                    $ext = strtolower ( substr(  $_FILES[ $postfield ]
                      ['name'], $i+1, $l ) );

                    if( in_array( $ext, $this->uploadExtentions ) )
                    {
                       if( in_array( $_FILES[ $postfield ]['type'], $this-
                         >uploadTypes ) )
                       {

                            $name = str_replace( ' ', '', $_FILES[
                              $postfield ]['name'] );
                            $this->name = $name_prefix . $name;
                            $path = $moveto . $name_prefix.$name;
                          move_uploaded_file( $_FILES[ $postfield ]
                            ['tmp_name'] , $path );
                            $this->loadFromFile( $path );
                            return true;

                       }
                       else
                       {
                          // 'invalid type';
                          return false;
                       }
                    }
                    else
                    {
                       // 'invalid extention';
                       return false;
                    }
             }

        }
        else
        {
           // 'not uploaded file';
           return false;
        }
    }
```

```
/**
 * Get the image name
 * @return String
 */
public function getName()
{
    return $this->name;
}
```

When we have finished processing an image, the save method finds the appropriate image function for the format of the image, and then saves the file.

```
/**
 * Save changes to an image e.g. after resize
 * @param String $location location of image
 * @param String $type type of the image
 * @param int $quality image quality /100
 * @return void
 */
public function save( $location, $type='', $quality=100 )
{
    $type = ( $type == '' ) ? $this->type : $type;

    if( $type == IMAGETYPE_JPEG )
    {
        imagejpeg( $this->image, $location, $quality);
    }
    elseif( $type == IMAGETYPE_GIF )
    {
        imagegif( $this->image, $location );
    }
    elseif( $type == IMAGETYPE_PNG )
    {
        imagepng( $this->image, $location );
    }
}
}

?>
```

Back to the controller

Now, we have an excellent class available to process our profile image uploads, which should make things much easier for us; let's look at actually allowing the user to edit their profile page, with a new function in our profile information controller (`controllers/profile/profileinformationcontroller.php`).

```
/**
 * Edit your profile
 * @return void
 */
private function editProfile()
{
    if ( $this->registry->getObject('authenticate')->isLoggedIn() ==
        true )
    {
```

We first check that the user is logged into the site, and if they are, we get their user ID.

```
$user = $this->registry->getObject('authenticate')->getUser()-
    >getUserID();
if( isset( $_POST ) && count( $_POST ) > 0 )
{
```

If the edit form has been submitted, include the model and set the new values.

```
// edit form submitted
$profile = new Profile( $this->registry, $user );
$profile->setBio( $this->registry->getObject('db')-
    >sanitizeData( $_POST['bio'] ) );
$profile->setName( $this->registry->getObject('db')-
    >sanitizeData( $_POST['name'] ) );
$profile->setDinoName( $this->registry->getObject('db')-
    >sanitizeData( $_POST['dino_name'] ) );
$profile->setDinoBreed( $this->registry->getObject('db')-
    >sanitizeData( $_POST['dino_breed'] ) );
$profile->setDinoGender( $this->registry->getObject('db')-
    >sanitizeData( $_POST['dino_gender'] ), false );
$profile->setDinoDOB( $this->registry->getObject('db')-
    >sanitizeData( $_POST['dino_dob'] ), false );
```

If a profile picture was uploaded, call the image manager, check that the image is an image, upload it, resize it, and set the profile picture field.

```
if( isset( $_POST['profile_picture'] ) )
{
    require_once( FRAMEWORK_PATH . 'lib/images/imagemanager.
        class.php' );
```

```
$im = new Imagemanager();
$im->loadFromPost( 'profile_picture', $this->registry-
    >getSetting('uploads_path') .'profile/', time() );
if( $im == true )
{
    $im->resizeScaleHeight( 150 );
    $im->save( $this->registry->getSetting('uploads_path')
      .'profile/' . $im->getName() );
    $profile->setPhoto( $im->getName() );
}
}
```

We then save the profile, and redirect the user back to the edit page after informing them that the profile has been saved.

```
$profile->save();
$this->registry->redirectUser( array('profile', 'view',
    'edit' ), 'Profile saved', 'The changes to your profile
    have been saved', false );
}
else
{
```

If the user hasn't submitted the edit form, show them the form and populate it with profile data from the profile model.

```
// show the edit form
$this->registry->getObject('template')->buildFromTemplates(
    'header.tpl.php', 'profile/information/edit.tpl.php',
    'footer.tpl.php' );
// get the profile information to pre-populate the form
    fields
require_once( FRAMEWORK_PATH . 'models/profile.php' );
$profile = new Profile( $this->registry, $user );
$profile->toTags( 'p_' );
}
}
else
{
```

If the user isn't logged in, they shouldn't be trying to edit a profile, so show them an error message.

```
$this->registry->errorPage('Please login', 'You need to be
    logged in to edit your profile');
}
}
```

We also need a switch statement at the top of our profile information controller, to either call the `viewProfile` method or the `editProfile` method, depending on the user's request.

```
$urlBits = $this->registry->getObject('url')->getURLBits();
    if( isset( $urlBits[3] ) )
    {
        switch( $urlBits[3] )
        {
            case 'edit':
                $this->editProfile();
                break;
            default:
                $this->viewProfile( $user );
                break;
        }
    }
    else
    {
        $this->viewProfile( $user );
    }
```

Template

Next, we need a template file for our edit page. This needs to contain a form, with template variables as the values for the form fields, to be pre-populated with the user's profile information.

The template file

The template file should be similar to that of the view profile template, as the name, picture, and selection of friends will still be generated and inserted into the view. The code for the template (`views/default/templates/profile/information/edit.tpl.php`) is below, with the form highlighted:

```
<div id="main">

    <div id="rightside">
        <div style="text-align:center; padding-top: 5px;">
            <img src="uploads/profile/{profile_photo}" />
        </div>
        <div style="padding: 5px;">
            <h2>Friends</h2>
            <ul>
                <!-- START profile_friends_sample -->
                <li><a href="profile/view/{ID}">{users_name}</a></li>
                <!-- END profile_friends_sample -->
```

```
            <li><a href="relationships/all/{p_user_id}">View all</a>
            </li>
            <li><a href="relationships/mutual/{p_user_id}">View mutual
            friends</a></li>
        </ul>
        <h2>Rest of my profile</h2>
        <ul>
            <li><a href="profile/statuses/{ID}">Status updates</a>
            </li>
        </ul>
    </div>
</div>

<div id="content"><h1>{profile_name}: Edit Profile</h1>
    <form action="profile/view/{p_user_id}/edit" method="post"
    enctype="multipart/form-data">
    <label for="name">Name</label><br />
    <input type="text" id="name" name="name" value="{p_name}"
    /><br />
    <label for="profile_picture">Photograph</label> <br />
    <input type="file" id="profile_picture" name="profile_
    picture" />
    <br />
    <label for="bio">Biography</label>
    <textarea id="bio" name="bio" cols="40" rows="6">{p_bio}</
    textarea>
    <label for="dino_name">Dinosaur Name</label><br />
    <input type="text" id="dino_name" name="dino_name" value="
    {p_dino_name}" /><br />
    <label for="dino_breed">Dinosaur Breed</label><br />
    <input type="text" id="dino_breed" name="dino_breed"
    value="{p_dino_breed}" /><br />
    <label for="dino_dob">Dinosaur Date of Birth</label><br />
    <input type="text" id="dino_dob" class="selectdate"
    name="dino_dob" value="{p_dino_dob}" /><br />
    <label for="dino_gender">Dinosaur Gender</label><br />
    <select id="dino_gender" name="dino_gender">
        <option value="">Please select</option>
        <option value="male">Male</option>
        <option value="female">Female</option>
    </select>
    <br />
    <input type="submit" id="" name="" value="Save profile" />
    </form>

</div>
</div>
```

Datepicker

The date format is something users are likely to get confused with, being unsure of how to format the date correctly or putting in incorrect details. To make this easier, we should use the jQuery datepicker plugin, which can take a textbox, and present the user with a nice calendar popup to select the date from.

We will need jQuery, jQuery UI, and the datepicker plugin, which can be downloaded from: `http://jqueryui.com/download`.

With the files downloaded and placed suitably within our framework, we need to edit our `views/default/templates/header.tpl.php` file to include the files, and assign certain textboxes with the datepicker plugin. The code below shows referencing the new files, and some JavaScript that links textboxes with a class of `selectdate` to the datepicker plugin:

```
<link type="text/css" href="external/ui-lightness/jquery-ui-
  1.7.1.custom.css" rel="stylesheet" />
  <script type="text/javascript" src="external/jquery-1.3.2.min.
    js"></script>
  <script type="text/javascript" src="external/jquery-ui-
    1.7.2.custom.min.js"></script>
  <script type="text/javascript">
    $(function() {
      $('.selectdate').datepicker({
        numberOfMonths: 1,
        showButtonPanel: false
      });
      $('.selectdate').datepicker('option', 'dateFormat', 'dd/mm/
        yy');

    });
  </script>
```

In action

If we now take a look at the edit screen, we have our form as shown in the following screenshot:

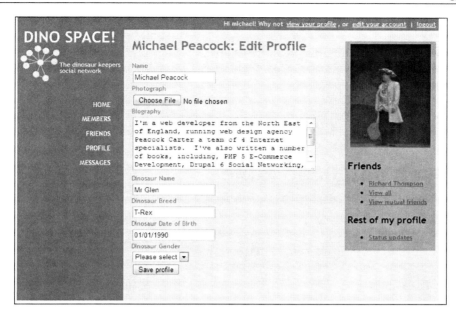

And if we click the date, a datepicker is displayed as shown in the following screenshot:

Statuses

If we assume for the moment that statuses are not the only things we would want to display on our users profiles, this can help us plan out this feature more appropriately.

Because of this, we would want to have a single database table that keeps a central record of all the different types of content, and the profiles it relates to.

Statuses database table

Below is a suitable structure for the statuses database table.

Field	Type	Description
ID	Integer, Primary Key, Auto-increment	ID of the status
Update	Longtext	The content of the update
Type	Integer	Reference to the status types table
Creator	Integer	The ID of the poster
Created	Timestamp	Time status was posted
Profile	Integer	Profile the status was posted on
Approved	Boolean	If the status is approved or notIf the status is approved or not

Statuses types database table

We also need a status types table, to relate to the type field, giving a name of the type of status update (for example, if it is a posted URL, an image, and so on), and a reference for the template bit to be used for that status update (we will discuss that shortly).

Field	Type	Description
ID	Integer, Primary Key, Auto-increment	ID of the status type
Type_name	Varchar	The name of the type of status
Type_reference	Varchar	A machine readable name for the type, used as the file name of template bits (that is, no spaces or punctuation)
Active	Boolean	Indicates whether the status type is active or not

Different types of status

Each type of profile update, if appropriate, would have its own database table to store data specific to that type of update. For instance, if the user posted a URL we would use the status text as a description of the URL and include the user's comment about it, but we would also want to store the URL itself; this is where we would use another table to extend the status. This keeps a central table of statuses that we can query to provide our status list, while allowing us to have specialist tables to contain only the data required for different types of status.

We will look into different types of status, in *Chapter 8, Statuses — Other Media*.

Template improvements

Depending on posted comments, messages, and statuses on a user's profile, we may need to insert different template bits to the page, for instance one for a status update, one for a public post, one for an image posted on the profile and so on. And, for each of these, we may need to display a number of comments, a number of likes, and a number of dislikes.

To facilitate this, we would need to upgrade our template system. For instance, the first stage would be to create a template loop of updates to a user's profile, then each of these would require a new template bit to be inserted within. However, since we may have more than one of each type, for example, three status updates, the template bit would need to have a unique template tag within there, for example, status-message-1, status-message-2. Otherwise, the three statuses will all be the same. We need to allow the template system to dynamically update some of its template variables on the fly, as it is inserted into the page.

To do this, we simply add a new optional parameter to the addTemplateBit method, which is an array of template variables assigned specifically with that instance of the template bit.

This new parameter, $replacements, needs to be passed to the appropriate addTemplateBit method in the page object too.

```
/**
 * Add a template bit from a view to our page
 * @param String $tag the tag where we insert the template e.g.
 {hello}
 * @param String $bit the template bit (path to file, or just the
 filename)
 * @param Array $replacements template bit specific replacements
 * @return void
 */
```

```
public function addTemplateBit( $tag, $bit, $replacements=array() )
{
   if( strpos( $bit, 'views/' ) === false )
   {
       $bit = 'views/' . $this->registry->getSetting('view') . '/
          templates/' . $bit;
   }
   $this->page->addTemplateBit( $tag, $bit, $replacements );
}
```

As mentioned above, we need to take this parameter in the method in the page object; this method also needs to be changed to assign both the template bit and the replacements array with the template tag, and not just assign the template bit with the template tag, as it previously did. This can be achieved by putting the template bit and replacements array into an array, and assigning them with the template tag in the bits array. This is highlighted in the code below:

```
/**
 * Add a template bit to the page, doesnt actually add the content
   just yet
 * @param String the tag where the template is added
 * @param String the template file name
 * @param Array the replacements array
 * @return void
 */
public function addTemplateBit( $tag, $bit, $replacements=array() )
{
    $this->bits[ $tag ] = array( 'template' => $bit,
       'replacements' => $replacements);
}
```

Now that we have the additional information being stored where we need it, we need to process it when we actually insert the template bit into the page. This simply involves iterating through the tags, and performing a simple find and replace on the content of the template bit (importantly, only on the template bit), then placing the content generated into the main template as before. The highlighted code below illustrates the changes:

```
/**
 * Take the template bits from the view and insert them into our page
   content
 * Updates the pages content
 * @return void
 */
private function replaceBits()
{
```

```
$bits = $this->page->getBits();
// loop through template bits
foreach( $bits as $tag => $template )
{
    $templateContent = file_get_contents( $template['template'] );
    $tags = array_keys( $template['replacements'] );
    $tagsNew = array();
    foreach( $tags as $taga )
    {
        $tagsNew[] = '{' . $taga . '}';
    }
    $values = array_values( $template['replacements'] );
    $templateContent = str_replace( $tagsNew, $values,
        $templateContent );
    $newContent = str_replace( '{' . $tag . '}', $templateContent,
        $this->page->getContent() );
    $this->page->setContent( $newContent );
}
}
```

Listing statuses

As discussed earlier, we are going to extend this system to include more types of
statuses, and also show activity by the user on the profiles of others, but for now,
we are just focusing on the users own status updates. Here is what we need to do:

1. Query the statuses.

2. Cache the statuses, and send them to the template. This populates a loop of
   status updates, and for each update, we get a template tag such as {update-1}
   based off a template variable of {update-{ID}}.

3. For each status update, we add a template bit (as we may have different
   types of update shortly, they will use different templates).

4. Along with each template bit, we pass the status details, so the template bit
   can be populated too.

```
/**
 * List recent statuses on a users profile
 * @param int $user the user whose profile we are viewing
 * @return void
 */
private function listRecentStatuses( $user )
{
    // load the template
    $this->registry->getObject('template')->buildFromTemplates(
```

```
     'header.tpl.php', 'profile/statuses/list.tpl.php', 'footer.tpl.php');
        $updates = array();
        $ids = array();

        // query the updates
        $sql = "SELECT t.type_reference, t.type_name, s.*, p.name as
           poster_name FROM statuses s, status_types t, profile p WHERE
           t.ID=s.type AND p.user_id=s.poster AND p.user_id={$user}
           ORDER BY s.ID DESC LIMIT 20";
        $this->registry->getObject('db')->executeQuery( $sql );
        if( $this->registry->getObject('db')->numRows() > 0 )
        {
           // populate the updates and ids arrays with the updates
           while( $row = $this->registry->getObject('db')->getRows() )
           {
               $updates[] = $row;
               $ids[$row['ID']] = $row;
           }
        }

        // cache the updates to build the loop which gives us a template
           tag for each status updates, for a template bit to go in
        $cache = $this->registry->getObject('db')->cacheData( $updates
        );
```

Add the updates to the template:

```
        $this->registry->getObject('template')->getPage()->addTag(
           'updates', array( 'DATA', $cache ) );
```

Add the template bits:

```
        foreach( $ids as $id => $data )
        {
           // iterate through the statuses, adding the update template
             bit, and populating it with the status information.
           // remember: the idea is we can extend the query to include
             other updates, which include different template bits
           $this->registry->getObject('template')->addTemplateBit(
             'update-' . $id, 'profile/updates/' . $data['type_
             reference'] . '.tpl.php', $data);
        }

    }
```

Templates

We need a status list template (`views/default/templates/profile/statuses/list.tpl.php`).

```html
<div id="main">

    <div id="rightside">
        <div style="text-align:center; padding-top: 5px;">
            <img src="uploads/profile/{profile_photo}" />
        </div>
        <div style="padding: 5px;">
        <h2>{profile_name}</h2>
            <h2>Friends</h2>
            <ul>
                <!-- START profile_friends_sample -->
                <li><a href="profile/view/{ID}">{users_name}
                    </a></li>
                <!-- END profile_friends_sample -->
                <li><a href="relationships/all/{p_user_id}">
                    View all</a></li>
                <li><a href="relationships/mutual/{p_user_
                    id}">View mutual friends</a></li>
            </ul>
            <h2>Rest of my profile</h2>
            <ul>
                <li><a href="profile/statuses/{p_user_id}">
                    Status updates</a></li>
            </ul>
        </div>
    </div>

    <div id="content"><h1>Recent updates</h1>
        <!-- START updates -->
        {update-{ID}}
        <!-- END updates -->
    </div>
</div>
```

And, we need a standard update template (`views/default/templates/updates/update.tpl.php`).

```html
<p><strong>{poster_name}</strong>: {update}</p>
<!-- START comments-{ID} -->
<!-- we will put comments here! -->
<!-- END comments-{ID} -->
```

In action

If we add some test status updates to the database and take a look, this is what we have now:

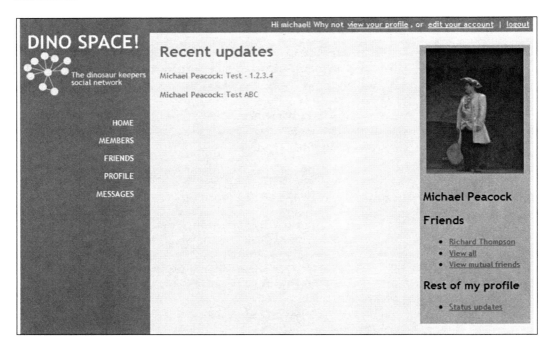

Likes, dislikes, and comments

In addition to showing statuses, messages, and other profile posts, we would want to allow friends to comment on these and indicate whether they like or dislike the posts.

Comments

There are two main options for comments:

- Class all comments on a status as a direct reply to the status
- Have a hierarchical structure of comments, allowing users to comment on comments

For Dino Space, we will look at the first option, as this is simpler, and will leave us with a more focused profile where comments focus on the user whose profile we are viewing. After creating the table, we should create some test comments that we will be able to see in the template shortly.

Field	Type	Description
ID	Integer, Primary Key, Auto-increment	ID of the comment
Comment	Longtext	The comment
Profile_post	Integer	The profile post the comment relates to
Creator	Integer	The creator of the comment
Created	Timestamp	The date the comment was posted
Approved	Boolean	If the comment is approved

We need to query the comments table for any related comments, cache them, and assign them to the appropriate status update.

Template

The update template needs to be extended to include comments posted on that update.

```
<p><strong>{poster_name}</strong>: {update}</p>
<!-- START comments-{ID} -->
<p> Comments:</p>
<p> {comment} by {commenter}</p>
<!-- END comments-{ID} -->
```

Code

The code to generate the comments goes in the `listRecentStatuses` method before we cache the updates. It needs to check whether there are status updates, and if there are:

1. Query the comments table for comments related to any of the updates that have happened.

2. Iterate through the comments, sorting them into arrays related to the profile update.

3. Iterate through the profile updates, and for each of them cache an empty array and assign it to the comments loop for that update — this ensures if there are no comments, the template tags don't display to the user.

4. Iterate through the profile updates that have comments, and cache the comments array associated with it, and send it to the template.

```
$post_ids = array_keys( $ids );
```

Check whether there are status updates:

```
if( count( $post_ids ) > 0 )
{
    $post_ids = implode( ',', $post_ids );
    $pids =  array_keys( $ids );
```

Cache an empty array for each update—blanking out comments by default:

```
foreach( $pids as $id )
{

    $blank = array();
    $cache = $this->registry->getObject('db')-
      >cacheData( $blank );
    $this->registry->getObject('template')->getPage()-
      >addPPTag( 'comments-' . $id, array( 'DATA', $cache ) );
}
```

Query the comments table for comments related to any of the updates that have happened:

```
$sql = "SELECT p.name as commenter, c.profile_post, c.comment
    FROM profile p, comments c WHERE p.user_id=c.creator AND
    c.approved=1 AND c.profile_post IN ({$post_ids})";
$this->registry->getObject('db')->executeQuery( $sql );
if( $this->registry->getObject('db')->numRows() > 0 )
{
```

Iterate through the comments, putting them into appropriate arrays:

```
$comments = array();
while( $comment = $this->registry->getObject('db')-
    >getRows() )
{
    if( in_array( $comment['profile_post'], array_keys(
        $comments ) ) )
    {
        $comments[ $comment['profile_post'] ][] = $comment;
    }
    else
    {
        $comments[ $comment['profile_post'] ] = array();
        $comments[ $comment['profile_post'] ][] = $comment;
    }
}
```

Cache the comments:

```
foreach( $comments as $pp => $commentlist )
{
    $cache = $this->registry->getObject('db')->cacheData(
        $commentlist );
    $this->registry->getObject('template')->getPage()-
     >addPPTag( 'comments-' .
     $pp, array( 'DATA', $cache ) );
}
}

}
```

In action

If we now take a look at our status updates, we have a comment!

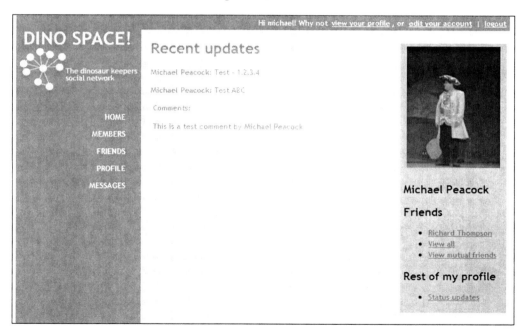

Try it yourself

Now that we have got this far, why not try and implement the following yourself. If you have difficulties, the code for the next chapter includes suitable implementations of the following features:

- Posting comments
- Liking and disliking a post
- Displaying likes and dislikes
- Posting profile updates

Summary

In this chapter, we created a profile screen for our members to display information about themselves to other members, as well as basic provisions for them to manage who has access to that information. We also created a profile status and message system, so that our users can update their network with what they are currently doing, and their network of contacts can respond by commenting on the status, indicating that they like or dislike it, or by writing their own message on that users profile.

With profiles, statuses, and public messages in place, the next stage for us is to allow users to see a stream of activity from their network, showing new updates from their contacts.

6
Status Stream

With users on Dino Space able to create profiles and post their statuses, we need to provide a way for users to see the statuses of their contacts at a glance.

In this chapter, you will learn:

- How to create a stream of status updates for users to see what their personal network is up to at any given time. The system will need to be extendable to allow users to see a stream of other content as we extend the site.

- How to make the times these statuses were posted more relevant to the user.

With more of an idea of the functionality we are going to create in this chapter, let's get started.

What is a status stream?

Most social networks provide functionality for their users to see the buzz of activity which is happening within the user's own network of contacts. This is typically a list of status updates, posts on other users' profiles, and the sharing of media such as images, videos, and links.

At this stage, Dino Space only has support for simple status updates, though we will look at this again in Chapter 7 and extend it to include other media, such as images, links, and video. This means that our user's status stream, at present, only needs to include:

- Status updates
- Statuses posted by users on another user's profile
- Comments on these statuses
- Likes and dislikes of these statuses

The concept is very similar to the statuses section of a user's profile we created in Chapter 5 except that instead of relating to one specific user, this should combine the activity of all users directly connected to the logged-in user.

Although at this stage it is primarily simple statuses, this will involve some logic to determine the context of the status. There will, after all, be five different types of status to list in the stream, all of which will require different wording to present to the user:

- The user's own status update
- The logged-in user posting a status update on the profile of another user
- A contact posting a status update on the profile of the logged-in user
- A contact updating their status
- A contact posting a status update on the profile of another contact

Stream model

We will require a stream model to build the status stream from the database. The functionalities required are:

- Looking up an activity in the user's network
- Formatting the time of these updates to make them more relevant; for example, 5 minutes ago
- Retuning the stream
- Knowing if the stream is empty

Code for the model is saved in the `models/stream.php` file.

Building the stream

Let's walk through the logic of how building a stream of updates would work:

1. We will need to get the IDs of users the current user is connected to.
2. As the IDs will be imploded and used as part of an IN condition, the list of IDs cannot be empty. So in case it is, we should add an ID of zero to the list.
3. We then need to query the database, pulling in the 20 most recent statuses that have been posted by the user, posted onto the user's profile, or posted between two contacts of the user.
4. If there are rows, we update our empty variable to `false`, so the object knows if the stream is empty or not.

5. We then iterate through the results making the time the status was posted more friendly and relevant, and store them in the object's stream variable.

6. Since the IDs of the status updates will be required to build our initial template loop, we should add the IDs to a separate array, which can be retrieved from outside the object (via a getter method).

The following code does this for us:

```
/**
 * Build a users stream
 * @param int $user the user whose network we want to stream
 * @param int $offset - useful if we add in an AJAX based "view more
statuses" feature
 * @return void
 */
public function buildStream( $user, $offset=0 )
{
  // prepare an array
  $network = array();
```

Step 1: Get the ID's of connected users.

```
  // use the relationships model to get relationships
  require_once( FRAMEWORK_PATH . 'models/relationships.php' );
  $relationships = new Relationships( $this->registry );
  $network = $relationships->getNetwork( $user );
  // Add a zero element; so if network is empty the IN part of the
    query won't fail
```

Step 2: Add an extra element to the array for safety.

```
  $network[] = 0;
  $network = implode( ',', $network );
```

Step 3: Query the database. The offset variable the method takes is used here. So if we were to have a "view more" link at the bottom of the status stream, we could get the previous 20 statuses by providing a suitable offset.

```
  // query the statuses table
  $sql = "SELECT t.type_reference, t.type_name, s.*,
    UNIX_TIMESTAMP(s.posted) as timestamp, p.name as poster_name,
    r.name as profile_name FROM statuses s, status_types t,
    profile p, profile r WHERE t.ID=s.type AND p.user_id=s.poster
    AND r.user_id=s.profile AND ( p.user_id={$user} OR
    r.user_id={$user} OR ( p.user_id IN ({$network}) AND r.user_id
    IN ({$network}) ) ) ORDER BY s.ID DESC LIMIT {$offset}, 20";
  $this->registry->getObject('db')->executeQuery( $sql );
```

Step 4: If there are rows, we set the empty variable to `false`, so the object knows the stream isn't empty, as the default for this variable is `true`.

```
if( $this->registry->getObject('db')->numRows() > 0 )
{
  $this->empty = false;
```

Steps 5 and 6: Iterate through the results getting a friendly version of the time (from another method within the object, which we will discuss shortly), and add the status ID to the status' variable.

```
// iterate through the statuses, adding the ID to the IDs array,
   making the time friendly, and saving the stream
while( $row = $this->registry->getObject('db')->getRows() )
{
  $row['friendly_time'] = $this->generateFriendlyTime(
    $row['timestamp'] );
  $this->IDs[] = $row['ID'];
  $this->stream[] = $row;
}
}
}
```

This simple method does most of the work we need to get a status stream from the database, requiring the help of two additional methods, one to get the IDs of connected users (a modification to the relationships model) and another to make the time string more friendly and relevant. Let's look now at creating those methods, and complete the groundwork for this feature.

Relationships—get the IDs!

Our relationships model (`models/relationships.php`) is currently used to query the database when it relates to user connections and relationships on the site. At present however, the queries this object performs are more complex than we require, and are cached, with the cache returned. Since this object is related purely with relationships, it makes sense for us to add a new method to this object to retrieve only the IDs of users who are connected to another user. We will call this method `getNetwork`, as it essentially gets the network of contacts related to a user.

Very simply, this method queries the database, puts the IDs of the users the user is connected to into an array, and returns the array. Since the user the logged-in user is connected to could be stored in either of two fields (with the currently logged-in user being stored in the other), there is some additional logic in the query (as with the other queries in this model) to ensure it returns the correct field, resulting in the users the user is connected to. This is illustrated by the `if` statement within the query. If `usera` is the current user, then we join the query against `userb` to ensure we don't end up listing the current user instead of the user they have a relationship with.

```
/**
 * Get relationship IDs (network) by user
 * @param int $user the user whose relationships we wish to list
 * @return array the IDs of profiles in the network
 */
public function getNetwork( $user )
{
  $sql = "SELECT u.ID FROM users u, profile p, relationships r,
    relationship_types t WHERE t.ID=r.type AND r.accepted=1 AND
    (r.usera={$user} OR r.userb={$user}) AND IF(
    r.usera={$user},u.ID=r.userb,u.ID=r.usera) AND p.user_id=u.ID";
  $this->registry->getObject('db')->executeQuery( $sql );
  $network = array();
  if( $this->registry->getObject('db')->numRows() > 0 )
  {
    while( $r = $this->registry->getObject('db')->getRows() )
    {
      $network[] = $r['ID'];
    }
  }
  return $network;
}
```

We now have a method that gives us the data behind a user's contact network on the site!

Friendly times

The time that a status update or profile status post is made is recorded in the database. If we simply convert this time to a date and time, it doesn't really provide much context for the user, as they simply see the date and time. This is especially true with a social networking site, as we would expect the status stream to be updated frequently, with most of the most recent updates being from the same day. We could make this more user friendly, by taking any updates from the last 24 hours (which as mentioned, should hopefully be the majority of any user's status stream) and making them relative to the current time.

For example:

- Posted less than a minute ago
- Posted 7 minutes ago

- Posted just over an hour ago
- Posted 5 hours ago

Times like these mean the user can make more sense out of when the statuses were posted.

A method to make the times more user friendly is quite straightforward and, for now, can be stored within the stream model. We simply take the time (as a UNIX timestamp, which is simply the number of seconds since the UNIX epoch) and add a specific time interval to it (as illustrated by the code) and compare the result to the current time (again a UNIX timestamp), depending on what we have added. If it exceeds the current time, then we know what to display.

If the time the status was posted plus 60 seconds is a larger number than the current time, then we know the status was posted within the last minute, and can return that accordingly.

```
/**
 * Generate a more user friendly time
 * @param int $time - timestamp
 * @return String - friendly time
 */
private function generateFriendlyTime( $time )
{
  $current_time = time();
  if( $current_time < ( $time + 60 ) )
  {
    // the update was in the past minute
    return "less than a minute ago";
  }
```

If the above wasn't true, then if we add 120 seconds to the time the status was posted, and this is greater than the current time, we know that it was posted between 1 and 2 minutes ago. This isn't too useful, except for the fact that any number of minutes other than 1 would be written as x minutes; with 1, we write 1 minute. We can make this time more friendly by returning "just over a minute ago".

```
  elseif( $current_time < ( $time + 120 ) )
  {
    // it was less than 2 minutes ago, more than 1, but we don't want
      to say 1 minute ago do we?
    return "just over a minute ago";
  }
```

If the above wasn't true, and we add an hour worth of seconds to the time it was posted, and this is greater than the current time, then we know it was within the last hour, but not within the last 1 minute 59 seconds, so we can say "x minutes ago".

```
elseif( $current_time < ( $time + ( 60*60 ) ) )
{
  // it was less than 60 minutes ago: so say X minutes ago
  return round( ( $current_time - $time ) / 60 ) . " minutes ago";
}
```

If the above isn't true but adding two hours to the time makes it greater than the current time, we can say "just over an hour ago". Again, this is the same reason for "just over a minute ago".

```
elseif( $current_time < ( $time + ( 60*120 ) ) )
{
  // it was more than 1 hour ago, but less than two, again we dont
    want to say 1 hourS do we?
  return "just over an hour ago";
}
```

If the status was posted within the last day, work out how many hours ago, and return that.

```
elseif( $current_time < ( $time + ( 60*60*24 ) ) )
{
  // it was in the last day: X hours
  return round( ( $current_time - $time ) / (60*60) ) . " hours
    ago";
}
```

Otherwise, we simply return a nice format of the date, which isn't as useful, but hopefully these statuses will be old and buried in the user's stream.

```
else
{
  // longer than a day ago: give up, and display the date / time
  return "at " . date( 'h:ia \o\n l \t\h\e jS \o\f M',$time);
}
}
```

We now have a really handy function that makes the time more friendly for our users.

> **Save some CPU cycles**
>
> In the above calculations, the time offset is broken down as multiples of a minute, to make them clearer. If these pages become popular, these additional calculations can add to our servers load. You may wish to replace them with their actual values.

The rest...

Finally, our stream model requires a few extra methods so that we can interact with it more easily, including:

- A getter method for the stream array
- A getter method for the IDs array
- A check to see if the stream is empty

Following is the required code:

```
/**
 * Get the stream
 * @return array
 */
public function getStream()
{
  return $this->stream;
}

/**
 * Get the status IDs in the stream
 * @return array
 */
public function getIDs()
{
  return $this->IDs;
}

/**
 * Is the stream empty?
 * @return bool
 */
public function isEmpty()
{
  return $this->empty;
}
```

With our model complete, we can create our controller to tie the data to the user interface.

Stream controller

What does our stream controller need to do? Let's walk through how we can take our model and turn it into a stream for the user to see.

1. Require the stream model class, and instantiate the object.

2. If the stream is empty, display an empty stream template.

3. If the stream isn't empty, we display the main template and carry on.

4. We take the status IDs and turn them into an array we can cache and send to the template. This gives us a list in the template of status IDs. In itself, this isn't useful, but it will be used to duplicate the template tag (where we will insert the status itself), the comments list, and the like / dislike list for each of the statuses, ready for the data to be pushed to the template later.

5. We then need to iterate through the stream, and depending on the type of status we have to add a specific template to the page (so a status update and a status post by someone on someone else's post show up differently in the list), and the stream data needs to be pushed directly into that template.

6. Comments, likes, and dislikes can then be looked up and inserted into the template too.

However, before we implement these features, we need a constructor. This needs to check if the user is a logged-in user, and if so, call the method we are going to create. If the user isn't an authenticated user, then we should show them an error page. This is the first bit of code for our `controllers/stream/controller.php` file.

```php
/**
 * Controller constructor - direct call to false when being embedded
   via another controller
 * @param Registry $registry our registry
 * @param bool $directCall - are we calling it directly via the
   framework (true), or via another controller (false)
 */
public function __construct( Registry $registry, $directCall )
{
  $this->registry = $registry;
  if( $this->registry->getObject('authenticate')->isLoggedIn() )
  {
    $this->generateStream();
  }
  else
  {
    $this->registry->errorPage( 'Please login', 'You need to be
      logged in to see what is happening in your network' );
  }
}
```

Generating the stream

With the constructor in place, let's look at creating the `generateStream` method.

```
private function generateStream( $offset=0 )
{
```

We start by requiring the stream model class and instantiating the object.

```
require_once( FRAMEWORK_PATH . 'models/stream.php' );
$stream = new Stream( $this->registry );
```

We then build the stream, based off the user's ID, and any offset that has been defined.

```
$stream->buildStream( $this->registry->getObject('authenticate')-
    >getUser()->getUserID(), $offset );
if( ! $stream->isEmpty() )
{
```

If the stream isn't empty, we use the main stream template.

```
$this->registry->getObject('template')->buildFromTemplates(
    'header.tpl.php', 'stream/main.tpl.php', 'footer.tpl.php');
```

We then retrieve our stream data and status IDs from the model.

```
$streamdata = $stream->getStream();

$IDs = $stream->getIDs();
```

Since we need to cache the IDs to make a loop of template tags, we need to restructure them into a new, cacheable array, which we then cache and send to the template engine.

```
$cacheableIDs = array();
foreach( $IDs as $id )
{
  $i = array();
  $i['status_id'] = $id;
  $cacheableIDs[] = $i;
}

$cache = $this->registry->getObject('db')->cacheData(
    $cacheableIDs );
$this->registry->getObject('template')->getPage()->addTag(
    'stream', array( 'DATA', $cache ) );
```

We then begin iterating through the stream of data.

```
foreach( $streamdata as $data )
{
```

We prepare the data from the status to go into the template shortly.

```
$datatags = array();
foreach( $data as $tag => $value )
{
   $datatags[ 'status' . $tag ] = $value;
}
```

Depending on the type of update this is we use different templates, as defined by the status type itself. This should make adding in new media types in Chapter 7 much easier. Also, depending on the context of the status, that is who made the update and on whose profile was the update, we need to use a different template for these too. We then add the stream data directly into the template bit, and assign the template bit to one of the template tags generated by the loop of cached IDs earlier. The following is a handy bit of re-use from our template engine extensions in Chapter 5.

```
// your own status updates
if( $data['profile'] == $this->registry-
   >getObject('authenticate')->getUser()->getUserID()
   && $data['poster'] == $this->registry->getObject('
   authenticate')->getUser()->getUserID() )
{
   // it was a present...from me to me!
   // http://www.imdb.com/title/tt0285403/quotes?qt0473119
   $this->registry->getObject('template')->addTemplateBit(
      'stream-' . $data['ID'], 'stream/types/' .
      $data['type_reference'] . '-Spongebob-Squarepants-Costume-
      gift.tpl.php', $datatags );
}
elseif( $data['profile'] == $this->registry-
   >getObject('authenticate')->getUser()->getUserID() )
{
   // updates to you
   $this->registry->getObject('template')->addTemplateBit(
      'stream-' . $data['ID'], 'stream/types/' .
      $data['type_reference'] . '-toself.tpl.php', $datatags );
}
elseif( $data['poster'] == $this->registry-
   >getObject('authenticate')->getUser()->getUserID() )
{
   // updates by you
   $this->registry->getObject('template')->addTemplateBit(
```

```
            'stream-' . $data['ID'], 'stream/types/' .
            $data['type_reference'] . '-fromself.tpl.php', $datatags );
        }
        elseif( $data['poster'] == $data['profile'] )
        {
          $this->registry->getObject('template')->addTemplateBit(
            'stream-' . $data['ID'], 'stream/types/' .
            $data['type_reference'] . '-user.tpl.php', $datatags );
        }
        else
        {
          // network updates
          $this->registry->getObject('template')->addTemplateBit(
            'stream-' . $data['ID'], 'stream/types/' .
            $data['type_reference'] . '.tpl.php', $datatags );
        }
      }
    }
  }
  else
  {
```

If there were no updates, we display the none template.

```
    $this->registry->getObject('template')->buildFromTemplates(
      'header.tpl.php', 'stream/none.tpl.php', 'footer.tpl.php');
  }
}
```

So, if we had our templates in place at this stage, bringing all of this together, adding the controller to our database, and viewing /stream what would we see?

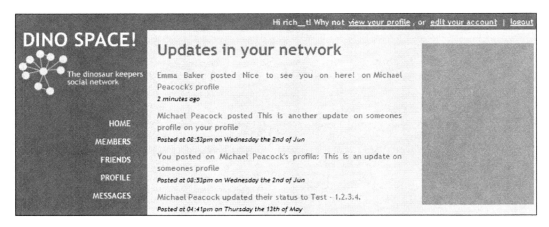

This is the basics of our status stream. We can now look at adding comments, likes, and dislikes to the stream.

Comments, likes, and dislikes

The functionality behind adding comments, likes, and dislikes is very similar to the work we did in Chapter 5 in developing the statuses on a user's profile.

The concept to adding these to the stream is fairly straightforward. Firstly, we create an empty array of comments / likes / dislikes for each status. This way, if a post has no comments, likes, or dislikes, then by caching the empty array and sending it to the template, we don't see a blank list where comments should be. If there are comments, they are added to the empty array (making it non-empty), cached, and sent to the template.

Although the method is the same for the three aspects, comments require one database query, whereas likes and dislikes combined require another, so let's add in support one at a time.

Comments

Take the status IDs we retrieved earlier, and create empty arrays for each of them.

```
$status_ids = implode( ',', $IDs );
$start = array();
foreach( $IDs as $id )
{
   $start[ $id ] = array();
}
```

Copy our new array of empty arrays to be used for comments.

```
// comments
$comments = $start;
```

Query the database for comments.

```
$sql = "SELECT p.name as commenter, c.profile_post, c.comment FROM
   profile p, comments c WHERE p.user_id=c.creator AND c.approved=1
   AND c.profile_post IN ({$status_ids})";
$this->registry->getObject('db')->executeQuery( $sql );
if( $this->registry->getObject('db')->numRows() > 0 )
{
```

If there are comments, iterate through them and add them to the appropriate bucket
(or array) for the status it relates to.

```
while( $comment = $this->registry->getObject('db')->getRows() )
{
  $comments[ $comment['profile_post'] ][] = $comment;
}
}
```

For each of the comments arrays, we cache the data and send them to the
template engine.

```
foreach( $comments as $status => $comments )
{
  $cache = $this->registry->getObject('db')->cacheData( $comments );
  $this->registry->getObject('template')->getPage()->addTag(
    'comments-' . $status, array( 'DATA', $cache )  );
}
```

Likes and dislikes

Likes and dislikes are stored in the same table. So we query it, and depending
on the result, put the result in a different array.

```
$likes = $start;
$dislikes = $start;
$sql = "SELECT i.status, p.name as iker, i.iker as iker_id, i.type as
  type FROM profile p, ikes i WHERE p.user_id=i.iker AND i.status IN
  ({$status_ids}) ";
$this->registry->getObject('db')->executeQuery( $sql );
if( $this->registry->getObject('db')->numRows() > 0 )
{
  while( $ike = $this->registry->getObject('db')->getRows() )
  {
    if( $ike['type'] == 'likes' )
    {
      $likes[ $ike['status'] ][] = $ike;
    }
    else
    {
      $dislikes[ $ike['status'] ][] = $ike;
    }
  }
}
foreach( $likes as $status => $likeslist )
{
```

```
  $cache = $this->registry->getObject('db')->cacheData( $likeslist );
  $this->registry->getObject('template')->getPage()->addTag( 'likes-'
    . $status, array( 'DATA', $cache )  );
}
foreach( $dislikes as $status => $dislikeslist )
{
  $cache = $this->registry->getObject('db')->cacheData(
    $dislikeslist );
  $this->registry->getObject('template')->getPage()->addTag(
    'dislikes-' . $status, array( 'DATA', $cache )  );
}
```

Views

Now we need our template files to provide us with the view.

Main template

The main template contains an outer template loop, which is populated based on the cached status IDs. Once this is populated, we have a unique template tag for each status, ready for the status template to be inserted. It also generates three inner loops—one for comments, one for likes, and one for dislikes.

```
<div id="main">

<div id="rightside">
</div>

<div id="content">
<h1>Updates in your network</h1>
<!-- START stream -->
  {stream-{status_id}}
  <!-- START comments-{status_id} -->
    <p> {comment} by {commenter}</p>
  <!-- END comments-{status_id} -->
  <!-- START likes-{status_id} -->
    <p>{iker} likes this</p>
  <!-- END likes-{status_id} -->
  <!-- START dislikes-{status_id} -->
    <p>{iker} dislikes this</p>
  <!-- END dislikes-{status_id} -->
<!-- END stream -->
</div>
</div>
```

Status type templates

For each status type (we have only one at the moment) we need a template for each context (user's own status, user posting on someone else's profile, someone posting on a user's profile, and two users in a contact's network posting on their profile). These templates are stored in the `views/default/templates/stream/types` folder. Below is the template used when showing the status the logged-in user posted on the profile of another user:

```
<p>You posted on {statusprofile_name}'s profile: {statusupdate}</p>
<p class="postedtime">Posted {statusfriendly_time}</p>
```

In action

Now that we have the model, controller, and views in place, all that leaves us to do is create a controller record in the database for stream, and visit `/stream` as a logged-in user.

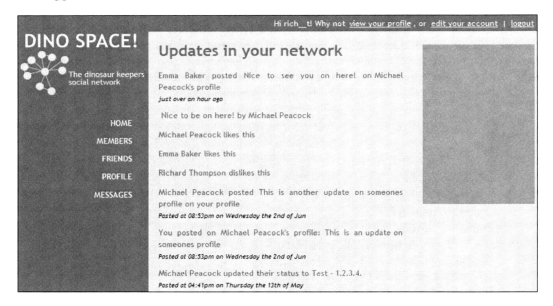

Room for improvement

We have developed a powerful status stream in this chapter, but as with anything there is always room for improvement. Let's discuss how this might be improved and extended.

Firstly, there is some overlap in terms of logic and queries with the user's profile and the status' delegator within the profile. It may be possible for us to centralize this functionality and use it in both these instances, perhaps generating a stream for a profile or generating a stream for a network, depending on methods called in the object.

Secondly, we are doing a few small queries in the controller. This is generally best avoided, and instead models should be used to generate the comments, likes, and dislikes. We could create models for these, which this and the user's profile could make use of.

Plural names are currently hardcoded within the templates. So if Bill posts on Ben's profile, the text is generated by adding 's to the user's name. Some names may only require an apostrophe, so we could look at making this more dynamic.

The final obvious area for improvement is the data it pulls in; it currently pulls in the 20 most recent updates, taking an offset into account. We may wish to detect more recent updates since then, so a user could load in (perhaps through AJAX) more recent status updates that have occurred while they have been viewing the stream page.

A system stream for administrators

While not as straightforward, as these events won't be centrally stored, we could also create a stream of system events for the administrator. These could include:

- Logins / logouts / signups
- Statuses
- Relationship formations
- When passwords are sent
- When e-mails are sent via the site, and so on

This isn't an essential feature, but could be a nice feature to have depending on the size of the network and the size of the administrative team running the site.

Summary

In this chapter we have taken the statuses that users were able to update and post thanks to our work in Chapter 5 and created a stream of these statuses that the user can see, based on the activity and contacts within their network on Dino Space. This includes:

- Status updates
- Posting on other user's profiles
- Comments relating to these updates
- Likes / dislikes related to these updates

We've also looked at potential ways to improve and enhance this feature, as well as what we might wish to consider adding for administrators to see an overview of the system.

With all of this now in place, let's move on to supporting new types of media on the site, with images, videos, and links being posted onto the profiles of our users!

Public and Private Messages

7

On Dino Space, we have a new status stream for our users to display the activity happening in their network. One of the things included in the stream was postings on other users' wall posts, something which our database supports, but at the moment, our site doesn't!

In this chapter, you will learn:

- How to allow users to post messages on each other's profiles
- How to allow users to post private messages to each other

Most social networking sites support two types of messages: public and private messages. Private messages are generally sent in a similar fashion to e-mails, and public messages being posted on user's profiles for other users to see.

Let's get started with extending our profiles and the status stream!

Public messages

Our status stream from Chapter 6 fully supports public messages and streaming them to the Dino Space members. What we don't yet have, however, is support for users to post messages on the profiles of other users, so, let's add that in now.

Controller

A user should only be able to post a message on another user's profile if they are connected. The post message form should only be displayed if the users are connected. Similarly, a public message post should only be processed if the two users are connected. The controller also needs to display messages that have been posted on a user's profile too.

Displaying profile messages

If we look at our `Profilestatusescontroller` (`controllers/profile/profilestatusescontroller.php`), in the `listRecentStatuses` method, we have our query for listing recent profile statuses:

```
$sql = "SELECT t.type_reference, t.type_name, s.*, p.name as
    poster_name FROM statuses s, status_types t, profile p
    WHERE t.ID=s.type AND p.user_id=s.poster AND p.user_id={$user}
    ORDER BY s.ID DESC LIMIT 20";
```

At the moment, this query pulls in any posts on a user's profile by the user whose profile it is. If that user has made a post on someone else's profile, the message instead shows on the user's own profile, which we don't want.

We need to change this to pull in the profiles table twice, once for the user who made the post, and again for the user whose profile is being viewed. We will also want to only pull in posts made on the user's profile, and not posts made by the user on another user's profile (though this is something we can expand on in the future, perhaps to indicate that a user has made a post on the profile of another user). The following query should meet our requirements nicely:

```
$sql = "SELECT t.type_reference, t.type_name, s.*, pa.name as
    poster_name FROM statuses s, status_types t, profile p,
    profile pa WHERE t.ID=s.type AND p.user_id=s.profile
    AND pa.user_id=s.poster AND p.user_id={$user}
    ORDER BY s.ID DESC LIMIT 20";
```

Now, if we view a user's profile, we see their own status updates, and messages posted on their profile by other users, as shown in the following screenshot:

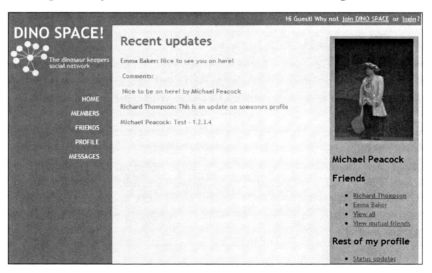

Displaying the post message box

The `listRecentStatuses` method we were just editing is the method we need to edit to display the post message box. This box should only be displayed if the user is logged in, and is connected to the user. If the user is viewing their own profile, then they should see a box to update their own status:

```
// post status / public message box
if( $this->registry->getObject('authenticate')->isLoggedIn() == true )
{
    $loggedInUser = $this->registry->getObject('authenticate')-
        >getUser()->getUserID();
```

If the logged in user is viewing their own profile, then we add the update template to the view, so they can update their status:

```
    if( $loggedInUser == $user )
    {
        $this->registry->getObject('template')->addTemplateBit( 'status_
            update', 'profile/statuses/update.tpl.php' );
    }
    else
    {
```

If the user isn't viewing their own profile, but is logged in, we get any connections the user has:

```
        require_once( FRAMEWORK_PATH . 'models/relationships.php' );
        $relationships = new Relationships( $this->registry );
        $connections = $relationships->getNetwork( $user, false );
        if( in_array( $loggedInUser, $connections ) )
        {
```

If the user is connected to the user whose profile they are viewing, then we allow them to post a message on the users profile with the post template:

```
            $this->registry->getObject('template')->addTemplateBit(
                'status_update', 'profile/statuses/post.tpl.php' );
        }
        else
        {
```

If the user isn't connected to the user, or isn't logged in, then we simply remove the template tag from the view so they don't see any update or post box on the page:

```
            $this->registry->getObject('template')->getPage()-
                >addTag( 'status_update', '' );
        }
    }
}
else
{
    $this->registry->getObject('template')->getPage()-
        >addTag( 'status_update', '' );
}
```

Now, we need to process status updates and profile posts, and create the templates that make up the final aspect of our view.

Process a new message

The same logic that we used to determine whether the user should see a post form is what we need to use to determine if we should process a status update, or public message submission.

Status model

To save the status update or public profile post in the database, we will need a status model; as with our previous models, this simply needs to represent the fields from the database, with setter methods for these fields, and a save method to insert a new record into the database. In the future, we may wish to extend this to pull in statuses from the database, and save changes to them, as well as deleting statuses, perhaps if the owner of the message or the owner of the profile the message was posted on wishes to edit or delete it.

The following is suitable code for our status model (`models/status.php`):

```
<?php
/**
 * Status model
 */
class Status {

    /**
     * The registry object
     */
    private $registry;
```

```php
/**
 * Statuses ID
 */
private $id;

/**
 * Poster of the status update / profile message
 */
private $poster;

/**
 * The profile the status update / profile message was posted on
 */
private $profile;

/**
 * Type of status
 */
private $type;

/**
 * The update / profile message itself
 */
private $update;

/**
 * Reference for the type of status
 */
private $typeReference = 'update';

/**
 * Constructor
 * @param Registry $registry the registry object
 * @param int $id ID of the status update / profile message
 * @return void
 */
public function __construct( Registry $registry, $id=0 )
{
    $this->registry = $registry;
    $this->id = 0;
}

/**
 * Set the poster of the status / profile message
```

```
 * @param int $poster the id of the poster
 * @return void
 */
public function setPoster( $poster )
{
    $this->poster = $poster;
}


/**
 * Set the profile that the message / status is posted on
 * @param int $profile the profile ID
 * @return void
 */
public function setProfile( $profile )
{
    $this->profile = $profile;
}


/**
 * Set the status / profile message itself
 * @param String $status
 * @return void
 */
public function setStatus( $status )
{
    $this->status = $status;
}


/**
 * Set the type of status / profile message
 * @param int $type
 * @return void
 */
public function setType( $type )
{
    $this->type = $type;
}


/**
 * Set the type reference, so we can get the type ID from the
   database
 * @param String $typeReference the reference of the type
 * @return void
 */
```

```
public function setTypeReference( $typeReference )
{
    $this->type = $typeReference;
}

/**
 * Generate the type of status based of the type reference
 * @return void
 */
public function generateType()
{
    $sql = "SELECT * FROM status_types WHERE
        type_reference='{$this->typeReference}'";
    $this->registry->getObject('db')->executeQuery( $sql );
    $data = $this->registry->getObject('db')->getRows();
    $this->type = $data['ID'];
}

/**
 * Save the status / profile message
 * @return void
 */
public function save()
{
    if( $this->id == 0 )
    {
        $insert = array();
        $insert['update'] = $this->status;
        $insert['type'] = $this->type;
        $insert['poster'] = $this->poster;
        $insert['profile'] = $this->profile;
        $this->registry->getObject('db')-
            >insertRecords( 'statuses', $insert );
        $this->id = $this->registry->getObject('db')->lastInsertID();
    }
}
}
```

```
?>
```

Now that we have some functionality to easily insert the status into the database, we need to update our profile controller to process the new status update.

Controller additions

As we discussed earlier, we need to take the same logic we used for displaying the status form, to determine whether we should process a status submission. We can then combine our new status model to insert the status.

Within the `listRecentStatuses` method in the `profilestatusescontroller`, under the authentication check line, we can check for any `$_POST` data being submitted, and if there is, we can call a new method to process the submission:

```
// post status / public message box
if( $this->registry->getObject('authenticate')->isLoggedIn() == true )
{
    if( isset( $_POST ) && count( $_POST ) > 0 )
    {
        $this->addStatus( $user );
    }
}
```

Since we have placed this within our `listRecentStatuses` method, once any processing has been done, the user is presented with the list of statuses and public profile messages for that user.

The `addStatus` method only inserts the status into the database if the user is posting the status either to their own profile, or the profile of one of their contacts:

```
/**
 * Process a new status submission / profile message
 * @param int $user the profile the message is being posted on
 * @return void
 */
private function addStatus( $user )
{
    $loggedInUser = $this->registry->getObject('authenticate')-
        >getUser()->getUserID();
    if( $loggedInUser == $user )
    {
        require_once( FRAMEWORK_PATH . 'models/status.php' );
        $status = new Status( $this->registry, 0 );
        $status->setProfile( $user );
        $status->setPoster( $loggedInUser );
        $status->setStatus( $this->registry->getObject('db')-
            >sanitizeData( $_POST['status'] ) );
        $status->generateType();
        $status->save();
        // success message display
    }
```

```
else
{
    require_once( FRAMEWORK_PATH . 'models/relationships.php' );
    $relationships = new Relationships( $this->registry );
    $connections = $relationships->getNetwork( $user, false );
    if( in_array( $loggedInUser, $connections ) )
    {
        require_once( FRAMEWORK_PATH . 'models/status.php' );
        $status = new Status( $this->registry, 0 );
        $status->setProfile( $user );
        $status->setPoster( $loggedInUser );
        $status->setStatus( $this->registry->getObject('db')-
            >sanitizeData( $_POST['status'] ) );
        $status->generateType();
        $status->save();
        // success message display
    }
    else
    {
        // error message display
    }
}
```

Displaying a confirmation message

Once the user has posted their message on another user's profile, they are redirected to the profile. Although the profile now has their message on it, there isn't a direct confirmation message to the user, so let's look at adding a notification to confirm to the user that their post was successful.

As we won't always wish to display a message, such as if the user hasn't submitted the form, then we either need to clear the template tag, or simply place it within some HTML comments, for example:

```
<!-{status_update_message} -->
```

If we do this, we simply need to start the contents of the message template with `-->` and end it with `<!--` to ensure the message itself isn't commented out. Since we have used the same logic to process the form as we used to display the form, we can also customize the message based on the context of the submission, for example, **You have updated your status**, or **You have posted on John's wall**.

We can then add the message to the view, like so:

```
$this->registry->getObject('template')->addTemplateBit( 'status_
    update_message', 'profile/statuses/update_confirm.tpl.php' );
```

View

We need to add two template tags to our statuses list file (`views/default/
templates/profile/statuses/list.tpl.php`), one for the status update/profile
message submit form, and the other (wrapped in HTML comments) for the success
or error message to use:

```
{status_update}
<!-- {status_update_message} -->
```

Five small new templates are required, for:

- Form to update your own status
- Form to post a message on someone else's profile
- Success confirmation message when your own status is updated
- Success confirmation message when you post on someone else's profile
- Error message, if you try to post on the profile of someone you are
  not connected to (although the lack of a form for this should prevent
  this happening)

Updating your own status: `views/default/templates/profile/statuses/
update.tpl.php`.

```
<p>Tell your network what you are up to</p>
<form action="profile/statuses/{profile_user_id}" method="post">
<textarea id="status" name="status"></textarea>
<br />
<input type="submit" id="updatestatus" name="updatestatus"
value="Update" />
</form>
```

Posting on someone else's profile: `views/default/templates/profile/statuses/
post.tpl.php`.

```
<p>Post a message on {profile_name}'s profile</p>
<form action="profile/statuses/{profile_user_id}" method="post">
<textarea id="status" name="status"></textarea>
<br />
<input type="submit" id="postmessage" name="postmessage"
value="Update" />
</form>
```

Success message after updating your own status: `views/default/templates/profile/statuses/update_confirm.tpl.php`.

```
-->
<p style="border: 1px solid #000; padding: 5px;">Your status
   has been saved</p>
<!--
```

Success message after posting on someone else's profile: `views/default/templates/profile/statuses/post_confirm.tpl.php`.

```
-->
<p style="border: 1px solid #000; padding: 5px;">Your message
   has been posted on {profile_name}'s profile</p>
<!--
```

Error message after trying to post on the profile of an unconnected user: `views/default/templates/profile/statuses/error.tpl.php`.

```
-->
<p style="border: 1px solid #000; padding: 5px;">You are not
   connected to {profile_name}, so your message was not saved.</p>
<!--
```

In action

With the new logic and templates in place, let's try updating our own status. We now have a form to allow us to update our status as shown in the following screenshot:

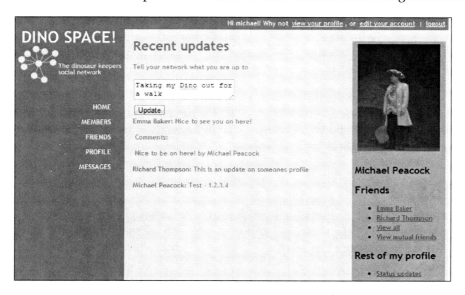

After submitting the form, we have a new status in our updates stream, and a confirmation message is displayed as shown in the following screenshot:

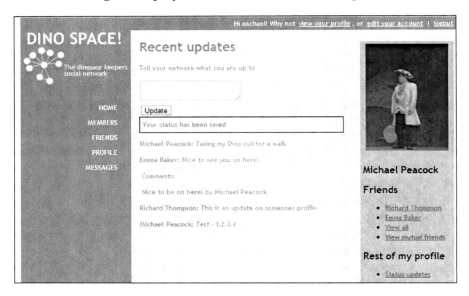

Private messages

We obviously need to keep private messages separate from the rest of the site, and ensure that they are only accessible to the sender and the receiver. While we could alter the public messages feature developed earlier, this would raise a few issues, such as being more difficult to tell whether the message being sent or read was private, and when using the Internet in a public area, the message would be shown on the area of the social network the user would most likely be visiting, which isn't ideal for private information.

Because private messages will be separate from statuses, and won't need to make use of other media types to make them more interesting (though, we could set them up to make use of other media if we wanted), it makes sense for us to also use separate database tables and models for this feature.

Database

Our database needs provisions for the sender of the message, the recipient of the message, the subject of the message, and of course the message itself. We should also provide for if the message has been read, when the message was sent, and an ID for the message.

The following illustrates a suitable structure for a messages table in our database:

Field	Type	Description
ID	Integer, Auto-increment, Primary Key	Reference ID for the message
Sender	Integer	The sender of the message
Recipient	Integer	The recipient of the message
Subject	Varchar	The subject the message relates to
Sent	Timestamp	When the message was sent
Message	Longtext	The contents of the message itself
Read	Boolean	Indicates whether the message has been read or not

More than one recipient?

This database structure, and the code that follows, only supports one recipient per message. Our users might want to send to more than one recipient—feel free to add this functionality if you wish.

Message model

As with the majority of our database access, we require a model (`models/message.php`) to create, update, and retrieve message-related data from the database and encapsulate it within itself.

It would also be helpful if the model pulled in a little more information from the database, including:

- A more user friendly representation of the date (we can get this via the MySQL `DATE_FORMAT` function)
- The name of the sender, by joining the messages table to the profile table
- The name of the recipient, by joining the messages table to the profile table again

The first part of our model simply defines the class variables:

```php
<?php
/**
 * Private message class
 */
class Message {
```

```
/**
 * The registry object
 */
private $registry;

/**
 * ID of the message
 */
private $id=0;

/**
 * ID of the sender
 */
private $sender;

/**
 * Name of the sender
 */
private $senderName;

/**
 * ID of the recipient
 */
private $recipient;

/**
 * Name of the recipient
 */
private $recipientName;

/**
 * Subject of the message
 */
private $subject;

/**
 * When the message was sent (TIMESTAMP)
 */
private $sent;

/**
 * User readable, friendly format of the time the message was sent
 */
```

```
    private $sentFriendlyTime;

    /**
     * Has the message been read
     */
    private $read=0;

    /**
     * The message content itself
     */
    private $message;
```

The constructor takes the registry and ID of the message as parameters, if the ID has been defined, then it queries the database and sets the class variables. The database query here also formats a copy of the date into a friendlier format, and looks up the names of the sender and recipient of the message:

```
    /**
     * Message constructor
     * @param Registry $registry the registry object
     * @param int $id the ID of the message
     * @return void
     */
    public function __construct( Registry $registry, $id=0 )
    {
        $this->registry = $registry;
        $this->id = $id;
        if( $this->id > 0 )
        {
            $sql = "SELECT m.*, DATE_FORMAT(m.sent, '%D %M %Y') as
                sent_friendly, psender.name as sender_name, precipient.name
                as recipient_name FROM messages m, profile psender, profile
                precipient WHERE precipient.user_id=m.recipient AND
                psender.user_id=m.sender AND m.ID=" . $this->id;
            $this->registry->getObject('db')->executeQuery( $sql );
            if( $this->registry->getObject('db')->numRows() > 0 )
            {
                $data = $this->registry->getObject('db')->getRows();
                $this->sender = $data['sender'];
                $this->recipient = $data['recipient'];
                $this->sent = $data['sent'];
                $this->read = $data['read'];
                $this->subject = $data['subject'];
                $this->message = $data['message'];
```

```
                  $this->sentFriendlyTime = $data['sent_friendly'];
                  $this->senderName = $data['sender_name'];
                  $this->recipientName = $data['recipient_name'];


              }
              else
              {
                  $this->id = 0;
              }
          }
      }
```

Next, we have setter methods for most of the class variables:

```
    /**
     * Set the sender of the message
     * @param int $sender
     * @return void
     */
    public function setSender( $sender )
    {
        $this->sender = $sender;
    }


    /**
     * Set the recipient of the message
     * @param int $recipient
     * @return void
     */
    public function setRecipient( $recipient )
    {
        $this->recipient = $recipient;
    }


    /**
     * Set the subject of the message
     * @param String $subject
     * @return void
     */
    public function setSubject( $subject )
    {
        $this->subject = $subject;
    }


    /**
```

```
 * Set if the message has been read
 * @param boolean $read
 * @return void
 */
public function setRead( $read )
{
    $this->read = $read;
}

/**
 * Set the message itself
 * @param String $message
 * @return void
 */
public function setMessage( $message )
{
    $this->message = $message;
}
```

The save method takes the class variables that directly relate to the messages table in the database and either inserts them as a new record, or updates the existing record:

```
/**
 * Save the message into the database
 * @return void
 */
public function save()
{
    if( $this->id > 0 )
    {
        $update = array();
        $update['sender'] = $this->sender;
        $update['recipient'] = $this->recipient;
        $update['read'] = $this->read;
        $update['subject'] = $this->subject;
        $update['message'] = $this->message;
        $this->registry->getObject('db')->updateRecords( 'messages',
          $update, 'ID=' . $this->id );
    }
    else
    {
        $insert = array();
        $insert['sender'] = $this->sender;
        $insert['recipient'] = $this->recipient;
        $insert['read'] = $this->read;
```

```
            $insert['subject'] = $this->subject;
            $insert['message'] = $this->message;
            $this->registry->getObject('db')->insertRecords( 'messages',
                $insert );
            $this->id = $this->registry->getObject('db')->lastInsertID();
        }
    }
```

One getter method that we need, is to return the user ID of the recipient, so we can check that the currently logged in user has permission to read the message:

```
/**
 * Get the recipient of the message
 * @return int
 */
public function getRecipient()
{
return $this->recipient;
}
```

We should also provide a method to delete the message from the database, should the user wish to delete a message:

```
/**
 * Delete the current message
 * @return boolean
 */
public function delete()
{
    $sql = "DELETE FROM messages WHERE ID=" . $this->id;
    $this->registry->getObject('db')->executeQuery( $sql );
    if( $this->registry->getObject('db')->affectedRows() > 0 )
    {
        $this->id =0;
        return true;
    }
    else
    {
        return false;
    }
}
```

Finally, we have a `toTags` method, which converts all of the non-object and non-array variables into template tags, so when we create a view message method in the controller, we simply need to construct the message object and call the `toTags` method:

```php
/**
 * Convert the message data to template tags
 * @param String $prefix prefix for the template tags
 * @return void
 */
public function toTags( $prefix='' )
{
    foreach( $this as $field => $data )
    {
        if( ! is_object( $data ) && ! is_array( $data ) )
        {
            $this->registry->getObject('template')->getPage()->addTag(
                $prefix.$field, $data );
        }
    }
}

}

?>
```

Messages model

Similar to how we have a model for representing a single relationship and another for representing a number of relationships, we also need a model to represent a number of messages within the site. This is to handle the lookup of a user's private message inbox.

```php
<?php

/**
 * Messages model
 */
class Messages {

/**
 * Messages constructor
 * @param Registry $registry
 * @return void
```

```
    */
    public function __construct( Registry $registry )
    {
      $this->registry = $registry;
    }


    /**
    * Get a users inbox
    * @param int $user the user
    * @return int the cache of messages
    */
    public function getInbox( $user )
    {
      $sql = "SELECT IF(m.read=0,'unread','read') as read_style,
        m.subject, m.ID, m.sender, m.recipient, DATE_FORMAT(m.sent, '%D
        %M %Y') as sent_friendly, psender.name as sender_name FROM
        messages m, profile psender WHERE psender.user_id=m.sender AND
        m.recipient=" . $user . " ORDER BY m.ID DESC";
      $cache = $this->registry->getObject('db')->cacheQuery( $sql );
      return $cache;

    }
}
?>
```

Controllers and views

Our controller needs functionality for:

- Listing a user's private messages
  - Indicating which messages have been read, and which ones are unread

- Reading a message
- Deleting a message
- Composing a new message

And we need three templates, for:

- Our inbox
- Viewing a message
- Creating a new message

Listing messages

To list our messages, we simply require our messages controller, call the `getInbox` method, and send the cache to the template engine. The `read_style` field in the results of the query can be used to highlight rows in the messages table (HTML table in the view), which represent unread messages:

```
/**
 * View your inbox
 * @return void
 */
private function viewInbox()
{
    require_once( FRAMEWORK_PATH . 'models/messages.php' );
    $messages = new Messages( $this->registry );
    $cache = $messages->getInbox( $this->registry-
        >getObject('authenticate')->getUser()->getUserID() );
    $this->registry->getObject('template')-
        >buildFromTemplates('header.tpl.php', 'messages/inbox.tpl.php',
        'footer.tpl.php');
    $this->registry->getObject('template')->getPage()-
        >addTag( 'messages', array( 'SQL', $cache ) );

}
```

Inbox

The inbox template (`views/default/templates/messages/inbox.tpl.php`)) simply requires a table with a template loop to contain the messages. Notice that the class of the table row is set based on whether the message has been read or not:

```
<div id="main">

    <div id="rightside">

    <ul>
        <li><a href="messages/create">Create a new message</a></a>
    </ul>
    </div>

    <div id="content">
        <h1>Your inbox</h1>
        <table>
            <tr>
                <th>From</th>
                <th>Subject</th>
```

```
            <th>Sent</th>
        </tr>
        <!-- START messages -->
        <tr class="{read_style}">
            <td>{sender_name}</td>
            <td><a href="messages/view/{ID}">{subject}</a></td>
            <td>{sent_friendly}</td>
        </tr>
        <!-- END messages -->
    </table>
    </div>

</div>
```

The following screenshot shows the Inbox feature:

Reading a message

To read a message we need to require our message model, construct the message object with the registry and message ID, check that the recipient is the currently logged in user, load the template, and send the message information to the template:

```
/**
 * View a message
 * @param int $message the ID of the message
 * @return void
 */
private function viewMessage( $message )
{
    require_once( FRAMEWORK_PATH . 'models/message.php' );
    $message = new Message( $this->registry, $message );
```

```
    if( $message->getRecipient() == $this->registry-
      >getObject('authenticate')->getUser()->getUserID() )
    {
      $this->registry->getObject('template')-
        >buildFromTemplates('header.tpl.php', 'messages/view.tpl.php',
        'footer.tpl.php');
      $message->toTags( 'inbox_' );
    }
    else
    {
      $this->registry->errorPage( 'Access denied', 'Sorry, you are not
        allowed to view that message');
    }
}
```

View message template

The view message template (`views/default/templates/messages/view.tpl.
php`) simply contains template tags for the message properties, and a few
additional links:

```
<div id="main">

    <div id="rightside">

    <ul>
       <li><a href="messages/">Your inbox</a></a>
       <li><a href="messages/create/{inbox_id}">
         Reply to this message</a></a>
       <li><a href="messages/delete/{inbox_id}">
         Delete this message</a></a>
       <li><a href="messages/create">Create a new message</a></a>
    </ul>
    </div>

    <div id="content">
       <h1>View message</h1>
       <table>
          <tr>
             <th>Subject</th>
             <td>{inbox_subject}</td>
          </tr>
          <tr>
             <th>From</th>
             <td>{inbox_senderName}</td>
          </tr>
```

```
      <tr>
         <th>Sent</th>
         <td>{inbox_sentFriendlyTime}</td>
      </tr>
      <tr>
         <th>Message</th>
         <td>{inbox_message}</td>
      </tr>
   </table>
</div>

</div>
```

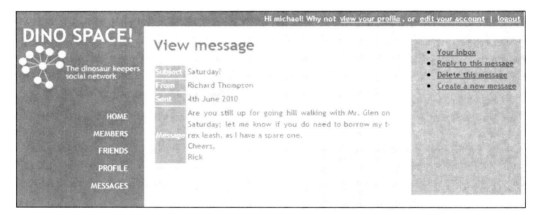

Mark as read

Once a user has read a message, we should update the database to indicate that the message has been read, so that the user can see at a glance which of their messages are new and unread, and which ones have already been read. However, for privacy reasons, we shouldn't show this information to the sender of the message.

To do this, we simply set the read property on the model to 1, and save the record, as illustrated by the changes to `viewMessage` highlighted below:

```
/**
 * View a message
 * @param int $message the ID of the message
 * @return void
 */
private function viewMessage( $message )
{
    require_once( FRAMEWORK_PATH . 'models/message.php' );
```

```
$message = new Message( $this->registry, $message );
if( $message->getRecipient() == $this->registry-
   >getObject('authenticate')->getUser()->getUserID() )
{
   $this->registry->getObject('template')-
      >buildFromTemplates('header.tpl.php', 'messages/view.tpl.php',
      'footer.tpl.php');
   $message->toTags( 'inbox_' );
   $message->setRead(1);
   $message->save();
}
else
{
   $this->registry->errorPage( 'Access denied',
      'Sorry, you are not allowed to view that message');
}
}
```

Now once the user reads a message, the database records the message as having been read.

Deleting a message

To delete a message, we simply call the model's `delete` method, provided the message was sent to the logged in user of course!

What about the sender?

These deletes will remove the message completely, even from the sender, but what if we want to have the sender keep their copy, or have the sender be able to delete their copy? Feel free to extend this to have an additional field to indicate whether the message has been deleted by the sender, and add the functionality in.

```
/**
 * Delete a message
 * @param int $message the message ID
 * @return void
 */
private function deleteMessage( $message )
{
   require_once( FRAMEWORK_PATH . 'models/message.php' );
   $message = new Message( $this->registry, $message );
   if( $message->getRecipient() == $this->registry-
```

```
>getObject('authenticate')->getUser()->getUserID() )
    {
        if( $message->delete() )
        {
            $url = $this->registry->getObject('url')->buildURL( array(),
              'messages', false );
            $this->registry->redirectUser( $url, 'Message deleted',
              'The message has been removed from your inbox');
        }
```

If the message wasn't sent to the logged in user, or if there was a problem deleting the message, we should display an appropriate error message to the user:

```
        else
        {
            $this->registry->errorPage( 'Sorry...', 'An error occured
              while trying to delete the message');
        }
    }
    else
    {
        $this->registry->errorPage( 'Access denied',
          'Sorry, you are not allowed to delete that message');
    }
}
```

Composing a new message

Composing a new message is the most complicated aspect for the feature, as there are a number of aspects to consider (and change, depending on the needs of the social network). Let's discuss these as we walk through the code:

```
/**
 * Compose a new message, and process new message submissions
 * @parm int $reply message ID this message is in reply to [optional]
   only used to pre-populate subject and recipient
 * @return void
 */
private function newMessage( $reply=0 )
{
$this->registry->getObject('template')->buildFromTemplates('header.
  tpl.php', 'messages/create.tpl.php', 'footer.tpl.php');
```

The two strands of this feature (displaying the new message form, and processing the new message) require knowing a list of members that the message can be sent to (provided we wish to restrict sending to contacts only). As this is the case, it makes sense for us to require the relationships model, and instantiate it before progressing:

```
require_once( FRAMEWORK_PATH . 'models/relationships.php' );
$relationships = new Relationships( $this->registry );

if( isset( $_POST ) && count( $_POST ) > 0 )
{
```

If the user has submitted a new message, we need to check that the recipient they have selected is in their network (that is, that they are allowed to send them a message):

```
$network = $relationships->getNetwork( $this->registry-
    >getObject('authenticate')->getUser()->getUserID() );
$recipient = intval( $_POST['recipient'] );
if( in_array( $recipient, $network ) )
{
```

If the recipient is in the user's network, then we create an instance of the message model, populate it with the data the user has submitted, and then save the message and redirect the user after displaying a confirmation message:

```
// this additional check may not be something we require for
    private messages?
require_once( FRAMEWORK_PATH . 'models/message.php' );
$message = new Message( $this->registry, 0 );
$message->setSender( $this->registry-
    >getObject('authenticate')->getUser()->getUserID() );
$message->setRecipient( $recipient );
$message->setSubject( $this->registry->getObject('db')-
    >sanitizeData( $_POST['subject'] ) );
$message->setMessage( $this->registry->getObject('db')-
    >sanitizeData( $_POST['message'] ) );
$message->save();
// email notification to the recipient perhaps??

// confirm, and redirect
$url = $this->registry->getObject('url')->buildURL( array(),
    'messages', false );
$this->registry->redirectUser( $url, 'Message sent', 'The
    message has been sent');
}
else
{
```

If the recipient isn't in their network, we display an error page. Alternatively, we could check the recipient's privacy settings to see if they allow messages from any user—something to consider when implementing privacy controls:

```
        $this->registry->errorPage('Invalid recipient',
            'Sorry, you can only send messages to your recipients');
    }
}
else
{
```

If the user hasn't submitted the form, then we need to display the new message form to them. We can get the list of potential recipients (to go in a drop down) from the relationships model, which we associate with a template variable.

```
        $cache = $relationships->getByUser( $this->registry-
            >getObject('authenticate')->getUser()->getUserID() );
        $this->registry->getObject('template')->getPage()-
            >addTag( 'recipients', array( 'SQL', $cache ) );
        if( $reply > 0 )
        {
```

If the message is in reply to another message, then we can provide some basic support for this, such as pre-selecting the recipient, and pre-completing the subject line based off the message this is in reply to:

```
        require_once( FRAMEWORK_PATH . 'models/message.php' );
        $message = new Message( $this->registry, $reply );
        if( $message->getRecipient() == $this->registry-
            >getObject('authenticate')->getUser()->getUserID() )
        {
            $this->registry->getObject('template')-> getPage()-
                >addAdditionalParsingData( 'recipients', 'ID',
                $message->getSender(), 'opt', "selected='selected'");
            $this->registry->getObject('template')->getPage()-
                >addTag( 'subject', 'Re: ' . $message->getSubject() );
        }
        else
        {
            $this->registry->getObject('template')->getPage()-
                >addTag( 'subject', '' );
        }
```

```
        }
        else
        {
            $this->registry->getObject('template')->getPage()-
              >addTag( 'subject', '' );
        }
    }


}
```

Creating a message template

For the new message template (`views/default/templates/messages/create.tpl.php`), we have a template loop for possible recipients. If the message is a reply, the recipient is selected via the `additionalParsingData` set in the controller. The subject is also pre-populated for us:

```
<div id="main">

    <div id="rightside">

    <ul>
        <li><a href="messages/">Your inbox</a></a>
    </ul>
    </div>

    <div id="content">
        <h1>Compose message</h1>
        <form action="messages/create" method="post">
        <label for="recipient">To:</label><br />
        <select id="recipient" name="recipient">
            <!-- START recipients -->
            <option value="{ID}" {opt}>{users_name}</option>
            <!-- END recipients -->
        </select><br />
        <label for="subject">Subject:</label><br />
        <input type="text" id="subject" name="subject"
          value="{subject}" /><br />
        <label for="message">Message:</label><br />
        <textarea id="message" name="message"></textarea><br />
```

```
<input type="submit" id="create" name="create" value="Send
   message" />
</form>

</div>

</div>
```

In action

If we visit our message centre /messages, we can see our inbox (once the controller is added to the controllers table in the database!), as shown in the screenshots earlier in the chapter.

If we click reply, we are taken to the same screen as with creating a new message, except the recipient is pre-selected and the subject is the subject of the previous message prefixed with **Re:**.

Room for improvement?

There are three particular areas that can be improved significantly:

- Sent items
- Replies
- Group messages

Sent items

At the moment, we can't see sent items, and while in principle this could be added easily, the problem lies if a user deletes the message. We would need to add two columns to the database, one indicating that the recipient has deleted it from their inbox, and one indicating the sender has deleted it from their sent items, as we discussed earlier in the chapter.

Replies

Our replies are not linked together; they are all stored as standalone messages, which is something we could improve.

Group messages

At the moment, private messages are only between two users, but we may wish to extend this in the future to support any number of users.

Summary

In this chapter, we have taken extended statuses on our users' profiles to support public messages between users. These public messages can use the comments system we have in place to form public conversations. We have also created a private messages area that allows users to communicate with one another in private.

Next, we can look at further extending the statuses system to support more types of message.

8
Statuses—Other Media

With our status stream now supporting simple-text updates from the profile owner, and public messages from other users, it is time for us to integrate other types of media into these statuses.

In this chapter, you will learn how to integrate other types of media in profile posts, including:

- Images
- Videos
- Links

The core information to our current statuses is held within the statuses table. We will keep this the same. However, depending on the type of status update, we may call upon other database tables to extend the information available to us.

Since different status types will use different status tables, we should use a left join to connect the tables, so we can keep just a single query to look up the statuses. It also pulls in the extra information when it is required.

Let's get started with extending our profiles and the status stream!

Why support other media types?

The following are the potential uses of supporting other media types for Dino Space users:

- Sharing videos of their pet dinosaurs
- Sharing photographs with other users
- Sharing relevant links with their contacts

Changes to the view

Since all of the media types we are going to support require at least one additional database field in a table that extends the statuses table, we are going to need to display any additional fields on the post status form. The standard type of status doesn't require additional fields, and new media types that we haven't discussed, which we may wish to support in the future, may require more than one additional field. To support a varying number of additional fields depending on the type, we could use some JavaScript (in this case, we will use the jQuery framework) to change the form depending on the context of the status. Beneath the main status box, we can add radio buttons for each of the status types, and depending on the one the user selects, the JavaScript can show or hide the additional fields, making the form more relevant.

Template

Our update status template needs a few changes:

- We need to set the `enctype` on the form, so that we can upload files (for posting images)
- We need radio buttons for the new types of statuses
- We need additional fields for those statuses

The changes are highlighted in the following code segment:

```
<p>Tell your network what you are up to</p>
<form action="profile/statuses/{profile_user_id}" method="post"
  enctype="multipart/form-data">
<textarea id="status" name="status"></textarea>
<br />
<input type="radio" name="status_type" id="status_checker_update"
  class="status_checker" value="update"  />Update
<input type="radio" name="status_type" id="status_checker_video"
  class="status_checker" value="video"  />Video
<input type="radio" name="status_type" id="status_checker_image"
  class="status_checker" value="image"  />Image
<input type="radio" name="status_type" id="status_checker_link"
  class="status_checker" value="link"  />Link
<br />
<div class="video_input  extra_field">
<label for="video_url" class="">YouTube URL</label>
<input type="text" id="" name="video_url" class="" /><br />
</div>
<div class="image_input  extra_field">
```

```
<label for="image_file" class="">Upload image</label>
<input type="file" id="" name="image_file" class="" /><br />
</div>
<div class="link_input  extra_field">
<label for="link_url" class="">Link</label>
<input type="text" id="" name="link_url" class="" /><br />
<label for="link_description" class="">Description</label>
<input type="text" id="" name="link_description" class="" /><br />
</div>
<input type="submit" id="updatestatus" name="updatestatus"
   value="Update" />
</form>
```

These changes also need to be made to the post template, for posting on another user's profile.

jQuery to enhance the user experience

For accessibility purposes, we need this form to function regardless of whether the user has JavaScript enabled on their browser. To that end, we should use JavaScript to hide the unused form elements. So, even if the user has JavaScript disabled, they can still use all aspects of the form. We can then use JavaScript to enhance the user experience, toggling which aspects of the form are hidden or shown.

```
<script type="text/javascript">
$(function() {
```

First, we hide all of the extended status fields.

```
$('.extra_field').hide();
$("input[name='status_type']").change(function(){
```

When the user changes the type of status, we hide all of the extended fields.

```
$('.extra_field').hide();
```

We then show the fields directly related to the status type they have chosen.

```
$('.'+ $("input[name='status_type']:checked").val() +
   '_input').show();
});
});
</script>
```

View in action

If we now take a look at our status updates page for our profile, we have some radio buttons that we can use to toggle elements of the form.

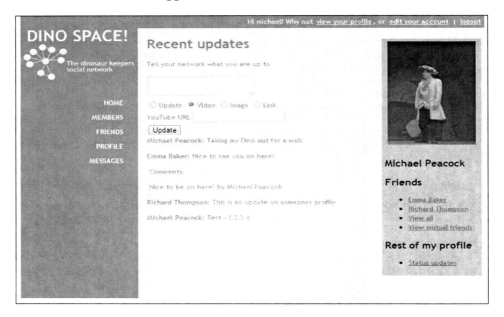

Images

To process images as a new status type, we will need a new database table and a new model to extend from the main status model. We will also need some new views, and to change the profile and status stream controllers (though we will make those changes after adding the three new status types).

Database table

The database table for images simply needs two fields:

Field	Type	Description
ID	Integer, Primary key	To relate to the main statuses table
Image	Varchar	The image filename

These two fields will be connected to the statuses table via a left join, to bring in the image filename for statuses that are images.

Model

The model needs to extend our statuses model, providing setters for any new fields, call the parent constructor, call the parent `setTypeReference` method to inform that it is an image, call the parent save method to save the status, and then insert a new record into the image status table with the image information.

Class, variable, and constructor

Firstly, we define the class as an extension of the status class. We then define a variable for the image, and construct the object. The constructor calls the parent `setTypeReference` method to ensure it generates the correct type ID for an image, and then calls the parent constructor so it too has reference to the registry object. This file is saved as `/models/imagestatus.php`.

```php
<?php
/**
 * Image status object
 * extends the base status object
 */
class Imagestatus extends status {
  private $image;

  /**
   * Constructor
   * @param Registry $registry
   * @param int $id
   * @return void
   */
  public function __construct( Registry $registry, $id = 0 )
  {
    $this->registry = $registry;
    parent::setTypeReference('image');
    parent::__construct( $this->registry, $id );
  }
```

 To call a method from an object's parent class, we use the `parent` keyword, followed by the scope resolution operator, followed by the method we wish to call.

Processing the image upload

When dealing with image uploads, resizing, and saving, there are different PHP functions that should be used depending on the type of the image. To make this easier and to provide a centralized place for dealing with image uploads and other image-related tasks, we should create a library file (`lib/images/imagemanager.class.php`) to make this easier.

Let's discuss what an image manager library file should do to make our lives easier:

- Process uploading of an image from `$_POST` data
  - Verify the type of file and the file extension

- Process images from the file system so that we can modify them
- Display an image to the browser
- Resize an image
- Rescale an image by resizing either the x or y co-ordinate, and scaling the other co-ordinate proportionally
- Get image information such as size and name
- Save the changes to the image

The following is the code required to perform the above-mentioned tasks:

```php
<?php
/**
 * Image manager class
 * @author Michael Peacock
 */
class Imagemanager
{
  /**
   * Type of the image
   */
  private $type = '';

  /**
   * Extensions that the user can upload
   */
  private $uploadExtentions = array( 'png', 'jpg', 'jpeg', 'gif' );

  /**
   * Mime types of files the user can upload
   */
  private $uploadTypes = array( 'image/gif', 'image/jpg',
    'image/jpeg', 'image/pjpeg', 'image/png' );
```

```
/**
 * The image itself
 */
private $image;

/**
 * The image name
 */
private $name;

public function __construct(){}
```

We need a method to load a local image, so that we can work with images saved on the servers file system.

```
/**
 * Load image from local file system
 * @param String $filepath
 * @return void
 */
public function loadFromFile( $filepath )
{
```

Based on the path to the image, we can get information on the image including the type of image (getimagesize gives us an array of information on the image; the second element in the array is the type).

```
$info = getimagesize( $filepath );
$this->type = $info[2];
```

We can then compare the image type to various PHP constants, and depending on the image type (JPEG, GIF, or PNG) we use the appropriate imagecreatefrom function.

```
if( $this->type == IMAGETYPE_JPEG )
{
  $this->image = imagecreatefromjpeg($filepath);
}
elseif( $this->type == IMAGETYPE_GIF )
{
  $this->image = imagecreatefromgif($filepath);
}
elseif( $this->type == IMAGETYPE_PNG )
{
  $this->image = imagecreatefrompng($filepath);
}
}
```

We require a couple of getter methods to return the height or width of the image.

```
/**
 * Get the image width
 * @return int
 */
public function getWidth()
{
  return imagesx($this->image);
}

/**
 * Get the height of the image
 * @return int
 */
public function getHeight()
{
  return imagesy($this->image);
}
```

We use a simple `resize` method that resizes the image to the dimensions we request.

```
/**
 * Resize the image
 * @param int $x width
 * @param int $y height
 * @return void
 */
public function resize( $x, $y )
{
  $new = imagecreatetruecolor($x, $y);
  imagecopyresampled($new, $this->image, 0, 0, 0, 0, $x, $y,
    $this->getWidth(), $this->getHeight());
  $this->image = $new;
}
```

Here we use a scaling function that takes a height parameter to resize to and scales the width accordingly.

```
/**
 * Resize the image, scaling the width, based on a new height
 * @param int $height
 * @return void
 */
public function resizeScaleWidth( $height )
{
```

```
    $width = $this->getWidth() * ( $height / $this->getHeight() );
    $this->resize( $width, $height );
}
```

Similar to the above method, this method takes a width parameter, resizes the width, and rescales the height based on the width.

```
/**
 * Resize the image, scaling the height, based on a new width
 * @param int $width
 * @return void
 */
public function resizeScaleHeight( $width )
{
    $height = $this->getHeight() * ( $width / $this->getWidth() );
    $this->resize( $width, $height );
}
```

The following is another scaling function, this time to rescale the image to a percentage of its current size:

```
/**
 * Scale an image
 * @param int $percentage
 * @return void
 */
public function scale( $percentage )
{

    $width = $this->getWidth() * $percentage / 100;
    $height = $this->getheight() * $percentage / 100;
    $this->resize( $width, $height );
}
```

To output the image to the browser from PHP, we need to check the type of the image, set the appropriate header based off the type, and then use the appropriate image function to render the image. After calling this method, we need to call exit() to ensure the image is displayed correctly.

```
/**
 * Display the image to the browser - called before output is sent,
   exit() should be called straight after.
 * @return void
 */
public function display()
{
    if( $this->type == IMAGETYPE_JPEG )
```

```
    {
      $type = 'image/jpeg';
    }
    elseif( $this->type == IMAGETYPE_GIF )
    {
      $type = 'image/gif';
    }
    elseif( $this->type == IMAGETYPE_PNG )
    {
      $type = 'image/png';
    }

    header('Content-Type: ' . $type );

    if( $this->type == IMAGETYPE_JPEG )
    {
      imagejpeg( $this->image );
    }
    elseif( $this->type == IMAGETYPE_GIF )
    {
      imagegif( $this->image );
    }
    elseif( $this->type == IMAGETYPE_PNG )
    {
      imagepng( $this->image );
    }
  }
```

To load an image from $_POST data, we need to know the post field the image is being sent through, the directory we wish to place the image in, and any additional prefix we may wish to add to the image's name (to prevent conflicts with images with the same name).

```
    /**
     * Load image from postdata
     * @param String $postfield the field the image was uploaded via
     * @param String $moveto the location for the upload
     * @param String $name_prefix a prefix for the filename
     * @return boolean
     */
    public function loadFromPost( $postfield, $moveto,
      $name_prefix='' )
    {
```

Before doing anything, we should check that the file requested is actually a file that has been uploaded (and that this isn't a malicious user trying to access other files).

```
if( is_uploaded_file( $_FILES[ $postfield ]['tmp_name'] ) )
{
  $i = strrpos( $_FILES[ $postfield ]['name'], '.');
  if (! $i )
  {
    //'no extention';
    return false;
  }
  else
  {
```

We then check that the extension of the file is in our allowed extensions array.

```
    $l = strlen(  $_FILES[ $postfield ]['name'] ) - $i;
    $ext = strtolower ( substr(  $_FILES[ $postfield ]['name'],
      $i+1, $l ) );
    if( in_array( $ext, $this->uploadExtentions ) )
    {
```

Next, we check if the file type is an allowed file type.

```
      if( in_array( $_FILES[ $postfield ]['type'],
      $this->uploadTypes ) )
      {
```

Then, we move the file, as it has already been uploaded to our server's `temp` folder, to our own uploads directory and load it into our image manager class for any further processing we wish to make.

```
        $name = str_replace( ' ', '', $_FILES[
          $postfield ]['name'] );
        $this->name = $name_prefix . $name;
        $path = $moveto . $name_prefix.$name;
        move_uploaded_file( $_FILES[ $postfield ]['tmp_name'] ,
          $path );
        $this->loadFromFile( $path );
        return true;
      }
      else
      {
        // 'invalid type';
        return false;
      }
    }
```

```
        else
        {
          // 'invalid extention';
          return false;
        }
      }
    }
    else
    {
      // 'not uploaded file';
      return false;
    }
  }
```

The following getter method is used to return the name of the image we are working with:

```
/**
 * Get the image name
 * @return String
 */
public function getName()
{
  return $this->name;
}
```

Finally, we have our save method, which again must detect the type of image, to work out which function to use.

```
/**
 * Save changes to an image e.g. after resize
 * @param String $location location of image
 * @param String $type type of the image
 * @param int $quality image quality /100
 * @return void
 */
public function save( $location, $type='', $quality=100 )
{
  $type = ( $type == '' ) ? $this->type : $type;
  if( $type == IMAGETYPE_JPEG )
  {
    imagejpeg( $this->image, $location, $quality);
  }
  elseif( $type == IMAGETYPE_GIF )
  {
```

```
         imagegif( $this->image, $location );
      }
      elseif( $type == IMAGETYPE_PNG )
      {
         imagepng( $this->image, $location );
      }
   }
}
?>
```

Using the image manager library to process the file upload

Now that we have a simple, centralized way of processing file uploads and resizing them, we can process the image the user is trying to upload as their extended status.

```
/**
 * Process an image upload and set the image
 * @param String $postfield the $_POST field the image was uploaded
   through
 * @return boolean
 */
public function processImage( $postfield )
{
   require_once( FRAMEWORK_PATH .
      'lib/images/imagemanager.class.php' );
   $im = new Imagemanager();
   $prefix = time() . '_';
   if( $im->loadFromPost( $postfield, $this->registry-
      >getSetting('upload_path') . 'statusimages/', $prefix ) )
   {
      $im->resizeScaleWidth( 150 );
      $im->save( $this->registry->getSetting('upload_path') .
         'statusimages/' . $im->getName() );
      $this->image = $im->getName();
      return true;
   }
   else
   {
      return false;
   }
}
```

Saving the status

This leaves us with the final method for saving the status. This calls the parent object's save method to create the record in the statuses table. Then it gets the ID, and inserts a new record into the images table with this ID as the ID.

```
/**
 * Save the image status
 * @return void
 */
public function save()
{
  // save the parent object and thus the status table
  parent::save();
  // grab the newly inserted status ID
  $id = $this->getID();
  // insert into the images status table, using the same ID
  $extended = array();
  $extended['id'] = $id;
  $extended['image'] = $this->image;
  $this->registry->getObject('db')->insertRecords(
    'statuses_images', $extended );
  }
 }
?>
```

Video (via YouTube)

To support video (via YouTube), we need one additional field on the form for the user to paste in the YouTube URL. From the URL, we can automatically generate code to play the video, and we can also look up the thumbnail image of the video from YouTube, from the data contained within the URL.

Database

As with our image's status type, we only require two fields in our new table:

Field	Type	Description
ID	Integer, Primary key	To relate to the main statuses table
Video_id	Varchar	The YouTube video ID

Model

The model needs to be very similar to our image's model. Firstly, the class extends the status class. Then, we have our variable for the video ID, after which we construct the object by calling the parent object's `setTypeReference` and `__construct` methods.

```php
<?php
/**
 * Video status object
 * extends the base status object
 */
class Videostatus extends status {
  private $video_id;

  /**
   * Constructor
   * @param Registry $registry
   * @param int $id
   * @return void
   */
  public function __construct( Registry $registry, $id = 0 )
  {
    $this->registry = $registry;
    parent::__construct( $this->registry, $id );
    parent::setTypeReference('video');
  }
```

We then have a setter method to set the video ID (assuming we know what the video ID is).

```php
  public function setVideoId( $vid )
  {
    $this->video_id = $vid;
  }
```

Then, we have a useful setter method that parses the YouTube URL, extracts the video ID from it, and sets the class variable accordingly. In this case, if no video ID is found in the URL, it uses a clip from the TV series "Dinosaurs" as a default video.

```php
  public function setVideoIdFromURL( $url )
  {
    $data = array();
    parse_str( parse_url($url, PHP_URL_QUERY), $data );
    $this->video_id = $this->registry->getObject('db')-
      >sanitizeData(isset( $data['v'] ) ? $data['v']
      : '7NzzcOWPH0');
  }
```

Finally we have our save method, which works in the same way as the image model.

```
/**
 * Save the video status
 * @return void
 */
public function save()
{
  // save the parent object and thus the status table
  parent::save();
  // grab the newly inserted status ID
  $id = $this->getID();
  // insert into the video status table, using the same ID
  $extended = array();
  $extended['id'] = $id;
  $extended['video_id'] = $this->video_id;
  $this->registry->getObject('db')->insertRecords(
    'statuses_videos', $extended );
  }
}
?>
```

Links

When sharing links with other users we need to at least store the URL itself. We could also store a brief description of the link or even an image from the site. If we wished, we could automatically populate this information from the link. However, for the moment, we will stick to just storing the link and a brief description of it.

Database

Our video statuses table requires three fields: an ID, the URL of the link, and the name or description of the link.

Field	Type	Description
ID	Integer, Primary key	To relate to the main statuses table
URL	Varchar	The link itself
Description	Varchar	Description of the link

Model

As with the video and image types, we require a simple model to extend our statuses model (`models/videostatus.php`).

```php
<?php
/**
 * Link status object
 * extends the base status object
 */
class Linkstatus extends status {

  private $url;
  private $description;
```

Our constructor needs to set the registry, call the parent class' constructor, and then set the type of status by calling the parent's `setTypeReference` method.

```php
/**
 * Constructor
 * @param Registry $registry
 * @param int $id
 * @return void
 */
public function __construct( Registry $registry, $id = 0 )
{
  $this->registry = $registry;
  parent::__construct( $this->registry, $id );
  parent::setTypeReference('link');
}
```

We then have setters for the variables we are extending onto the class.

```php
/**
 * Set the URL
 * @param String $url
 * @return void
 */
public function setURL( $url )
{
  $this->url = $url;
}

/**
 * Set the description of the link
 * @param String $description
```

```
   * @return void
   */
  public function setDescription( $description )
  {
    $this->description = $description;
  }
```

Finally, our save method needs to call the parent object's save method, to save the status record. It then gets the ID of the status and creates a record in the `statuses_links` table, relating the core status with the custom link data.

```
  /**
   * Save the link status
   * @return void
   */
  public function save()
  {
    // save the parent object and thus the status table
    parent::save();
    // grab the newly inserted status ID
    $id = $this->getID();
    // insert into the link status table, using the same ID
    $extended = array();
    $extended['id'] = $id;
    $extended['URL'] = $this->url;
    $extended['description'] = $this->description;
    $this->registry->getObject('db')->insertRecords(
      'statuses_links', $extended );
  }
}
?>
```

Extending the profiles

With new database tables, status forms, and models in place for the new status types of Dino Space, we need to extend our profiles to save these new statuses, and also to include the information from these additional tables in the profile's statuses. We already have provisions for including different templates depending on the type of the status (as per Chapter 6), so we just need to alter our status stream query.

Processing the new status posts

In our profile statuses controller (`controllers/profile/
profilestatusescontroller.php`) in the `addStatus` method, in the two instances
where we construct the status object, we instead need to check which type of status
is being posted, and if it is a different status type, we must also include that file, and
instead construct that object.

```php
if( isset( $_POST['status_type'] ) && $_POST['status_type'] !=
  'update' )
    {
      if( $_POST['status_type'] == 'image' )
      {
        require_once( FRAMEWORK_PATH . 'models/imagestatus.php' );
        $status = new Imagestatus( $this->registry, 0 );
        $status->processImage( 'image_file' );
      }
      elseif( $_POST['status_type'] == 'video' )
      {
        require_once( FRAMEWORK_PATH . 'models/videostatus.php' );
        $status = new Videostatus( $this->registry, 0 );
        $status->setVideoIdFromURL( $_POST['video_url'] );
      }
      elseif( $_POST['status_type'] == 'link' )
      {
        require_once( FRAMEWORK_PATH . 'models/linkstatus.php' );
        $status = new Linkstatus( $this->registry, 0 );
        $status->setURL( $this->registry->getObject('db')-
          >sanitizeData( $_POST['link_url'] ) );
        $status->setDescription( $this->registry->getObject('db')-
          >sanitizeData( $_POST['link_description'] ) );
      }
    }
    else
    {
      $status = new Status( $this->registry, 0 );
    }
```

Altering our profile status' query

Our updates query (in the profile statuses controller) needs to be altered to left join onto the various extended statuses tables, pulling in additional information where appropriate, like the following code:

```
$sql = "SELECT t.type_reference, t.type_name, s.*, pa.name as
    poster_name, i.image, v.video_id, l.URL, l.description FROM
    status_types t, profile p, profile pa, statuses s LEFT JOIN
    statuses_images i ON s.ID=i.id LEFT JOIN statuses_videos v ON
    s.ID=v.id LEFT JOIN statuses_links l ON s.ID=l.id WHERE t.ID=s.type
    AND p.user_id=s.profile AND pa.user_id=s.poster AND
    p.user_id={$user} ORDER BY s.ID DESC LIMIT 20";
```

Status views

Next, we need to create the various template files to be included to display the relevant status information.

Images

It is saved as `views/default/templates/profile/updates/image.tpl.php`.

```
<p><strong>{poster_name}</strong>: posted an image "{update}"</p>
<img src="uploads/statusimages/{image}" alt="Image" />
<!-- START comments-{ID} -->
<p> Comments:</p>
<p> {comment} by {commenter}</p>
<!-- END comments-{ID} -->
```

Video

It is saved as `views/default/templates/profile/updates/video.tpl.php`.

```
<p><strong>{poster_name}</strong>: posted an video "{update}"</p>
<object width="200" height="164"><param name="movie"
    value="http://www.youtube.com/v/{video_id}&amp;hl=en_GB&amp;fs=1?
    rel=0&amp;border=1"></param><param name="allowFullScreen"
    value="true"></param><param name="allowscriptaccess"
    value="always"></param><embed
    src="http://www.youtube.com/v/{video_id}&amp;hl=en_GB&amp;fs=1?rel=
    0&amp;border=1" type="application/x-shockwave-flash"
    allowscriptaccess="always" allowfullscreen="true" width="200"
    height="164"></embed></object>
<!-- START comments-{ID} -->
<p> Comments:</p>
<p> {comment} by {commenter}</p>
<!-- END comments-{ID} -->
```

Links

It is saved as `views/default/templates/profile/updates/link.tpl.php`.

```
<p><strong>{poster_name}</strong>: posted an link "{update}"</p>
<a href="{URL}">{description}</a>
<!-- START comments-{ID} -->
<p> Comments:</p>
<p> {comment} by {commenter}</p>
<!-- END comments-{ID} -->
```

In action

Let's now take a look at our profile with these new status types on!

Images

After posting a status update with an image, the image is resized and displayed beneath the status.

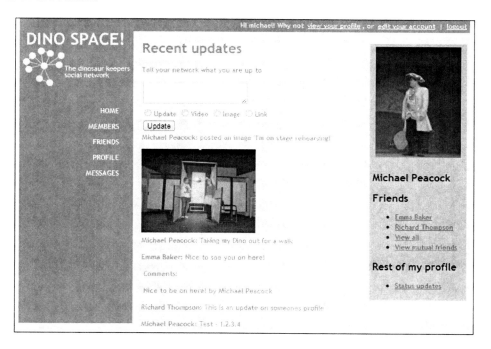

Videos

A nice YouTube player is embedded with the video we selected when we posted a new video.

Links

If we post a status with a link attached, the link is shown beneath our status.

Repeat!

We also need to extend our status stream to work in the same way as our profiles, pulling in extended data from the extended status types. As we have discussed thoroughly how to update the profile view, you should be able to tackle the status stream on your own, applying the knowledge from this chapter.

Summary

In this chapter we have taken our simple status stream and user profiles and extended them to support statuses and messages that make use of other media including images, videos, and links.

Next up, is creating calendars and providing provisions for creating and displaying events and birthdays.

9
Events and Birthdays

Our social network is nearing completion; we now have not only a status stream of updates for our users, but also support for a number of different types of media, including video and images. One of the two main remaining features (the other being groups) is events. No social network would be complete without support for events and of course, birthdays.

In this chapter, you will learn:

- How to dynamically generate innovative calendars
- How to use these calendars to display specific dates
- How to re-use this calendar feature in other areas of the site
- How to notify users of the birthday of their contacts
- How to manage event invitations and RSVPs
- How to send reminders via the site, e-mail, and SMS

Let's plan

So, we want to store, manage, and display user-organized events and the birthdays of our members on the site. In itself, this is fairly trivial; we can simply list any events occurring within the next X days, and allow our users to paginate through the results. This of course, isn't a very user friendly approach; a more user friendly approach would be to display the events within a calendar, which is somewhat more complicated.

Because a calendar is something we will most likely want to reuse throughout our network, and because of the complexities that come with it, it is important for us to plan what we need it to do. We will create a calendar library file, a class that can be re-used throughout Dino Space, while we will also create controllers to display the primary calendar. The library file will do most of the work for us, so that we can re-use it in any number of other controllers we need.

Calendars: what do we need to be able to do?

We need our calendar library to:

- Generate a friendly interface for the current month

- Be capable of generating a friendly interface for other months

- Be aware of the next and previous months, and their years if they differ from the current year, as in most cases, a user will browse through months starting at the current month, moving forward or backwards a month at a time

- Be capable of indicating which day is the current day, and days with events within them

- Work out how many days there are in a particular month

Calendar library

We will save our calendar library file as `/lib/calendar/calendar.class.php`. The first thing for us to do in our file, is create a number of variables, and the constructor.

We need variables for:

- The year the calendar represents

- The day the calendar represents

- The month the calendar represents

- The day of the week we want our calendar to start with

- Days of the week, ordered so we can change them using our start day of the week as an offset

- Days of the week ordered with respect to our offset

- The name of the month represented by the calendar

- Dates of the month

- Styles associated with each of the days of the month

- Data associated with each of the days of the month, that is, the events on those days

```php
<?php
/**
 * Calendar object
 */
class Calendar{
```

```
/**
 * The year represented within the calendar
 */
private $year;

/**
 * The current day being represented within the calendar, if
     appropriate
 */
private $day;

/**
 * The current month being represented within the calendar
 */
private $month;

/**
 * Tells the calendar which day of the month weeks start at.
   Sunday is standard for UK calendars.
 */
private $startDay = 0;

/**
 * Array of days...as if we didn't already know...
 */
private $days = array('Sun','Mon','Tue','Wed','Thu','Fri', 'Sat');

/**
 * Array of months
 */
private $months = array(    0=> '',
                            1 => 'January',
                            2 => 'February',
                            3 => 'March',
                            4 => 'April',
                            5 => 'May',
                            6 => 'June',
                            7 => 'July',
                            8 => 'August',
                            9 => 'September',
                            10 => 'October',
                            11 => 'November',
                            12 => 'December'
                        );
```

```php
/**
 * Days of the week, ordered by our chosen start day
 */
private $orderedDays;

/**
 * Name of the current month
 */
private $monthName;

/**
 * Dates of the month
 */
private $dates=array();

/**
 * Styles for each day of the month
 */
private $dateStyles=array();

/**
 * List of days with events associated with them
 */
private $daysWithEvents = array();

/**
 * Data to associate with dates
 */
private $data=array();

/**
 * Data associated with dates, in corresponding 42 record array
 */
private $datesData = array();
```

With our variables in place, we now need a constructor that takes the day, month, and year, which we wish to represent in calendar form, and then set the appropriate values of our object. If an empty string is passed for any of the values, they default to today's date.

```php
/**
 * Calendar constructor
 * @param int $day selected day in the calendar
```

```
 * @param int $month month being represented in calendar
 * @param int $year the year being represented in the calendar
 * @return void
 */
public function __construct( $day, $month, $year )
{
    $this->year = ( $year == '' ) ? date('y') : $year;
    $this->month =  ( $month == '' ) ? date('m') : $month;
    $this->day = ( $day == '' ) ? date('d') : $day;
    $this->monthName =  $this->months[ ltrim( $this->month, '0') ];
}
```

Generating the month

From a computational perspective, and with the way our template engine works, it is best to think of a month as a grid of 42 squares. No month has 42 days in it; however, if a month starts on the last day of the week, then the grid may need to have 42 squares, 31 for the month itself, and the remaining 11 for the un-used grids on the first week, and last week of the month.

With this in mind, all we need our calendar library to do, is iterate 42 times and work out if the current grid is for a valid date for that month, and also, whether the date has any events associated with it, or if the date is the current date.

This method in itself won't return anything; instead, it will set various variables within the object that we can use, including:

- An ordered list of days of the week (ordered based off the desired start day of the week, allowing for US users to have weeks starting on Monday, and UK users to have weeks starting on Sunday)

- The name of the current month

- The days of the month, in an array corresponding to the 42 square grid for the calendar

- The styles (CSS classes to be used) of the days of the month, also in a corresponding array

- The data for each calendar day, also in a corresponding array

  ```
  /**
   * Builds the month being represented by the calendar object
   * @return void
   */
  public function buildMonth()
  {
  ```

First, we generate a list of the days in order, with respect to our chosen first day of the week. Then, we look up the string representation of the current month and set that:

```
$this->orderedDays = $this->getDaysInOrder();


$this->monthName =  $this->months[ ltrim( $this->month, '0') ];
```

Since we need to know the day of the first of the month, so we know which of our 42 boxes is to contain data for the first, we need to look up which day of the week the first of the month is:

```
// start of whichever month we are building
$start_of_month = getdate( mktime(12, 0, 0, $this->month, 1,
  $this->year ) );


$first_day_of_month = $start_of_month['wday'];
```

With the day of the first of the month looked up, we now need to work out an offset with respect to the first day of the week, so we know after how many days the first of the month appears. For example, if our calendar is set to display Sunday as the first of the week, and the 1st of the month is Wednesday, the first three boxes in the calendar will be empty, so we need to know how many to "pass over":

```
$days = $this->startDay - $first_day_of_month;

if( $days > 1 )
{
   // get an offset
   $days -= 7;

}

$num_days = $this->daysInMonth($this->month, $this->year);
// 42 iterations
$start = 0;
$cal_dates = array();
$cal_dates_style = array();
$cal_events = array();
```

Next, we loop 42 times, for each of the boxes in our calendar grid. Using the offset ($days), we skip the first empty boxes, setting an appropriate class for them:

```
while( $start < 42 )
{
   // off set dates
```

```
if( $days < 0 )
{
    $cal_dates[] = '';
    $cal_dates_style[] = 'calendar-empty';
    $cal_dates_data[] = '';
}
else
{
```

Once we have passed the offset dates, the next "number of days in the month" cycles are valid dates in the calendar, so we look to see if we have events assigned to the dates, and if so, we put them in the appropriate array and set an appropriate class for the day. We also put the day of the month in an array of calendar dates. We created empty values for the previous iterations, so we know the dates will be appropriately offset.

```
if( $days < $num_days )
{
    // real days
    $cal_dates[] = $days+1;
    if( in_array( $days+1, $this->daysWithEvents ) )
    {
        $cal_dates_style[] = 'has-events';
        $cal_dates_data[] = $this->data[ $days+1 ];
    }
    else
    {
        $cal_dates_style[] = '';
        $cal_dates_data[] = '';
    }

}
else
{
```

After the offset days, and the days of the month, we set an appropriate class indicating that the current box is not an actual date in the month:

```
    // surplus
    $cal_dates[] = '';
    $cal_dates_style[] = 'calendar-empty';
    $cal_dates_data[] = '';
}

}
```

```
    // increment and loop
    $start++;
    $days++;
}

// done
$this->dates = $cal_dates;
$this->dateStyles = $cal_dates_style;
$this->dateData = $cal_dates_data;
}
```

Days in the month

Calculating the days in a month is a fairly simple task; all months have a set number of days in them, except for February, so for February, we simply need to check whether the current year is a leap year:

```
/**
 * How many days are in a month?
 * @param int $m month
 * @param int $y year
 * @return int the number of days in the month
 */
function daysInMonth($m, $y)
{
```

If we have been passed a month that isn't valid, simply return zero:

```
if( $m < 1 || $m > 12 )
{
    return 0;
}
else
{
```

September, April, June, and November have 30 days—so for these months, return 30:

```
// 30: 9, 4, 6, 11
if( $m == 9 || $m == 4 || $m == 6 || $m == 11 )
{
    return 30;
}
```

For any remaining month that isn't February (all the rest have 31), we return 31:

```
else if( $m != 2 )
{
    // all the rest have 31
    return 31;
}
else
{
```

A year isn't a leap year if the year isn't divisible by 4, so in this instance, we return 28:

```
// except for february alone
if( $y % 4 != 0 )
{
    // which has 28
    return 28;
}
else
{
```

If a year isn't divisible by 100, then it is a leap year, so we return 29:

```
if( $y % 100 != 0 )
{
    // and on leap years 29
    return 29;
}
else
{
```

If the year isn't divisible by 400, then it isn't a leap year, so we return 28:

```
if( $y % 400 != 0 )
{
    // deja vu: which has 28
    return 28;
}
else
{
```

If it is divisible by 400, then we return 29, as it is a leap year:

```
                    // deja vu: and on leap years 29
                    return 29;
            }
        }
    }
  }
}
}
```

And there we have a very handy function, as part of our calendar library, to determine the number of days in any given month.

Ordered days

As discussed earlier, our calendar is set to be customizable in terms of which day of the month is the start date. Because of this, our array of days (`private $days = array('Sun','Mon','Tue','Wed','Thu','Fri', 'Sat');`) needs to be re-ordered based on the chosen first day of the week:

```
/**
 * Get days in order
 * @return array array of days (as strings)
 */
function getDaysInOrder()
{
    $ordered_days = array();
    for( $i = 0; $i < 7; $i++ )
    {
        $ordered_days[] = $this->days[ ( $this->startDay + $i ) % 7
];
    }
    return $ordered_days;
}
```

Previous month

Most calendars display links to the next and previous month, making it easy for the user to navigate between months. For this to be done, we need to know the month and if appropriate, year, of the next month and previous month.

We can easily get this information in integer form, by incrementing or decrementing the current month, unless we are at an edge case, such as month 1, where we go to 12, and then decrease the year. To make this as flexible as possible, we can simply create a new calendar object, representing the previous month, and whichever controller requires it can simply look up the month, month name, and year from the object and display that to the user:

```
/**
 * Get previous month
 * @return Object calendar object
 */
public function getPreviousMonth()
{
    $pm = new Calendar( '', ( ( $this->month > 1 ) ?
      $this->month - 1 : 12 ), ( ( $this->month == 1 ) ?
      $this->year-1 : $this->year ) );
    return $pm;
}
```

Next month

As with the previous month, a method to return a calendar object for the next month:

```
/**
 * Get next month
 * @return Object calendar object
 */
public function getNextMonth()
{
    $nm = new Calendar( '', ( ($this->month < 12 ) ?
        $this->month + 1 : 1), ( ( $this->month == 12 ) ?
        $this->year + 1 : $this->year ) );
    return $nm;
}
```

Displaying a calendar

With our calendar library in place, we now need to look at how a controller would leverage the power of the library to generate a particular month, and display it to the user.

Generate and output

To actually display a calendar, we need some code which:

- Requires the calendar library
- Instantiates the object
- Generates the month
- Sends various bits of data to the template
- Outputs the template

We also need a template file with our 42 boxes in a calendar grid.

The following code can be used to generate a calendar (this isn't for a specific feature, you can find the code in the testOutput() method in the calendar controller):

```
// require the class
    require_once( FRAMEWORK_PATH . 'lib/calendar/calendar.class.php'
);
    // set the default month and year, i.e. the current month and
      year
    $m = date('m');
    $y = date('Y');
    // check for a different Month / Year (i.e. user has moved to
      another month)
    if( isset( $_GET['month'] ) )
    {
       $m = intval( $_GET['month']);
       if( $m > 0 && $m < 13 )
       {

       }
       else
       {
          $m = date('m');
       }
    }
    if( isset( $_GET['year'] ) )
    {
       $y = intval( $_GET['year']);
    }
    // Instantiate the calendar object
    $calendar = new Calendar( '', $m, $y );
    // Get next and previous month / year
    $nm = $calendar->getNextMonth()->getMonth();
```

```php
$ny = $calendar->getNextMonth()->getYear();
$pm = $calendar->getPreviousMonth()->getMonth();
$py = $calendar->getPreviousMonth()->getYear();

// send next / previous month data to the template
$this->registry->getObject('template')->getPage()-
    >addTag('nm', $nm );
$this->registry->getObject('template')->getPage()-
    >addTag('pm', $pm );
$this->registry->getObject('template')->getPage()-
    >addTag('ny', $ny );
$this->registry->getObject('template')->getPage()-
    >addTag('py', $py );
// send the current month name and year to the template
$this->registry->getObject('template')->getPage()-
    >addTag('month_name', $calendar->getMonthName() );
$this->registry->getObject('template')->getPage()-
    >addTag('the_year', $calendar->getYear() );
// Set the start day of the week
$calendar->setStartDay(0);
// Get how many days there are in the month


// build the month, generate some data
$calendar->buildMonth();
// days
$this->registry->getObject('template')->dataToTags( $calendar-
    >getDaysInOrder(),'cal_0_day_' );
// dates
$this->registry->getObject('template')->dataToTags( $calendar-
    >getDates(),'cal_0_dates_' );
// styles
$this->registry->getObject('template')->dataToTags( $calendar-
    >getDateStyles(),'cal_0_dates_style_' );
// data
$this->registry->getObject('template')->dataToTags( $calendar-
    >getDateData(),'cal_0_dates_data_' );

$this->registry->getObject('template')->buildFromTemplates(
    'test-calendar.tpl.php' );
```

In terms of the template, we need a grid of 42 potential calendar dates, each with a template tag for a class, and a template tag for the date, and a template tag for any potential data within.

The days of the week are also template tags, as we may wish to dynamically generate them based off an individual user's preference, as highlighted below:

```
<html>
<body>

    <h1> {month_name} {the_year}      </h1>
    <p><a href="calendar/?&amp;month={nm}&amp;year={ny}">Next</a>
    <a href="calendar/?&amp;month={pm}&amp;year={py}">Previous</a></p>

    <div>
        <table id="ccc">
            <tr>
                <th class="weekend">{cal_0_day_0}</th>
                <th class="">{cal_0_day_1}</th>
                <th class="">{cal_0_day_2}</th>
                <th class="">{cal_0_day_3}</th>
                <th class="">{cal_0_day_4}</th>
                <th class="">{cal_0_day_5}</th>
                <th class="weekend">{cal_0_day_6}</th>
            </tr>
            <tr>
```

If we take a look at how an individual week (highlighted below) needs to be represented, you can see that we prefix the template tag with cal_0_ (more on that later), and that they range from 0 to 41 (42 boxes):

```
                <td class="weekend {cal_0_dates_style_0}">
                    {cal_0_dates_0} {cal_0_dates_data_0}</td>
                <td class="{cal_0_dates_style_1}">{cal_0_dates_1}
                    {cal_0_dates_data_1}</td>
                <td class="{cal_0_dates_style_2}">{cal_0_dates_2}
                    {cal_0_dates_data_2}</td>
                <td class="{cal_0_dates_style_3}">{cal_0_dates_3}
                    {cal_0_dates_data_3}</td>
                <td class="{cal_0_dates_style_4}">{cal_0_dates_4}
                    {cal_0_dates_data_4}</td>
                <td class="{cal_0_dates_style_5}">{cal_0_dates_5}
                    {cal_0_dates_data_5}</td>
                <td class="weekend {cal_0_dates_style_6}">{cal_0_dates_6}
                    {cal_0_dates_data_6}</td>
            </tr>
            <tr>
                <td class="weekend {cal_0_dates_style_7}">{cal_0_dates_7}
                    {cal_0_dates_data_7}</td>
                <td class="{cal_0_dates_style_8}">{cal_0_dates_8}
                    {cal_0_dates_data_8}</td>
```

```
<td class="{cal_0_dates_style_9}">{cal_0_dates_9}
  {cal_0_dates_data_9}</td>
<td class="{cal_0_dates_style_10}">{cal_0_dates_10}
  {cal_0_dates_data_10}</td>
<td class="{cal_0_dates_style_11}">{cal_0_dates_11}
  {cal_0_dates_data_11}</td>
<td class="{cal_0_dates_style_12}">{cal_0_dates_12}
  {cal_0_dates_data_12}</td>
<td class="weekend {cal_0_dates_style_13}">
  {cal_0_dates_13} {cal_0_dates_data_13}</td>
  </tr>
  <tr>
<td class="weekend {cal_0_dates_style_14}">
  {cal_0_dates_14} {cal_0_dates_data_14}</td>
<td class="{cal_0_dates_style_15}">{cal_0_dates_15}
  {cal_0_dates_data_15}</td>
<td class="{cal_0_dates_style_16}">{cal_0_dates_16}
  {cal_0_dates_data_16}</td>
<td class="{cal_0_dates_style_17}">{cal_0_dates_17}
  {cal_0_dates_data_17}</td>
<td class="{cal_0_dates_style_18}">{cal_0_dates_18}
  {cal_0_dates_data_18}</td>
<td class="{cal_0_dates_style_18}">{cal_0_dates_19}
  {cal_0_dates_data_19}</td>
<td class="weekend {cal_0_dates_style_20}">
  {cal_0_dates_20} {cal_0_dates_data_20}</td>
  </tr>
  <tr>
<td class="weekend {cal_0_dates_style_21}">
  {cal_0_dates_21} {cal_0_dates_data_21}</td>
<td class="{cal_0_dates_style_22}">{cal_0_dates_22}
  {cal_0_dates_data_22}</td>
<td class="{cal_0_dates_style_23}">{cal_0_dates_23}
  {cal_0_dates_data_23}</td>
<td class="{cal_0_dates_style_24}">{cal_0_dates_24}
  {cal_0_dates_data_24}</td>
<td class="{cal_0_dates_style_25}">{cal_0_dates_25}
  {cal_0_dates_data_25}</td>
<td class="{cal_0_dates_style_26}">{cal_0_dates_26}
  {cal_0_dates_data_26}</td>
<td class="weekend {cal_0_dates_style_27}">
  {cal_0_dates_27} {cal_0_dates_data_27}</td>
  </tr>
  <tr>
<td class="weekend {cal_0_dates_style_28}">
  {cal_0_dates_28} {cal_0_dates_data_28}</td>
<td class="{cal_0_dates_style_29}">{cal_0_dates_29}
  {cal_0_dates_data_29}</td>
<td class="{cal_0_dates_style_30}">{cal_0_dates_30}
  {cal_0_dates_data_30}</td>
```

```
            <td class="{cal_0_dates_style_31}">{cal_0_dates_31}
              {cal_0_dates_data_31}</td>
            <td class="{cal_0_dates_style_32}">{cal_0_dates_32}
              {cal_0_dates_data_32}</td>
            <td class="{cal_0_dates_style_33}">{cal_0_dates_33}
              {cal_0_dates_data_33}</td>
            <td class="weekend {cal_0_dates_style_34}">
              {cal_0_dates_34} {cal_0_dates_data_34}</td>
              </tr>
              <tr>
            <td class="weekend {cal_0_dates_style_35}">
              {cal_0_dates_35} {cal_0_dates_data_35}</td>
            <td class="{cal_0_dates_style_36}">{cal_0_dates_36}
              {cal_0_dates_data_36}</td>
            <td class="{cal_0_dates_style_37}">{cal_0_dates_37}
              {cal_0_dates_data_37}</td>
            <td class="{cal_0_dates_style_38}">{cal_0_dates_38}
              {cal_0_dates_data_38}</td>
            <td class="{cal_0_dates_style_39}">{cal_0_dates_39}
              {cal_0_dates_data_39}</td>
            <td class="{cal_0_dates_style_40}">{cal_0_dates_40}
              {cal_0_dates_data_40}</td>
            <td class="weekend {cal_0_dates_style_41}">
              {cal_0_dates_41} {cal_0_dates_data_41}</td>
              </tr>

          </table>

  </body>
  </html>
```

If we now go to `/calendar/test/`, we should see the following:

Multiple calendars

As our calendar returns information as arrays, we simply send it to the template manager using the `dataToTags` method, with a prefix of our choice. If we have multiple instances of a calendar object, we can send them to different parts of a template by changing the prefix. For example, if we have a template with a large calendar display for the current month (prefixed with cal_0_), a small calendar for the previous month (prefixed with cal_1_) and a small calendar for the next month (prefixed with cal_2_), we can put the three on the calendar with code such as the following:

```
$calendar = new Calendar( '', $m, $y );
    // build the month, generate some data
    $calendar->buildMonth();
    // days
    $this->registry->getObject('template')->dataToTags( $calendar-
        >getDaysInOrder(),'cal_0_day_' );
    // dates
    $this->registry->getObject('template')->dataToTags( $calendar-
        >getDates(),'cal_0_dates_' );
    // styles
    $this->registry->getObject('template')->dataToTags( $calendar-
        >getDateStyles(),'cal_0_dates_style_' );
    // data
    $this->registry->getObject('template')->dataToTags( $calendar-
        >getDateData(),'cal_0_dates_data_' );

    $calendarPrevious = $calendar->getPreviousMonth();
    // build the month, generate some data
    $calendarPrevious->buildMonth();
    // days
    $this->registry->getObject('template')->dataToTags(
        $calendarPrevious->getDaysInOrder(),'cal_1_day_' );
    // dates
    $this->registry->getObject('template')->dataToTags(
        $calendarPrevious->getDates(),'cal_1_dates_' );
    // styles
    $this->registry->getObject('template')->dataToTags(
        $calendarPrevious->getDateStyles(),'cal_1_dates_style_' );
    // data
    $this->registry->getObject('template')->dataToTags(
        $calendarPreviousndar->getDateData(),'cal_1_dates_data_' );

    $calendarNext = $calendar->getNextMonth();
    // build the month, generate some data
```

```
$calendarNext->buildMonth();
// days
$this->registry->getObject('template')->dataToTags(
   $calendarNext->getDaysInOrder(),'cal_2_day_' );
// dates
$this->registry->getObject('template')->dataToTags(
   $calendarNext->getDates(),'cal_2_dates_' );
// styles
$this->registry->getObject('template')->dataToTags(
   $calendarNext->getDateStyles(),'cal_2_dates_style_' );
// data
$this->registry->getObject('template')->dataToTags(
   $calendarNext->getDateData(),'cal_2_dates_data_' );
```

With events

To display event information alongside dates in the calendar, we simply need to pass an array of data to our calendar library, indicating which days have events, and we can also pass the data itself for inclusion in the calendar:

```
// pass data to the calendar for inclusion
$calendar->setData( $data );
// tell the calendar which days should be highlighted
$calendar->setDaysWithEvents($days);
```

We simply pass an array of dates that have events, and an array of event data. Both arrays use the day of the month as the key.

Birthdays

Birthdays should be a fairly straightforward feature for us to implement. We need to:

- Add an additional profile field for the user's birthday
- Look up the date of birth of our user's contacts
- Calculate their age
- Send the data to the calendar
- Generate the calendar view
- Display a list of upcoming birthdays to our users

Getting relationship IDs

For us to quickly look up the birthdays of a user's connections, we need to quickly gain access to the IDs of users another user is connected to. We have some similar functionality in our relationships model (`models/relationships.php`); however, the following method will give us a query returning IDs. We can then use this as a sub query in our birthdays lookup query:

```
/**
 * Get IDs of users a user has a relationship with
 * @param int $user the user in question
 * @param bool $cache - cache the results, or return the query?
 * @return String / int
 */
public function getIDsByUser( $user, $cache=false )
{
    $sql = "SELECT u.ID FROM users u, profile p, relationships
      r, relationship_types t WHERE t.ID=r.type AND r.accepted=1 AND
      (r.usera={$user} OR r.userb={$user}) AND IF( r.usera={$user},u.
      ID=r.userb,u.ID=r.usera) AND p.user_id=u.ID";
        if( $cache == false )
        {
            return $sql;
        }
        else
        {
            $cache = $this->registry->getObject('db')-
              >cacheQuery( $sql );
            return $cache;
        }
    }
}
```

Setting up the calendar

As we have done before, we need to set up the calendar (`controllers/calendar/controller.php`); this simply involves requiring the class, instantiating the object, and setting the current date and month:

```
// require the class
    require_once( FRAMEWORK_PATH . 'lib/calendar/calendar.class.php' );
// set the default month and year, i.e. the current month and year
    $m = date('m');
    $y = date('Y');
// check for a different Month / Year (i.e. user has moved to
    another month)
```

```php
if( isset( $_GET['month'] ) )
{
   $m = intval( $_GET['month']);
   if( $m > 0 && $m < 13 )
   {

   }
   else
   {
      $m = date('m');
   }
}
if( isset( $_GET['year'] ) )
{
   $y = intval( $_GET['year']);
}
// Instantiate the calendar object
$calendar = new Calendar( '', $m, $y );
// Get next and previous month / year
$nm = $calendar->getNextMonth()->getMonth();
$ny = $calendar->getNextMonth()->getYear();
$pm = $calendar->getPreviousMonth()->getMonth();
$py = $calendar->getPreviousMonth()->getYear();

// send next / previous month data to the template
$this->registry->getObject('template')->getPage()-
   >addTag('nm', $nm );
$this->registry->getObject('template')->getPage()-
   >addTag('pm', $pm );
$this->registry->getObject('template')->getPage()-
   >addTag('ny', $ny );
$this->registry->getObject('template')->getPage()-
   >addTag('py', $py );
// send the current month name and year to the template
$this->registry->getObject('template')->getPage()-
   >addTag('month_name', $calendar->getMonthName() );
$this->registry->getObject('template')->getPage()-
   >addTag('the_year', $calendar->getYear() );
// Set the start day of the week
$calendar->setStartDay(0); // require the class
```

Getting the birthdays

With the calendar setup, and a method in our relationships model for us to get the IDs of connected users, we can get the birthdays.

First, we need to require the relationships model, instantiate the object, and get the IDs SQL:

```
require_once( FRAMEWORK_PATH . 'models/relationships.php');
$relationships = new Relationships( $this->registry );
$idsSQL = $relationships->getIDsByUser( $this->registry-
    >getObject('authenticate')->getUser()->getUserID() );
```

Next, we query the profile table, only selecting profiles that are in the result set of the IDs query. We look for users with birthdays in the currently selected month, and calculate the age by subtracting the year of birth from the current year:

```
$sql = "SELECT DATE_FORMAT(pr.user_dob, '%d' ) as profile_dob,
    pr.name as profile_name, pr.user_id as profile_id, ( ( YEAR(
    CURDATE() ) ) - ( DATE_FORMAT(pr.user_dob, '%Y' ) ) )
    as profile_new_age FROM profile pr WHERE pr.user_id IN
    (".$idsSQL.") AND pr.user_dob LIKE '%-{$m}-%'";
$this->registry->getObject('db')->executeQuery( $sql );
```

Passing them to the calendar

We then iterate through our results from the query, building an array of dates with events, and an array of event data:

```
$dates = array();
    $data = array();
    if( $this->registry->getObject('db')->numRows() > 0 )
    {
        while( $row = $this->registry->getObject('db')->getRows() )
        {
            $dates[] = $row['profile_dob'];
            $data[ intval($row['profile_dob']) ] = "<br />".
                $row['profile_name']." (". $row['profile_new_age'] .
                ")<br />";
        }
    }
```

The data is then passed to the calendar:

```
$calendar->setData( $data );
            // tell the calendar which days should be highlighted
            $calendar->setDaysWithEvents($dates);
```

With everything passed to the calendar, we can now build the month and pass everything to the template:

```
$calendar->buildMonth();
// days
$this->registry->getObject('template')-
  >dataToTags( $calendar->getDaysInOrder(),'cal_0_day_' );
// dates
$this->registry->getObject('template')-
  >dataToTags( $calendar->getDates(),'cal_0_dates_' );
// styles
$this->registry->getObject('template')-
  >dataToTags( $calendar->getDateStyles(),'cal_0_dates_style_' );
// data
$this->registry->getObject('template')-
  >dataToTags( $calendar->getDateData(),'cal_0_dates_data_' );

$this->registry->getObject('template')->buildFromTemplates(
  'header.tpl.php', 'bd-calendar.tpl.php', 'footer.tpl.php' );
```

The results

If we now visit our birthdays calendar (`calendar/birthdays`), we have a calendar with the birthdays of our contacts shown, along with their age on that date.

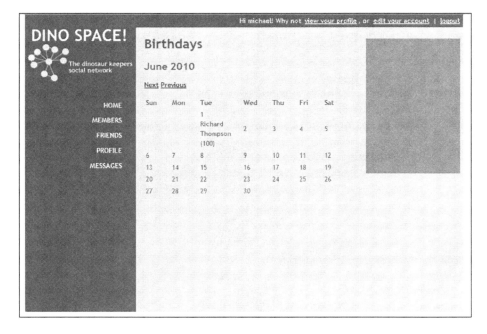

Events

With calendar functionality and birthday lookups in place, adding event functionality should be straightforward. Let's take a look at what we will need:

- An event model
    - To generate data from an event
    - To create and edit an event

- Integration with our calendar controller
- An event controller to display the event details, manage the creation of the event, and manage attendees and RSVPs

Event model

As with all of our models, the first stage is to define the variables, which relate to the registry, the fields for the event in the database, and an array of invitees to the event:

```php
<?php

/**
 * Event model
 */
class Event{

    /**
     * The registry
     */
    private $registry;

    /**
     * Event ID
     */
    private $ID;

    /**
     * Creators ID
     */
    private $creator;

    /**
     * Event name
     */
```

```
        private $name;

        /**
         * Description
         */
        private $description;

        /**
         * Event date
         */
        private $event_date;

        /**
         * start time
         */
        private $start_time;

        /**
         * End time
         */
        private $end_time;

        /**
         * Type
         */
        private $type;

        /**
         * Active
         */
        private $active;

        /**
         * Invitees
         */
        private $invitees = array();
```

Next, we have our constructor, which sets the registry, and if an ID is passed,
looks up the event and populates the model's fields with those from the database:

```
        /**
         * Event constructor
         * @param Registry $registry the registry
         * @param int $ID the event ID
         * @return voID
```

```
        */
    public function __construct( Registry $registry, $ID=0 )
    {
        $this->registry = $registry;
        if( $ID != 0 )
        {
            $this->ID = $ID;
            // if an ID is passed, populate based off that
            $sql = "SELECT * FROM events WHERE ID=" . $this->ID;
            $this->registry->getObject('db')->executeQuery( $sql );
            if( $this->registry->getObject('db')->numRows() == 1 )
            {
                $data = $this->registry->getObject('db')->getRows();
                // populate our fields
                foreach( $data as $key => $value )
                {
                    $this->$key = $value;
                }
            }

        }
    }
```

Next, we have setters for all of our fields, except for the ID:

```
    /**
     * Sets the events name
     * @param String $name
     * @return voID
     */
    public function setName( $name )
    {
        $this->name = $name;
    }


    /**
     * Sets the creator
     * @param int $creator the creator
     * @return voID
     */
    public function setCreator( $ID )
    {
        $this->creator = $ID;
    }
```

```php
public function setInvitees( $invitees )
{
    $this->invitees = $invitees;
}


/**
 * Set the events description
 * @param String $description the description
 */
public function setDescription( $description )
{
    $this->description = $description;
}
```

Our `setDate` method takes an additional parameter to check whether the controller formatted the date, if it didn't then we assume it was passed in a format such as the default jQuery datepicker format, and format it here:

```php
/**
 * Set the event date
 * @param String $date the date
 * @param boolean $formatted - indicates if the controller has
   formatted the date, or if we need to do it here
 */
public function setDate( $date, $formatted=true )
{
    if( $formatted == true )
    {
        $this->event_date = $date;
    }
    else
    {
        $temp = explode('/', $date );
        $this->event_date = $temp[2].'-'.$temp[1].'-'.$temp[0];
    }
}


/**
 * Sets the start time of the event
 * @param String $time
 * return voID
 */
public function setStartTime( $time )
{
    $this->start_time = $time;
```

```
    }

    /**
     * Sets the end time of the event
     * @param String $time
     * return voID
     */
    public function setEndTime( $time )
    {
        $this->end_time = $time;
    }
```

The `setType` method takes an additional parameter to check whether the controller validated the type or not; if it didn't, then we check it against our list of allowed types:

```
    /**
     * Set the type of the event
     * @param String $type the type
     * @param boolean $checked - indicates if the controller has
       valIDated the type, or if we need to do it
     * @return voID
     */
    public function setType( $type, $checked=true )
    {
        if( $checked == true )
        {
            $this->type = $type;
        }
        else
        {
            $types = array( 'public', 'private' );
            if( in_array( $type, $types ) )
            {
                $this->type = $type;
            }
        }
    }

    /**
     * Sets if the event is active
     * @param bool $active
     * @return voID
     */
    public function setActive( $active )
    {
        $this->active = $active;
    }
```

Next, we have our save method, which depending on whether an ID is set or not, either inserts a new record into the database or updates an existing one. If we are inserting a new record, it also iterates through the invitees, and adds them to the attendees table as an invitee. This would be where we may wish to add an e-mail notification to the user to inform them that they have been invited to the event:

```php
/**
 * Save the event
 * @return bool
 */
public function save()
{
  // handle the updating of a profile
  if( $this->registry->getObject('authenticate')->isLoggedIn() &&
    ( $this->registry->getObject('authenticate')-
    >getUser()->getUserID() ==  $this->creator || $this->registry-
    >getObject('authenticate')->getUser()->isAdmin() == true  ||
    $this->ID == 0 ) )
  {
    // we are either the user created the event, or we are the
      administrator, or the event is being created
    $event = array();
    foreach( $this as $field => $data )
    {
      if( ! is_array( $data ) && ! is_object( $data )
        && $field != 'ID'  )
        {
          $event[ $field ] = $this->$field;
        }

    }
    if( $this->ID == 0 )
    {
      $this->registry->getObject('db')->insertRecords( 'events',
        $event );
      $this->ID = $this->registry->getObject('db')-
        >lastInsertID();
      if( is_array( $this->invitees ) && count( $this-
        >invitees ) > 0 )
      {
        foreach( $this->invitees as $invitee )
        {
          $insert = array();
          $insert['event_id'] = $this->ID;
          $insert['user_id'] = $invitee;
```

```
                $insert['status'] = 'invited';
                $this->registry->getObject('db')->insertRecords(
                    'event_attendees', $insert );
                }
            }
            $insert = array();
            $insert['event_id'] = $this->ID;
            $insert['user_id'] = $this->creator;
            $insert['status'] = 'going';
            $this->registry->getObject('db')->insertRecords( 'event_
                attendees', $insert );
            return true;
        }
        else
        {
          $this->registry->getObject('db')->updateRecords( 'events',
              $event, 'ID=' . $this->ID );
          if( $this->registry->getObject('db')->affectedRows() == 1 )
          {
              return true;
          }
          else
          {
              return false;
          }
        }

    }
    else
    {
        return false;
    }
}
```

Next, we have the standard `toTags` method, which takes a prefix, and converts all of the data that isn't an object or an array to template tags:

```
/**
 * Convert the event data to template tags
 * @param String $prefix prefix for the template tags
 * @return voID
 */
public function toTags( $prefix='' )
{
    foreach( $this as $field => $data )
```

```
        {
            if( ! is_object( $data ) && ! is_array( $data ) )
            {
                $this->registry->getObject('template')->getPage()-
                    >addTag( $prefix.$field, $data );
            }
        }
    }
```

Finally, we have any getter methods that we may require:

```
    /**
     * Get the event name
     * @return String
     */
    public function getName()
    {
        return $this->name;
    }

    /**
     * Get the users ID
     * @return int
     */
    public function getID()
    {
        return $this->ID;
    }

}

?>
```

Events model

Now, let's look at creating the events model to generate a list of events that a user may be interested in (`models/events.php`):

```
<?php
/**
 * Events model
 * - builds lists of events
 */
class Events{
```

We need to define our registry, and construct the object:

```
/**
 * Registry object
 */
private $registry;

/**
 * Events constructor
 * @param Registry $registry
 * @return void
 */
public function __construct( Registry $registry )
{
    $this->registry = $registry;
}
```

To list events by connected users in a certain month, we simply use the relationships model, call the `getIDsByUser` method, and then query the events table, filtering by the results from the getIDs query, where the date is in a specific month and year:

```
/**
 * List events by connected users in specified month / year
 * @param int $connectedTo events of users connected to this user
 * @param int $month
 * @param int $year
 * @return int database cacehe
 */
public function listEventsMonthYear( $connectedTo, $month, $year )
{
    require_once( FRAMEWORK_PATH . 'models/relationships.php');
    $relationships = new Relationships( $this->registry );
    $idsSQL = $relationships->getIDsByUser( $connectedTo );
    $sql = "SELECT p.name as creator_name, e.* FROM events e,
        profile p WHERE p.user_id=e.creator AND e.event_date LIKE
        '{$year}-{$month}-%' AND e.creator IN ($idsSQL) ";
    $cache = $this->registry->getObject('db')->cacheQuery( $sql );
    return $cache;
}
```

Similar to the above query, here we use the DATE_ADD MySQL function to add X days to the current date, and return any events within the range between now and X days time:

```
/**
 * List events by connected users in specified time period
 * @param int $connectedTo events of users connected to this user
 * @param int $days days in the future
 * @return int database cacehe
 */
public function listEventsFuture( $connectedTo, $days )
{
    require_once( FRAMEWORK_PATH . 'models/relationships.php');
    $relationships = new Relationships( $this->registry );
    $idsSQL = $relationships->getIDsByUser( $connectedTo );
    $sql = "SELECT p.name as creator_name, e.* FROM events e,
        profile p WHERE p.user_id=e.creator AND e.event_date >=
        CURDATE() AND e.event_date <= DATE_ADD(CURDATE(),
        INTERVAL {$days} DAY ) AND e.creator IN ($idsSQL) ";
    $cache = $this->registry->getObject('db')->cacheQuery( $sql );
    return $cache;
}
```

This method lists any events X days in the future that were created by a specific user. This might be used on a user's profile, or for a user to see which events they had created:

```
/**
 * List events by a specific user within next X days
 * @param int $user user whose events to list
 * @param int $days
 * @return int database cache
 */
public function listEventsUserFuture( $user, $days )
{
    $sql = "SELECT p.name as creator_name, e.* FROM events e,
        profile p WHERE p.user_id=e.creator AND e.event_date >=
        CURDATE() AND e.event_date <= DATE_ADD(CURDATE(),
        INTERVAL {$days} DAY ) AND e.creator={$user} ";
    $cache = $this->registry->getObject('db')->cacheQuery( $sql );
    return $cache;
}
```

Finally, we have methods to return events that the current user was either invited to, is attending, isn't attending, or is maybe attending:

```
/**
 * List events in the future user is invited to
 * @param int $user the user
 * @return int database cache
 */
public function listEventsInvited( $user )
{
   $sql = "SELECT p.name as creator_name, e.* FROM events e,
      profile p WHERE p.user_id=e.creator AND e.event_date >=
      CURDATE() AND ( SELECT COUNT(*) FROM events_attendees a
      WHERE a.event_id=e.ID AND a.user_id={$user} AND
      a.status='invited' ) > 0";
   $cache = $this->registry->getObject('db')->cacheQuery( $sql );
   return $cache;
}


/**
 * List events in the future user is attending
 * @param int $user the user
 * @return int database cache
 */
public function listEventsAttending( $user )
{
   $sql = "SELECT p.name as creator_name, e.* FROM events e,
      profile p WHERE p.user_id=e.creator AND e.event_date >=
      CURDATE() AND ( SELECT COUNT(*) FROM events_attendees a
      WHERE a.event_id=e.ID AND a.user_id={$user} AND
      a.status='going' ) > 0";
   $cache = $this->registry->getObject('db')->cacheQuery( $sql );
   return $cache;
}


/**
 * List events in the future user is not attending
 * @param int $user the user
 * @return int database cache
 */
public function listEventsNotAttending( $user )
{
   $sql = "SELECT p.name as creator_name, e.* FROM events e,
      profile p WHERE p.user_id=e.creator AND e.event_date >=
      CURDATE() AND ( SELECT COUNT(*) FROM events_attendees a
      WHERE a.event_id=e.ID AND a.user_id={$user} AND
```

```
                          a.status='not going' ) > 0";
            $cache = $this->registry->getObject('db')->cacheQuery( $sql );
            return $cache;

        }


        /**
         * List events in the future user is maybe attending
         * @param int $user the user
         * @return int database cache
         */
        public function listEventsMaybeAttending( $user )
        {
            $sql = "SELECT p.name as creator_name, e.* FROM events e,
                profile p WHERE p.user_id=e.creator AND e.event_date >=
                CURDATE() AND ( SELECT COUNT(*) FROM events_attendees a
                WHERE a.event_id=e.ID AND a.user_id={$user} AND
                a.status='maybe' ) > 0";
            $cache = $this->registry->getObject('db')->cacheQuery( $sql );
            return $cache;

        }


    }


    ?>
```

Attendees, invitations, and RSVPs

To list who is attending, invited, maybe attending, and not attending an event, we can add some new methods to our event model (models/event.php). These methods query the database for users who are attending, not attending, maybe attending or invited, cache the results, and return the cache.

```
    /**
     * Get users attending the event
     * @return int cache id
     */
    public function getAttending()
    {
        $sql = "SELECT p.* FROM profile p, event_attendees
        WHERE p.user_id=a.user_id AND a.status='attending' AND
        a.event_id=" . $this->ID;
        $cache = $this->registry->getObject('db')->cacheQuery( $sql );
        return $cache;
    }
```

```
/**
 * Get users not attending the event
 * @return int cache id
 */
public function getNotAttending()
{
    $sql = "SELECT p.* FROM profile p, event_attendees WHERE
        p.user_id=a.user_id AND a.status='not attending' AND
        a.event_id=" . $this->ID;
    $cache = $this->registry->getObject('db')->cacheQuery( $sql );
    return $cache;
}


/**
 * Get users maybe attending the event
 * @return int cache id
 */
public function getMaybeAttending()
{
    $sql = "SELECT p.* FROM profile p, event_attendees WHERE
        p.user_id=a.user_id AND a.status='maybe' AND
        a.event_id=" . $this->ID;
    $cache = $this->registry->getObject('db')->cacheQuery( $sql );
    return $cache;
}


/**
 * Get users invited to the event
 * @return int cache id
 */
public function getInvited()
{
    $sql = "SELECT p.* FROM profile p, event_attendees WHERE
        p.user_id=a.user_id AND a.status='invited' AND
        a.event_id=" . $this->ID;
    $cache = $this->registry->getObject('db')->cacheQuery( $sql );
    return $cache;
}
```

RSVPs

To allow a user to change their attendance preference for an event, we need a method in our event controller (`controllers/event/controller.php`), which we are going to create in the next section. This takes the event ID as a parameter, and POST data is submitted indicating the user's new choice for the event:

```
private function changeAttendance( $event )
    {
        $sql = "SELECT * FROM event_attendees WHERE event_id={$event}
            AND user_id=" . $this->registry->getObject('authenticate')-
            >getUser()->getID();
        $this->registry->getObject('db')->executeQuery( $sql );
        if( $this->registry->getObject('db')->numRows() == 1 )
        {
            $data = $this->registry->getObject('db')->getRows();
            $changes = array();
            $changes['status'] = $this->registry->getObject('db')-
                >sanitizeData( $_POST['status'] );
            $this->registry->getObject('db')->updateRecords( 'event_
                attendees', $changes, 'ID=' . $data['ID'] );
            $this->registry->redirectUser( $this->registry-
                >buildURL(array( 'home' ), '', false ), 'Attendance
                updated', 'Thanks, your attendance has been updated for
                that event', false );
        }
        else
        {
            $this->registry->errorPage('Attendance not logged',
                'Sorry, we could not find any record of your attendance
                for that event, please try again');
        }
    }
```

Controller

With our event and events models in place, we now need a controller to allow the user to create, edit, view, and accept attendance of events.

Creating an event

To create an event, we need to see whether the user is submitting the form; if they are, we instantiate the event object, set the details, look for any invitees the user has added, set those, and create the event before redirecting them to the view event page. If no post data was submitted, we simply show the user the form. We may also want to provide a list of the users' connections on this page, so they can invite them to the event. After creating an event, you may wish to add functionality to e-mail those invitees:

```php
/**
 * Create an event
 * @return void
 */
private function createEvent()
{
  // if post data is set, we are creating an event
  if( isset( $_POST ) && count( $_POST ) > 0 )
  {
    require_once( FRAMEWORK_PATH . 'models/event.php' );
    $event = new Event( $this->registry, 0 );
    $event->setName( $this->registry->getObject('db')-
      >sanitizeData( $_POST['name'] ) );
    $event->setDescription( $this->registry->getObject('db')-
      >sanitizeData( $_POST['description'] ) );
    $event->setDate( $this->registry->getObject('db')-
      >sanitizeData( $_POST['date'] ), false );
    $event->setStartTime( $this->registry->getObject('db')-
      >sanitizeData( $_POST['start_time'] ) );
    $event->setEndTime( $this->registry->getObject('db')-
      >sanitizeData( $_POST['end_time'] ) );
    $event->setCreator( $this->registry->getObject('authenticate')-
      >getUser()->getID() );
    $event->setType( $this->registry->getObject('db')-
      >sanitizeData( $_POST['type'] ) );
    if( isset( $_POST['invitees'] ) && is_array( $_POST['invitees'] )
      && count( $_POST['invitees'] ) > 0 )
      {
        // assumes invitees are added to a table using javascript,
          with a hidden field with name invitees[] for the ID of
          invitee
        $is = array();
        foreach( $_POST['invitees'] as $i )
        {
          $is[] = intval( $i );
        }
          $event->setInvitees( $is );
      }
      $event->save();
      $this->registry->redirectUser( $this->registry-
        >buildURL(array( 'event', 'view', $event->getID() ), '',
        false ), 'Event created', 'Thanks, the event has been
        created', false );
    }
    else
    {
    $this->registry->getObject('template')->buildFromTemplates(
      'header.tpl.php', 'events/create.tpl.php', 'footer.tpl.php' );
    }
  }
```

Template for a new event

Our "Create event" template simply needs fields for the name, date, start time, end time, description, and checkboxes for all of the user's friends. We can give the date field a class of `selectdate`, to make use of the jQuery datepicker plug-in we used for profiles. We may also wish to use the time picker plug-in too, to make time selection easier. The friends loop is highlighted in the following code:

```
<div id="main">

    <div id="rightside">
    </div>

    <div id="content">
        <h1>Create an event</h1>
        <form action="event/create" method="post">
            <label for="">Name</label><br />
            <input type="text" name="name" /><br />

            <label for="">Type of event</label><br />
            <select name="type">
                <option value="public">Public event</option>
                <option value="private">Private event</option>
            </select><br />

            <label for="">Date</label><br />
            <input type="text" class="selectdate" name="date"
                /><br />

            <label for="">Start time</label><br />
            <input type="text" class="selecttime" name="start_
                time" /><br />

            <label for="">End time</label><br />
            <input type="text" class="selecttime" name="end_
                time" /><br />

            <label for="">Description</label><br />
            <textarea name="description" cols="45" rows="6">
            </ textarea><br />
            <h2>Invite friends?</h2>
            <p>Select any friends you would like to invite to
                the event.</p>
            <!-- START all --><input type="checkbox"
                name="invitees[]" value="{ID}" />{users_name}
            <!-- END all --><br />
```

```
        <input type="submit" name="" value="Create event" />

    </form>
  </div>

</div>
```

Now, if we visit the create event page (`event/create`), we see the form:

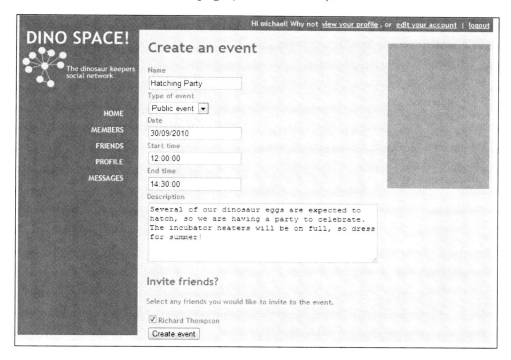

This makes use of the very helpful datepicker plugin:

Calendar of events

We looked earlier at integrating the calendar library with birthdays, so why not try and integrate the events with the calendar too? The code is in the download bundle for this book if you need help.

Viewing an event

To view an event, we simply call the `toTags` method on the model, and build the template. We should also list users who have been invited, are attending, are not attending, and who are maybe attending:

```
/**
 * View an event
 * @param int $id
 * @return void
 */
private function viewEvent( $id )
{
    require_once( FRAMEWORK_PATH . 'models/event.php' );
    $event = new Event( $this->registry, $id );
    $show = true;
    if( $event->getType() == 'private' )
    {
        // you may wish to add to support for private events here!
        $show = false;
    }
    if( $show == true )
    {
        $event->toTags( 'event_' );
        $this->registry->getObject('template')->buildFromTemplates(
          'header.tpl.php', 'events/view.tpl.php', 'footer.tpl.php' );
        $attendingCache = $event->getAttending();
        $this->registry->getObject('template')->getPage()->addTag(
          'attending', array('SQL', $attendingCache) );
        $notAttendingCache = $event->getNotAttending();
        $this->registry->getObject('template')->getPage()->addTag(
          'notattending', array('SQL', $notAttendingCache) );
        $maybeAttendingCache = $event->getMaybeAttending();
        $this->registry->getObject('template')->getPage()->addTag(
          'maybeattending', array('SQL', $maybeAttendingCache) );
        $invitedCache = $event->getInvited();
        $this->registry->getObject('template')->getPage()->addTag(
          'invited', array('SQL', $invitedCache) );
```

```
$sql = "SELECT * FROM event_attendees WHERE event_id={$id}
  AND user_id=" . $this->registry->getObject('authenticate')-
  >getUser()->getUserId();
$this->registry->getObject('db')->executeQuery( $sql );
if( $this->registry->getObject('db')->numRows() == 1 )
{
   $data = $this->registry->getObject('db')->getRows();
   if( $data['status'] == 'going' )
   {
      $s = 'attending';
   }
   elseif( $data['status'] == 'not going' )
   {
      $s = 'notattending';

   }
   elseif( $data['status'] == 'maybe' )
   {
      $s = 'maybeattending';
   }
   else
   {
      $s = 'unknown';
   }
   $this->registry->getObject('template')->getPage()-
      >addTag( $s . '_select', "selected='selected'");
}
else
{
   $this->registry->getObject('template')->getPage()-
      >addTag('unknown_select', "selected='selected'");
}

}
else
{
   // error handling
}

}
```

Event template

The template for viewing the event contains tags for the event, and template loops for the different types of attendee status:

```
<div id="main">

    <div id="rightside">
    </div>

    <div id="content">
        <h1>{event_name}</h1>
        <p>{event_description}</p>
        <p>{event_date}: {event_start_time} until
            {event_end_time}</p>
        <h2>Your attendance</h2>
        <p>You are currently recorded as:</p>
        <form action="event/change-attendance/{event_id}"
            method="post">
            <select name="status">
                <option value="" {unknown_select}>Unknown -
                    Please select...</option>
                <option value="going" {attending_
                    select}>Attending</option>
                <option value="not going" {notattending_
                    select}>Not attending</option>
                <option value="maybe" {maybeattending_
                    select}>Maybe attending</option>
            </select>
            <input type="submit" name="" value="Update
                attendance" />
        </form>
        <h2>Attending</h2>
        <ul>
            <!-- START attending --><li>{name}</li>
            <!-- END attending -->
        </ul>
        <h2>Invited / Awaiting Reply</h2>
        <ul>
            <!-- START invited --><li>{name}</li>
            <!-- END invited -->
        </ul>
        <h2>Maybe attending</h2>
        <ul>
            <!-- START maybeattending --><li>{name}</li>
            <!-- END maybeattending -->
        </ul>
        <h2>Not attending</h2>
        <ul>
            <!-- START notattending --><li>{name}</li>
```

```
                <!-- END notattending -->
            </ul>
        </div>
    </div>
```

Viewing an event in action

If we now view an event (`event/view/1`), we are presented with the view event screen:

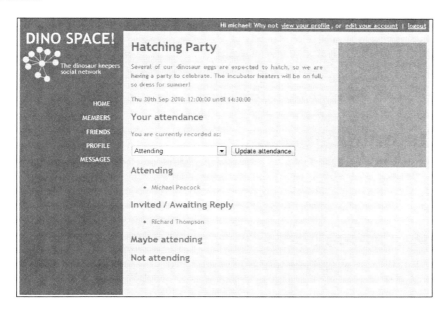

Upcoming events

Thanks to the `listUpcomingInNetwork` method in our events model, we can easily build a list of events in our user's network:

```
private function listUpcomingInNetwork()
    {
        require_once( FRAMEWORK_PATH . 'models/events.php' );
        $events = new Events( $this->registry );
        $cache = $events->listEventsFuture( $this->registry-
          >getObject('authenticate')->getUser()->getID(), 30 );
        $this->registry->getObject('template')->getPage()-
          >addTag( 'events', array( 'SQL', $cache ) );
        $this->registry->getObject('template')->buildFromTemplates(
          'header.tpl.php', 'events/upcoming.tpl.php',
          'footer.tpl.php' );
    }
```

Reminders

We may wish to remind users about specific events, either events created by their contacts, or events that they have indicated they wish to attend. We can easily remind them of the event either through:

- Notices on the site reminding them
- E-mails reminding them
- Text/SMS messages

Off-site reminders would need to work via a task-based system, for example a CRON job that is run each night, which looks up events a user is attending or may be attending X days in the future (those queries in the events model are looking extra handy now!) and sends them a reminder.

On-site notifications

On-site reminders would simply call the appropriate method in the events model, to see whether there are any events the user may be attending within the next X days, and if there are, list them on the screen.

E-mail notifications

We have an e-mail sending object in our registry; we can use this to e-mail out reminders to our users.

SMS notifications

For us to send SMS notifications, we need to use a mobile gateway, such as:

- **Clickatell:** Large international SMS/mobile gateway - `http://www. clickatell.com/`
- **Intellisoftware:** UK based SMS gateway — `http://www.intellisoftware. co.uk/`

Such gateways provide simple APIs where a text message can be sent via a simple HTTP request containing API credentials, sender number, recipient number, and the message. We can create a library to talk to the API, and use this to send messages to our users.

Packt have published a book called *Mobile Web Development* by Nirav Mehta (`https://www.packtpub.com/mobile-web-development/book`), which includes lots of great examples of clickatell, and well worth a read if you are considering implementing SMS integration. The Clickatell website and Intellisoftware websites both have in-depth information on working with their APIs too.

Summary

In this chapter, we have looked at developing a flexible calendar library to integrate calendar functionality into various aspects of our site. We created a calendar controller to display birthdays of our users' connections, along with their ages.

We then moved on to events, creating models and controllers for creating events, viewing events, listing events, and inviting connections to the events. With our calendar library, we are now able to integrate these events into the calendar.

Following from events, we looked at inviting contacts to events, and how they can update us on their intention to attend the event, and with a little extra development, we can integrate reminders too.

Now, we can move onto the final core feature of any social network—groups!

10
Groups

We only have one user-facing feature left to implement for our Dino Space website, and that is groups within the social network. Most social networking websites have the ability for users to form their own sub-groups, a small sub-set of users discussing or sharing information about specific things. Within our site, this could be to allow groups of users to privately discuss matters, or for users who share common interests to discuss things without cluttering up everyone else's network with information that may not interest them.

In this chapter you will learn:

- How to create a group area
- How to allow users to create groups
- How users can be invited to join these groups
- How to deal with the "ownership" of a particular group

Let's get started and add groups to our social network!

Some planning

Before we can start implementing this feature, we need to think about what information it needs to manage, how it will work, and what it will offer to our users.

Group information

There will need to be standard information saved for each group, so that groups have meaning to other users, and if appropriate can be found through the search feature. At a minimum, we need to store the following information:

- Name of the group
- Creator / owner of the group: So we know who has permission to manage it
- Description of the group: So users know what the group is about, in a little more detail than its name
- Permission structure of the group: So that the group can be shown if appropriate, and so that it is clear if and how new members can join that group
- Date the group was created: We could also store the creation date, so if one group becomes old and isn't participated in very often, a newer one may take priority in the search results

This information is what would be stored in the groups table in the database.

Types of groups

To make the groups system flexible, there need to be various types of groups available, with different permissions relating to who can have access to them. Typically, most social networks tend to provide the following options:

- Global / public groups: Open to everyone on the site
- Network specific: Only open to a section of the social network. For example, those from a particular geographical region, or working for one particular institution
- Private, with these options:
    ◦ Only available to those who have been explicitly invited by the group's creator
    ◦ Semi-private: Only available to those who have been explicitly invited by another member of the group
    ◦ Invite-only: Private groups where users can request membership (similar to friend requests), which is then decided by the group's creator or administrator

As our Dino Space network doesn't, in its current form, have any provisions for subsidiary networks, such as users based in the US or the UK, or users who work at a specific company, we will not look to implement this feature. The other types of groups seem appropriate, so we will look to implement those.

Ownership

There are a number of ways we could facilitate the ownership or management of a community group on our social network. Primarily there are two options:

- The creator is the owner / administrator of the group
- The creator can appoint owner / administrator(s) of the group

We will implement the first of these options. However, it shouldn't be too difficult to extend this to support appointed administrators, should you wish to extend this for your own social network.

In this sense, the creator of the group will be listed on the group's page, and they alone will have full control of the group.

Membership

Finally, we need to plan how membership will be organized, particularly in light of the types of groups that we may support. We need to be able to store and manage membership lists, lists of invited users who can become members of protected groups should they wish, and also users who have requested to be members of a group, but have not yet been granted access.

Features

Groups need to offer users a dedicated area where they can communicate and collaborate on specific topics related to the purpose of the group, including discussions.

A group

With an idea of what our group needs to do, the information it needs to contain, and how it will work, let's now create the functionality. This, as with other features, will involve creation of a model, a controller, and a series of template files to form the view.

Discussion

In order to facilitate communication and collaboration, groups require some new functionality that we don't yet have in Dino Space—discussion forum style topics. Let's create models for topics and discussion forum posts. Initially, we will tie these with groups; however, it would be easy for us to extend them to other areas of the social network should we wish.

We won't create controllers at this stage, as topics (for now) will only be accessed via groups. So either the group's controller will handle this, or the group's controller will delegate control to a group topic controller.

Discussion forums can be very complicated systems; there are numerous open source and commercial forum software products available with a wealth of features. Creating a fully-featured discussion forum would be the series of a number of books in itself. For the purposes of Dino Space, we are going to create a very simple discussion-style feature to plug into our social network.

Database

This discussion feature will require two new database tables, one for topics themselves, and one for the posts they relate to.

Topics

Topic records in the database will simply contain a name, who created it and when, and the group they are related to, as illustrated by the table below:

Field	Type	Description
ID	Integer, Auto-increment, Primary Key	Internal reference for the topic of conversation
Name	Varchar	The name of the topic
Creator	Integer	The user who created the topic
Created	Timestamp	The time the topic was created
Group	Integer	The group the topic was created within

Posts

Posts will contain the content of the post, who created it and when, and the topic that it relates to, as illustrated by the table below.

Field	Type	Description
ID	Integer, Auto-increment, Primary Key	Internal reference for the post within a topic
Topic	Integer	The topic the post is part of
Post	Longtext	The post itself
Creator	Integer	The user who created the post
Created	Timestamp	The time the post was created

Post

When a topic is created, in most cases so is the first post. Hence, we should link our post and topic models so that both are created at the same time. Since the topic will create the post, we should create the post model first.

Model

The post model (`models/post.php`) only needs to be basic: various properties for the object, a constructor to get the post from the database, some setter methods to update the properties, and a save method to create a new post or update an existing post.

```php
<?php
/**
 * Post model object
 */
class Post{
```

As usual we start with our class variables; these include a reference to the `registry` object itself, and the variables required for a post.

```php
/**
 * Registry object
 */
private $registry;

/**
 * ID of the post
 */
private $id;

/**
 * ID of the creator of the post
 */
private $creator;

/**
 * Name of the creator of the post
 */
private $creatorName;

/**
 * Timestamp of when the post was created
 */
private $created;
```

```
/**
 * Friendly representation of when the post was created
 */
private $createdFriendly;

/**
 * ID of the topic the post relates to
 */
private $topic;

/**
 * The post itself
 */
private $post;
```

The constructor takes the `registry` object as a parameter and, optionally, an ID for the post. If a post ID is supplied, then it queries the database for the post, and if a record exists, it populates the class variables with the results.

```
/**
 * Post constructor
 * @param Registry $registry the registry object
 * @param int $id the ID of the post
 * @return void
 */
public function __construct( Registry $registry, $id=0 )
{
  $this->registry = $registry;
  $this->id = $id;
  if( $this->id > 0 )
  {
    $sql = "SELECT p.*, DATE_FORMAT(p.created, '%D %M %Y') as
      created_friendly, pr.name as creator_name FROM posts p,
      profile pr WHERE pr.user_id=p.creator AND p.ID=" . $this->id;
    $this->registry->getObject('db')->executeQuery( $sql );
    if( $this->registry->getObject('db')->numRows() > 0 )
    {
      $data = $this->registry->getObject('db')->getRows();
      $this->creator = $data['creator'];
      $this->creatorName = $data['creator_name'];
      $this->createdFriendly = $data['created_friendly'];
      $this->topic = $data['topic'];
      $this->post = $data['post'];
    }
    else
```

```
        {
          $this->id = 0;
        }
      }
    }
  }
```

We have our setter methods to set the private class variables from outside the object.

```
    /**
     * Set the creator of the post
     * @param int $c the creator
     * @return void
     */
    public function setCreator( $c )
    {
      $this->creator = $c;
    }

    /**
     * Set the topic the post relates to
     * @param int $t the topic ID
     * @return void
     */
    public function setTopic( $t )
    {
      $this->topic = $t;
    }

    /**
     * Set the post content
     * @param String $p the post itself
     * @return void
     */
    public function setPost( $p )
    {
      $this->post = $p;
    }
```

Finally, we have our save method. If an ID is set, it updates an existing record; if no ID is set, then it inserts a record into the database.

```
    /**
     * Save the post in the database
     * @return void
     */
```

```php
public function save()
{
  if( $this->id > 0 )
  {
    $update = array();
    $update['topic'] = $this->topic;
    $update['post'] = $this->post;
    $update['creator'] = $this->creator;
    $this->registry->getObject('db')->updateRecords( 'posts',
      $update, 'ID=' . $this->id );
  }
  else
  {
    $insert = array();
    $insert['topic'] = $this->topic;
    $insert['post'] = $this->post;
    $insert['creator'] = $this->creator;
    $this->registry->getObject('db')->insertRecords( 'posts',
      $insert );
    $this->id = $this->registry->getObject('db')->lastInsertID();
  }
}
}
?>
```

Topic

Our topic model needs to link into the post model. So we should create a method
that creates a new instance of the post model and stores it publicly within the topic
model, so that our controllers can update the properties of both of these objects.
When it comes to saving the topic, if the post was created, it should pass the topic
ID to indicate the topic the post relates to.

Model

Because of what we discussed above, this model (`models/topic.php`) will be
slightly more complicated than the post model, but not by much.

```php
<?php
/**
 * Discussion topic class
 */
class Topic {
```

As usual, we have various properties within the object.

```
/**
 * The registry object
 */
private $registry;

/**
 * ID of the topic
 */
private $id=0;

/**
 * ID of the creator
 */
private $creator;

/**
 * Name of the creator
 */
private $creatorName;

/**
 * Name of the topic
 */
private $name;

/**
 * When the topic was created (TIMESTAMP)
 */
private $created;

/**
 * Friendly reference for the date the topic was created
 */
private $createdFriendly;
```

A few of these properties are of more than just data from the topics table. We also have the numPosts property, which is for the number of posts within a topic; we have a Boolean field, which determines if the topic should also save the first post, and in that instance, we also have a post object.

```
/**
 * Number of posts in the topic
 */
private $numPosts;

/**
 * If we are also saving the first post
 */
private $includeFirstPost;

/**
 * Post object - if saving the first post too
 */
private $post;

/**
 * Group the topic was posted within
 */
private $group;
```

We have our standard constructor, populating fields if the ID is valid.

```
/**
 * Topic constructor
 * @param Registry $registry the registry object
 * @param int $id the ID of the topic
 * @return void
 */
public function __construct( Registry $registry, $id=0 )
{
  $this->registry = $registry;
  $this->id = $id;
  if( $this->id > 0 )
  {
    $sql = "SELECT t.*, (SELECT COUNT(*) FROM posts po WHERE
      po.topic=t.ID) as posts, DATE_FORMAT(t.created, '%D %M %Y')
      as created_friendly, p.name as creator_name FROM topics t,
      profile p WHERE p.user_id=t.creator AND t.ID=" . $this->id;
    $this->registry->getObject('db')->executeQuery( $sql );
    if( $this->registry->getObject('db')->numRows() > 0 )
```

```
      {
        $data = $this->registry->getObject('db')->getRows();
        $this->creator = $data['creator'];
        $this->creatorName = $data['creator_name'];
        $this->createdFriendly = $data['created_friendly'];
        $this->name = $data['name'];
        $this->numPosts = $data['posts'];
        $this->group = $data['group'];
      }
      else
      {
        $this->id = 0;
      }
    }
  }

  /**
   * Get query of the posts in the topic (i.e. collection of posts ==
   * topic )
   */
  public function getPostsQuery()
  {
    $sql = "SELECT p.*, DATE_FORMAT() as friendly_created_post,
      pr.name as creator_friendly_post FROM posts p, profile pr WHERE
      pr.user_id=p.creator AND p.topic=" . $this->id;
    return $sql;
  }
```

We have a method to set if we are including the first post. If we are, we include the class, instantiate the object, and assign it to the post property in the topic object.

```
  /**
   * Set if this save should also save the first post
   * @param bool $ifp
   * @return void
   */
  public function includeFirstPost( $ifp )
  {
    $this->includeFirstPost = $ifp;
    require_once( FRAMEWORK_PATH . 'models/post.php' );
    $this->post = new Post( $this->registry, 0 );
  }
```

If we are setting the first post, our controllers can access this post object by calling the getFirstPost method, and then calling the appropriate public methods on the post object.

```
/**
 * Return the object for the first post, for setting fields
 * @return Object
 */
public function getFirstPost()
{
  return $this->post;
}
```

We have a number of setter methods, as standard.

```
/**
 * Set the group this topic should be part of
 * @param int $group
 * @return void
 */
public function setGroup( $group )
{
  $this->group = $group;
}

/**
 * Set the creator of the topic
 * @param int $creator
 * @return void
 */
public function setCreator( $creator )
{
  $this->creator = $creator;
}

/**
 * Set the name of the topic
 * @param String $name
 * @return void
 */
public function setName( $name )
{
  $this->name = $name;
}
```

We have our save method, which if appropriate, also saves the post once the topic
has been created.

```
/**
 * Save the topic into the database
 * @return void
 */
public function save()
{
  if( $this->id > 0 )
  {
    $update = array();
    $update['creator'] = $this->creator;
    $update['name'] = $this->name;
    $update['group'] = $this->group;
    $this->registry->getObject('db')->updateRecords( 'topics',
      $update, 'ID=' . $this->id );
  }
  else
  {
    $insert = array();
    $insert['creator'] = $this->creator;
    $insert['name'] = $this->name;
    $insert['group'] = $this->group;
    $this->registry->getObject('db')->insertRecords( 'topics',
      $insert );
    $this->id = $this->registry->getObject('db')->lastInsertID();
    if( $this->includeFirstPost == true )
    {
      $this->post->setTopic( $this->id );
      $this->post->save();
    }
  }
}
```

Next, we have a getter for the name property, and also a `toTags` method, which
is now almost a standard for most of our models.

```
/**
 * Get the name of the topic
 */
public function getName()
{
  return $this->name;
}
```

```
/**
 * Convert the topic data to template tags
 * @param String $prefix prefix for the template tags
 * @return void
 */
public function toTags( $prefix='' )
{
  foreach( $this as $field => $data )
  {
    if( ! is_object( $data ) && ! is_array( $data ) )
    {
      $this->registry->getObject('template')->getPage()->addTag(
        $prefix.$field, $data );
    }
  }
}

/**
 * Get the group this topic was posted within
 * @return int
 */
public function getGroup()
{
  return $this->group;
}
```

Finally, we have a `delete` method, which in addition to deleting the current topic from the database, also removes any posts related to it in the posts table.

```
/**
 * Delete the current topic
 * @return boolean
 */
public function delete()
{
  $sql = "DELETE FROM topics WHERE ID=" . $this->id;
  $this->registry->getObject('db')->executeQuery( $sql );
  if( $this->registry->getObject('db')->affectedRows() > 0 )
  {
    $sql = "DELETE FROM posts WHERE topic=" . $this->id;
    $this->registry->getObject('db')->executeQuery( $sql );
    $this->id =0;
    return true;
  }
```

```
    else
    {
      return false;
    }
  }
 }
}
?>
```

The group itself

With the models for topics and posts (which we will be using shortly) in place, we can now focus our attention on the group itself, as the group will need to make use of these models so that users of the groups can communicate and collaborate with one another.

Group table

The first stage, as with the other aspects of our social network, is the database table. We've already discussed what information the group needs to store; the following database structure simply formalizes that:

Field	Type	Description
ID	Integer, Auto-increment, Primary Key	Internal ID / reference for the group
Name	Varchar	Name of the group
Description	Longtext	Detailed description of the group
Type	ENUM	The type of the group
Creator	Integer	The user who created the group
Created	Timestamp	The time the group was created
Active	Boolean	If the group is active, gives us the ability to de-activate groups later without deleting them

Model

The model required for groups (`models/group.php`) is fairly standard with a few minor additions. We have some validation on the type of group, and we also have a method to cache a query of topics posted in the group.

```
<?php
/**
 * Group model object
 */
```

```php
class Group {
  /**
   * Types of group that are available
   */
  private $types = array('public', 'private', 'private-member-
    invite', 'private-self-invite');

  /**
   * The registry object
   */
  private $registry;

  /**
   * ID of the group
   */
  private $id;

  /**
   * The name of the group
   */
  private $name;

  /**
   * Description of the group
   */
  private $description;

  /**
   * The creator of the group
   */
  private $creator;

  /**
   * Name of the creator of the group
   */
  private $creatorName;

  /**
   * Time the group was created
   */
  private $created;

  /**
   * Friendly representation of when the group was created
```

```
 */
private $createdFriendly;

/**
 * Type of group
 */
private $type;

/**
 * If the group is active or not
 */
private $active=1;

/**
 * If the selected group is valid or not
 */
private $valid;

/**
 * Group constructor
 * @param Registry $registry the registry
 * @param int $id the ID of the group
 * @return void
 */
public function __construct( Registry $registry, $id=0 )
{
  $this->registry = $registry;
  if( $id > 0 )
  {
    $this->id = $id;
    $sql = "SELECT g.*, DATE_FORMAT(g.created, '%D %M %Y') as
      created_friendly, p.name as creator_name FROM groups g,
      profile p WHERE p.user_id=g.creator AND g.ID=" . $this->id;
    $this->registry->getObject('db')->executeQuery( $sql );
    if( $this->registry->getObject('db')->numRows() == 1 )
    {
      $data = $this->registry->getObject('db')->getRows();
      $this->name = $data['name'];
      $this->description = $data['description'];
      $this->creator = $data['creator'];
      $this->valid = true;
      $this->active = $data['active'];
      $this->type = $data['type'];
      $this->created = $data['created'];
```

```php
        $this->createdFriendly = $data['created_friendly'];
        $this->creator = $data['creator'];
        $this->creatorName = $data['creator_name'];
      }
      else
      {
        $this->valid = false;
      }
    }
    else
    {
      $this->id = 0;
    }
  }

  /**
   * Set the name of the group
   * @param String $name
   * @return void
   */
  public function setName( $name )
  {
    $this->name = $name;
  }

  /**
   * Set the description of the group
   * @param String $description the description
   * @return void
   */
  public function setDescription( $description )
  {
    $this->description = $description;
  }

  /**
   * Set the creator of the group
   * @param int $creator
   * @return void
   */
  public function setCreator( $creator )
  {
    $this->creator = $creator;
  }
```

When setting the type of the group, it is validated against an array of available group types.

```
/**
 * Set the type of the group
 * @param String $type
 * @return void
 */
public function setType( $type )
{
  if( in_array( $type, $this->types ) )
  {
    $this->type = $type;
  }
}

/**
 * Save the group
 * @return void
 */
public function save()
{
  if( $this->id > 0 )
  {
    $update = array();
    $update['description'] = $this->description;
    $update['name'] = $this->name;
    $update['type'] = $this->type;
    $update['creator'] = $this->creator;
    $update['active'] = $this->active;
    $update['created'] = $this->created;
    $this->registry->getObject('db')->updateRecords( 'groups',
      $update, 'ID=' . $this->id );
  }
  else
  {
    $insert = array();
    $insert['description'] = $this->description;
    $insert['name'] = $this->name;
    $insert['type'] = $this->type;
    $insert['creator'] = $this->creator;
    $insert['active'] = $this->active;
    $this->registry->getObject('db')->insertRecords( 'groups',
      $insert );
    $this->id = $this->registry->getObject('db')->lastInsertID();
  }
}
```

With the above code, we can easily populate our group page with topics related to it. We also have a method to cache a suitable query and return the cache.

```php
/**
 * Get a list of topics assigned to this group ( we could paginate
   this if we wanted to later)
 * @return int (database cache)
 */
public function getTopics()
{
  $sql = "SELECT t.*, (SELECT COUNT(*) FROM posts po WHERE
    po.topic=t.ID) as posts, DATE_FORMAT(t.created, '%D %M %Y')
    as created_friendly, p.name as creator_name FROM topics t,
    profile p WHERE p.user_id=t.creator AND t.group=" .
    $this->id . " ORDER BY t.ID DESC";
  $cache = $this->registry->getObject('db')->cacheQuery( $sql );
  return $cache;
}

/**
 * Get the ID of the group
 */
public function getID()
{
  return $this->id;
}

/**
 * Convert the group data to template tags
 * @param String $prefix prefix for the template tags
 * @return void
 */
public function toTags( $prefix='' )
{
  foreach( $this as $field => $data )
  {
    if( ! is_object( $data ) && ! is_array( $data ) )
    {
      $this->registry->getObject('template')->getPage()->addTag(
        $prefix.$field, $data );
    }
  }
}
}
?>
```

Creating a group

With our model in place, we now need to work on our group's controller, firstly to facilitate the creation of new groups. We will shortly also create a group controller, for viewing a group and performing tasks within a group.

Controller

Since we are creating a new controller (`controllers/groups/controller.php`), we need to put some skeleton code in there, in addition to our create group code. We need a constructor that detects if the user is logged in, and if they are not, reverts to displaying a list of public groups. If the user is logged in, the default still lists public groups, but they can also create a group (and shortly, also search groups).

The highlighted section of code shows how the group is created:

```php
<?php
class Groupscontroller {

  /**
    * Controller constructor - direct call to false when being
      embedded via another controller
    * @param Registry $registry our registry
    * @param bool $directCall - are we calling it directly via the
      framework (true), or via another controller (false)
    */
  public function __construct( Registry $registry, $directCall )
  {
    $this->registry = $registry;
    $urlBits = $this->registry->getObject('url')->getURLBits();

    if( $this->registry->getObject('authenticate')->isLoggedIn() )
    {
      if( isset( $urlBits[1] ) )
      {
        switch( $urlBits[1] )
        {
          case 'create':
            $this->createGroup();
            break;
          default:
            $this->listPublicGroups(0);
            break;
        }
      }
      else
      {
```

```
                                $this->listPublicGroups( 0 );
            }
        }
        else
        {
            if( isset( $urlBits[1] ) )
            {
                $this->listPublicGroups( intval( $urlBits[1] ) );
            }
            else
            {
                $this->listPublicGroups( 0 );
            }
        }
    }


    /**
     * Create a new group
     * @return void
     */
    private function createGroup()
    {
        if( isset( $_POST ) && is_array( $_POST ) && count( $_POST ) > 0
            )
        {
            require_once( FRAMEWORK_PATH . 'models/group.php');
            $group = new Group( $this->registry, 0 );
            $group->setCreator( $this->registry->getObject('authenticate')-
                >getUser()->getUserID() );
            $group->setName( $this->registry->getObject('db')-
                >sanitizeData( $_POST['name'] ) );
            $group->setDescription( $this->registry->getObject('db')-
                >sanitizeData( $_POST['description'] ) );
            $group->setType( $_POST['type'] );
            $group->save();
            $this->registry->errorPage('Group created', 'Thank you, your
                new group has been created');
        }
        else
        {
            $this->registry->getObject('template')->buildFromTemplates(
                'header.tpl.php', 'groups/create.tpl.php', 'footer.tpl.php' );
        }
    }
}
?>
```

View

The template for creating a group (`views/default/templates/groups/create.tpl.php`) is simply a form, with a text box for name and description and a drop-down list of types.

```html
<div id="main">

  <div id="rightside">
  </div>

  <div id="content">
    <h1>Create a new group</h1>
    <form action="groups/create" method="post">
    <label for="name">Name</label><br />
    <input type="text" id="name" name="name" value="" /><br />
    <label for="description">Description</label><br />
    <textarea id="description"
      name="description"></textarea><br />
    <label for="type">Type</label><br />
    <select id="type" name="type">
      <option value="public">Public Group</option>
      <option value="private">Private Group</option>
      <option value="private-member-invite">Private (Invite
        Only) Group</option>
      <option value="private-self-invite">Private (Self-Invite)
        Group</option>
    </select><br />

    <input type="submit" id="create" name="create"
      value="Create group" />
    </form>
  </div>


</div>
```

Creating a group—in action

If we navigate to groups/create, we see the create group form and are able to successfully create a new group.

Viewing a group

For us to view a group (and also participate in a group), we will need:

- A controller for the group
- A way of maintaining membership lists for groups, including:
    ○ A database table
    ○ A model

- A way of determining if a user is either a member of a group or the creator, and thus has permission to view the group

Membership

Maintaining a list of memberships is important so we know that a user can view a group, and more importantly, we know if a user is a member of a group, not a member of a group, or if they have requested to join or have been invited to join.

The following database structure would be a suitable `group_memberships` table for our site:

Field	Type	Description
ID	Integer, PK, Auto-increment	Internal reference for the membership
Group	Integer	The ID of the group
User	Integer	The ID of the user
Approved	Boolean	Indicates if the user's membership has been approved
Invited	Boolean	Indicates if the user has been invited to join
Requested	Boolean	Indicates if the user has requested to join
InvitedDate	Timestamp	Date the user was invited
RequestedDate	Timestamp	Date the user requested to join
JoinDate	Timestamp	Date the user joined
Inviter	Integer	The user who invited the user

Membership model

We also need a model (`models/groupmembership.php`) to represent a user's membership, pending membership, or lack of membership of a group. This model will be used to create memberships, create requests to join a group, and to create invites to a group. It will also be used to determine if a user has access to a group.

```php
<?php
/**
 * Group membership model
 */
class Groupmembership{
```

Our model starts with our class variables, including a reference to the `registry` object itself, and the properties related to an individual's membership of a group.

```php
/**
 * ID of the membership record
 */
private $id;

/**
 * ID of the user
 */
private $user;
```

```
/**
 * ID of the group
 */
private $group;

/**
 * Indicates if the membership is active / approved
 */
private $approved = 0;

/**
 * Indicates if the user was invited
 */
private $invited;

/**
 * Indicates if the user has requested to join
 */
private $requested;

/**
 * Date user was invited to join
 */
private $invitedDate;

/**
 * Date user requested to join
 */
private $requestedDate;

/**
 * Join date
 */
private $joinDate;

/**
 * User who invited the user to join the group
 */
private $inviter;
```

The constructor takes the `registry` object and an optional ID as a parameter. If the ID is passed, it queries the database, and if records are found, it assigns the relevant fields to the class variables.

```
/**
 * Constructor
 * @param Registry $registry
 * @param int $id
 * @return void
 */
public function __construct( Registry $registry, $id=0 )
{
  $this->registry = $registry;
  if( $id > 0 )
  {
    $sql = "SELECT * FROM group_membership WHERE ID={$id} LIMIT 1";
    $this->registry->getObject('db')->executeQuery( $sql );
    if( $this->registry->getObject('db')->numRows() == 1 )
    {
      $data = $this->registry->getObject('db')->getRows();
      $this->approved = $data['approved'];
      $this->invited = $data['invited'];
      $this->requested = $data['requested'];
      $this->invitedDate = $data['invited_date'];
      $this->requestedDate = $data['requested_date'];
      $this->joinDate = $data['join_date'];
      $this->inviter = $data['inviter'];
    }
  }
  else
  {
    $this->id = 0;
  }
}
```

If part of our code needs to look up a user's group membership but doesn't know the ID of the membership, we can instead call the following method, passing the user ID and group ID as parameters. The method will populate the class variables with results from the query:

```
/**
 * Get membership information by user and group
 * @param int $user
 * @param int $group
 * @return void
 */
public function getByUserAndGroup( $user, $group )
{
  $this->user = $user;
```

```
    $this->group = $group;
    $sql = "SELECT * FROM group_membership WHERE user={$user} AND
      `group`={$group} LIMIT 1";
    $this->registry->getObject('db')->executeQuery( $sql );
    if( $this->registry->getObject('db')->numRows() == 1 )
    {
      $data = $this->registry->getObject('db')->getRows();
      $this->approved = $data['approved'];
      $this->invited = $data['invited'];
      $this->requested = $data['requested'];
    }
  }
}
```

We have some of our standard getter methods to return some of the private
properties to other objects within the framework.

```
/**
 * Get if the membership is approved
 * @return boolean
 */
public function getApproved()
{
  return $this->approved;
}

/**
 * Get if the user was invited
 * @return boolean
 */
public function getInvited()
{
  return $this->invited;
}

/**
 * Get if the user requested to join
 * @return boolean
 */
public function getRequested()
{
  return $this->requested;
}

/**
 * Get the user who invited this user to the group
 * @return int
 */
```

```
public function getInviter()
{
  return $this->inviter;
}
```

Next, we have our setter methods, which set the relevant private properties of the class.

```
/**
 * Set membership to approved
 * @param boolean $approved
 * @return void
 */
public function setApproved( $approved )
{
  $this->approved = $approved;
}

/**
 * Set membership status to requested
 * @param boolean $requested
 * @return void
 */
public function setRequested( $requested )
{
  $this->requested = $requested;
}

/**
 * Set if the user was invited
 * @param boolean $invited
 * @return void
 */
public function setInvited( $invited )
{
  $this->invited = $invited;
}

/**
 * Set the inviter
 * @param int $inviter
 * @return void
 */
public function setInviter( $inviter )
{
  $this->inviter = $inviter;
}
```

Finally, we have our `save` method, which either creates a new record in the database, or updates an existing one.

```
/**
 * Save the membership record
 * @return void
 */
public function save()
{
  if( $this->id > 0 )
  {
    $update = array();
    $update['user'] = $this->user;
    $update['group'] = $this->group;
    $update['approved'] = $this->approved;
    $update['requested'] = $this->requested;
    $update['invited'] = $this->invited;
    $update['invited_date'] = $this->invitedDate;
    $update['requested_date'] = $this->requestedDate;
    $update['join_date'] = $this->joinDate;
    $update['inviter'] = $this->inviter;
    $this->registry->getObject('db')->updateRecords(
      'group_memberships', $update, 'ID=' . $this->id );
  }
  else
  {
    $insert = array();
    $insert['user'] = $this->user;
    $insert['group'] = $this->group;
    $insert['approved'] = $this->approved;
    $insert['requested'] = $this->requested;
    $insert['invited'] = $this->invited;
    $insert['invited_date'] = $this->invitedDate;
    $insert['requested_date'] = $this->requestedDate;
    $insert['join_date'] = $this->joinDate;
    $insert['inviter'] = $this->inviter;
    $this->registry->getObject('db')->insertRecords(
      'group_memberships', $insert );
    $this->id = $this->registry->getObject('db')->lastInsertID();
  }
}
}
?>
```

Controller

Our group controller (`controllers/group/controller.php`) needs to do a fair bit of logic to work out what it should do, even if the request is simply to view a group, as we want to do now.

```php
<?php
class Groupcontroller {

  /**
   * Controller constructor - direct call to false when being
     embedded via another controller
   * @param Registry $registry our registry
   * @param bool $directCall - are we calling it directly via the
     framework (true), or via another controller (false)
   */
  public function __construct( Registry $registry, $directCall )
  {
    $this->registry = $registry;
    $urlBits = $this->registry->getObject('url')->getURLBits();
```

Firstly, the controller checks that the current user is logged in.

```php
    if( $this->registry->getObject('authenticate')->isLoggedIn() )
    {
```

Secondly, the controller checks that there is at least one bit in the URL. The first bit of the URL should be the group ID.

```php
      if( isset( $urlBits[1] ) )
      {`
```

The group model is then included and instantiated, to determine if the requested group is valid / active.

```php
        require_once( FRAMEWORK_PATH . 'models/group.php');
        $this->group = new Group( $this->registry, intval(
          $urlBits[1] ) );
        $this->groupID = intval( $urlBits[1] );
        if( $this->group->isValid() && $this->group->isActive() )
        {
```

If the group is active, the next stage is to check that the currently logged in user is either the creator of the group, or is a member of the group.

```
require_once( FRAMEWORK_PATH .
  'models/groupmembership.php');
$gm = new Groupmembership( $this->registry );
$user = $this->registry->getObject('authenticate')-
  >getUser()->getUserID();
$gm->getByUserAndGroup( $user, $this->groupID );
if( $this->group->getCreator() == $user || $gm-
  >getApproved() )
{
```

If the currently logged in user is a member of the group, or its creator, then the controller looks up the full details of the user's request, and passes control to the appropriate method.

```
if( isset( $urlBits[2] ) )
{
  switch( $urlBits[2] )
  {
    case 'create-topic':
      $this->createTopic();
      break;
    case 'view-topic':
      $this->viewTopic( intval( $urlBits[3] ) );
      break;
    case 'reply-to-topic':
      $this->replyToTopic( intval( $urlBits[3] ) );
      break;
    case 'membership':
      $this->manageMembership( intval( $urlBits[3] ) );
      break;
    default:
      $this->viewGroup();
      break;
  }
}
else
{
  $this->viewGroup();
}
}
else
{
```

If the user isn't a member of the group, control is passed to a secondary controller (we will create it shortly) which, if appropriate, will provide a mechanism for the user to join the group.

```
            require_once( FRAMEWORK_PATH .
              'controllers/group/membership.php');
            $membership = new Membershipcontroller( $this->registry,
              $this->groupID );
            $membership->join();
          }
        }
        else
        {
          $this->registry->errorPage( 'Group not found', 'Sorry, the
            group you requested was not found' );
        }
      }
      else
      {
        $this->registry->errorPage( 'Group not found', 'Sorry, the
          group you requested was not found' );
      }
    }
    else
    {
      $this->registry->errorPage( 'Please login', 'Sorry, you must be
        logged in to view groups' );
    }
  }
```

If the user's request was to view a group, then the group model data is sent to the template engine, the template is built, and the cache of topics from the group is generated and also sent to the template engine.

```
  private function viewGroup()
  {
    $this->group->toTags( 'group_' );
    $this->registry->getObject('template')->buildFromTemplates(
      'header.tpl.php', 'groups/view.tpl.php', 'footer.tpl.php' );
    $cache = $this->group->getTopics();
    $this->registry->getObject('template')->getPage()->addTag(
      'topics', array( 'SQL', $cache ) );
  }

  private function viewTopic( $topic )
  {
```

```
    // next part of this chapter
  }


  private function replyToTopic( $topic )
  {
    // next part of this chapter
  }


  private function manageMembership()
  {
    if( $group->getCreator() == $this->registry-
      >getObject('authenticate')->getUser()->getUserID() )
    {
      require_once( FRAMEWORK_PATH .
        'controllers/group/membership.php');
      $membership = new Membershipcontroller( $this->registry, $this-
        >groupID );
      $membership->manage();
    }
    else
    {
      $this->registry->errorPage( 'Permission denied', 'Only the
        gorup creator can manage membership' );
    }
  }
}
?>
```

View

The template (`views/default/templates/groups/view.tpl.php`) for viewing a group is fairly straightforward, containing some information on the group and the topics within it.

```
<div id="main">

  <div id="rightside">
    <ul>
      <li><a href="group/{group_id}/create-topic">Create new
        topic</a></li>
    </ul>
  </div>

  <div id="content">
    <h1>{group_name}</h1>
```

```
        <p>{group_description}</p>
        <h2>Topics</h2>
        <table>
          <tr>
            <th>Topic</th><th>Creator</th>
            <th>Created</th><th>Posts</th>
          </tr>
          <!-- START topics -->
          <tr>
            <td><a href="group/{group_id}/view-
              topic/{ID}">{name}</a></td><td>{creator_name}</td>
            <td>{created_friendly}</td><td>{posts}</td>
          </tr>
          <!-- END topics -->
        </table>
      </div>


    </div>
```

In action

Let's take a look at viewing a group in action (`group/1/`):

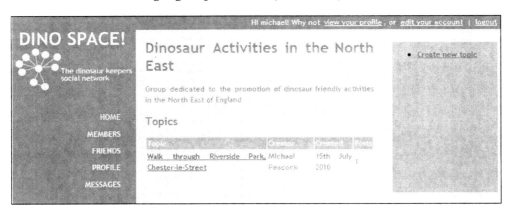

We have our group information displayed, with the topics listed underneath.

Discussing within a group

Now that we can create and view groups, we need to integrate the discussion features which will be facilitated thanks to our topic and post models.

Group controller additions

Most of this functionality can be added in by adding suitable code to our group controller.

Creating a topic

To create a topic, we simply add the following method to the controller:

```
/**
 * Create a new topic within the group
 * @return void
 */
private function createTopic()
{
  if( isset( $_POST ) && is_array( $_POST ) && count( $_POST ) >
    0 )
  {
    require_once( FRAMEWORK_PATH . 'models/topic.php' );
    $topic = new Topic( $this->registry, 0 );
    $topic->includeFirstPost( true );
    $user = $this->registry->getObject('authenticate')->getUser()-
      >getUserID();
    $topic->setCreator( $user );
    $topic->setGroup( $this->groupID );
    $topic->setName( $this->registry->getObject('db')-
      >sanitizeData( $_POST['name'] ) );
    $topic->getFirstPost()->setCreator( $user );
    $topic->getFirstPost()->setPost( $this->registry-
      >getObject('db')->sanitizeData( $_POST['name'] ) );
    $topic->save();
    $this->registry->redirectUser( $this->registry->buildURL(array(
      'group', $this->groupID ), '', false ), 'Topic created',
      'Thanks, the topic has been created', false );
  }
  else
  {
    $this->group->toTags( 'group_' );
    $this->registry->getObject('template')->buildFromTemplates(
      'header.tpl.php', 'groups/create-topic.tpl.php',
      'footer.tpl.php' );
  }
}
```

Viewing a topic

To view a topic, we simply add the following method to our controller:

```
/**
 * View a topic within the group
 * @return void
 */
private function viewTopic( $topic )
{
  $this->group->toTags( 'group_' );
  require_once( FRAMEWORK_PATH . 'models/topic.php' );
  $topic = new Topic( $this->registry, $topic );
  if( $topic->getGroup() == $this->groupID )
  {
    $topic->toTags( 'topic_' );
    $sql = $topic->getPostsQuery();
    $cache = $this->registry->getObject('db')->cacheQuery( $sql );
    $this->registry->getObject('template')->getPage()-
      >addTag('posts', array( 'SQL', $cache ) );
    $this->registry->getObject('template')->buildFromTemplates(
      'header.tpl.php', 'groups/view-topic.tpl.php',
      'footer.tpl.php' );
  }
  else
  {
    $this->registry->errorPage( 'Invalid topic', 'Sorry, you tried
      to view an invalid topic');
  }
}
```

Replying to a topic

To reply to a topic we simply add the following method to our controller:

```
/**
 * Reply to a topic within a group
 * @param int $topic
 * @return void
 */
private function replyToTopic( $topici )
{
  $this->group->toTags( 'group_' );
  require_once( FRAMEWORK_PATH . 'models/topic.php' );
  $topic = new Topic( $this->registry, $topici );
  if( $topic->getGroup() == $this->groupID )
```

```
{
   require_once( FRAMEWORK_PATH . 'models/post.php' );
   $post = new Post( $this->registry, 0 );
   $user = $this->registry->getObject('authenticate')->getUser()-
      >getUserID();
   $post->setPost( $this->registry->getObject('db')->sanitizeData(
      $_POST['post'] ) );
   $post->setCreator( $user );
   $post->setTopic( $topici );
   $post->save();
   $this->registry->redirectUser( $this->registry->buildURL(array(
      'group', $this->groupID, 'view-topic', $topici ), '',
      false ), 'Reply saved', 'Thanks, the topic topic reply has
      been saved', false );
}
else
{
   $this->registry->errorPage( 'Invalid topic', 'Sorry, you tried
      to view an invalid topic');
}
}
```

View

For each of the three methods we have created, we now need to create template files
for them (only two, as reply and view use the same template).

Creating a topic

This template file (`Views/default/templates/groups/create-topic.tpl.php`) is
simply a form with fields for the name of the topic and the contents of the first post.

```
<div id="main">

   <div id="rightside">
      <ul>
         <li><a href="group/{group_id}">{group_name}</a></li>
      </ul>
   </div>

   <div id="content">
      <h1>Create a new topic</h1>
      <form action="group/{group_id}/create-topic" method="post">
      <label for="name">Topic Name</label><br />
      <input type="text" id="name" name="name" value="" /><br />
      <label for="post">First Post</label><br />
```

```
    <textarea id="post" name="post"></textarea><br />
    <input type="submit" id="create" name="create"
      value="Create topic" />
  </form>
</div>

</div>
```

Viewing a topic

This template file (`Views/default/templates/groups/view-topic.tpl.php`) simply contains a loop of template tags representing the posts within the topic, as well as information on the topic itself.

```
<div id="main">

  <div id="rightside">
    <ul>
      <li><a href="group/{group_id}">{group_name}</a></li>
      <li><a href="group/{group_id}/create-topic">Create
        topic</a></li>
    </ul>
  </div>

  <div id="content">
    <h1>{topic_name}</h1>
    <!-- START posts -->
    <p>{post}</p>
    <p><em>Posted by {creator_friendly_post} on
      {friendly_created_post}</em></p>
    <hr />
    <!-- END posts -->
    <h2>Reply to this topic</h2>
    <form action="group/{group_id}/reply-to-topic/{topic_id}"
      method="post">
    <textarea id="post" name="post">
    </textarea>
    <input type="submit" id="np" name="np" value="Reply" />
    </form>
  </div>

</div>
```

Discussion in action—viewing a topic

Let's now take a look at viewing a topic from within one of our newly-created groups.

Joining a group

Now that our users can create groups, view groups, and communicate within groups, we need to provide users the ability to join groups, request admission to groups, or allow group members to send out invitations to join a group.

In this chapter we will simply look at members joining public groups. Feel free to extend this to meet the needs of your social network, and similarly include membership management options.

Joining (public) groups

Our group controller automatically passes control to a secondary controller if the user was not a member of the group, or was not the group's creator. This secondary controller can detect the type of group, and then display information regarding joining, or in the case of public groups, automatically sign them up.

This secondary controller is `controllers/group/membership.php`.

```php
<?php
class Membershipcontroller {
  private $registry;

  private $groupID;
```

```php
    private $group;

    public function __construct( Registry $registry, $groupID )
    {
        $this->registry = $registry;
        $this->groupID = $groupID;
        require_once( FRAMEWORK_PATH . 'models/group.php');
        $this->group = new Group( $this->registry, $this->groupID );
    }

    public function join()
    {
        $type = $this->group->getType();
        switch( $type )
        {
            case 'public':
                $this->autoJoinGroup();
                break;
        }
    }

    private function autoJoinGroup()
    {
        require_once( FRAMEWORK_PATH . 'models/groupmembership.php');
        $gm = new Groupmembership( $this->registry, 0 );
        $user = $this->registry->getObject('authenticate')->getUser()-
            >getUserID();
        $gm->getByUserAndGroup( $user, $this->groupID );
        if( $gm->isValid() )
        {
            $gm = new Groupmembership( $this->registry, $gm->getID() );
        }
        $gm->setApproved( 1 );
        $gm->save();
        $this->registry->errorPage('New membership', 'Thanks, you have
            now joined the group');
    }
}
?>
```

Groups

Now that we have functionality for groups in place, we need a facility to allow our users to be able to find and join groups. After all, if users can't find groups then there isn't much point in them being there. This can be enabled through two methods:

- Listing groups (where they are public)
- Searching groups (again, where they are public)

To facilitate this, we will need a new model and a new controller: groups. This will manage the listing and searching of groups.

Listing groups

Let's look at how we can list public groups, and also list our own group memberships to make it possible to find groups and easily access groups we are members of.

Group controller addition

We need to complete a method we referenced earlier in the chapter, to list public groups. As it takes an offset as a parameter, it should build a paginated list of public groups.

```
private function listPublicGroups( $offset )
{
  $sql = "SELECT * FROM groups WHERE active=1 AND type <>
    'private' ";
  require_once( FRAMEWORK_PATH .
    'lib/pagination/pagination.class.php');
  $pagination = new Pagination( $this->registry );
  $pagination->setQuery( $sql );
  $pagination->setOffset( $offset );
  $pagination->setLimit( 20 );
  $pagination->setMethod('cache');
  $pagination->generatePagination();
  if( $pagination->getNumRowsPage() == 0 )
  {
    $this->registry->getObject('template')->buildFromTemplates(
      'header.tpl.php', 'groups/no-public.tpl.php',
      'footer.tpl.php' );
  }
  else
  {
    $this->registry->getObject('template')->buildFromTemplates(
```

```
            'header.tpl.php', 'groups/public.tpl.php',
            'footer.tpl.php' );
        $this->registry->getObject('template')->getPage()->addTag(
            'groups', array( 'SQL', $pagination->getCache() ) );
        $this->registry->getObject('template')->getPage()->addTag(
            'page_number', $pagination->getCurrentPage() );
        $this->registry->getObject('template')->getPage()->addTag(
            'num_pages', $pagination->getNumPages() );
        if( $pagination->isFirst() )
        {
            $this->registry->getObject('template')->getPage()->addTag(
                'first', '');
            $this->registry->getObject('template')->getPage()->addTag(
                'previous', '' );
        }
        else
        {
            $this->registry->getObject('template')->getPage()->addTag(
                'first', "<a href='groups/'>First page</a>" );
            $this->registry->getObject('template')->getPage()->addTag(
                'previous', "<a href='groups/" . ( $pagination-
                >getCurrentPage() - 2 ) . "'>Previous page</a>" );
        }
        if( $pagination->isLast() )
        {
            $this->registry->getObject('template')->getPage()->addTag(
                'next', '' );
            $this->registry->getObject('template')->getPage()->addTag(
                'last', '' );
        }
        else
        {
            $this->registry->getObject('template')->getPage()->addTag(
                'first', "<a href='groups/" . $pagination->getCurrentPage()
                . "'>Next page</a>" );
            $this->registry->getObject('template')->getPage()->addTag(
                'previous', "<a href='groups/" . ( $pagination-
                >getNumPages() - 1 ) . "'>Last page</a>" );
        }
    }
}
```

Template

The template file for this list is `views/default/templates/groups/public.tpl.php`.

```
<div id="main">

  <div id="rightside">
    <ul>
      <li><a href="groups/create">Create a new group</a></li>
    </ul>
  </div>

  <div id="content">
    <h1>Public groups</h1>
    <!-- START groups -->
    <h2>{name}</h2>
    <p>{description}</p>
    <hr />
    <!-- END groups -->
    {first}{previous}{next}{last}
  </div>
</div>
```

In action

Let's look at the group's listing in action (`/groups`).

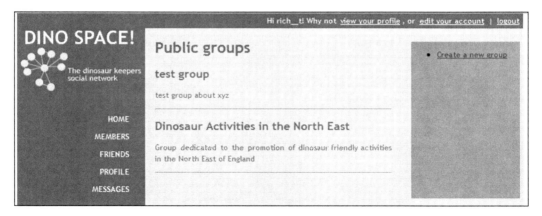

My groups

We now need an area in our social network where users can view groups which they are members of, so that they can quickly go into their groups.

Addition to the group's controller

Our final addition to the group's controller is a method listing our group memberships, either where we are a member (via the sub-query) or where we created the group.

```php
private function listMyGroups()
  {
    $user = $this->registry->getObject('authenticate')->getUser()-
      >getUserID();
    $sql = "SELECT * FROM groups WHERE creator={$user} OR ID IN
      (SELECT m.group FROM group_membership m WHERE m.user={$user}
      and m.approved=1 ) ";
    $cache = $this->registry->getObject('db')->cacheQuery( $sql );
    $this->registry->getObject('template')->getPage()->addTag(
      'my-groups', array('SQL', $cache ) );
    $this->registry->getObject('template')->buildFromTemplates(
      'header.tpl.php', 'groups/mine.tpl.php', 'footer.tpl.php' );
  }
```

Template file

The template file (`Views/default/templates/groups/mine.tpl.php`) simply contains a template loop of group names, descriptions, and links to the group itself.

```html
<div id="main">

  <div id="rightside">
    <ul>
      <li><a href="groups/create">Create a new group</a></li>
    </ul>
  </div>

  <div id="content">
    <h1>My groups</h1>
    <!-- START my-groups -->
    <h2><a href="group/{ID}">{name}</a></h2>
    <p>{description}</p>
    <hr />
    <!-- END my-groups -->
  </div>
</div>
```

In action

Let's take a look at this in action.

Summary

In this chapter, we have created a groups system that allows users of our social network to create either private or public sections for a sub-set of users to collaborate and communicate within on a number of different issues. We looked at permissions and features available to the creator of the group, as well as the ways in which other members could join the group, either by making them public, private, or private except for member's invitees.

With the final of our user-facing features in place on Dino Space, we can now create an API to allow other services and developers to interact with our social network, and the wealth of features it has to offer.

11
Developing an API

In order to extend and enhance social networks, most of them provide a suite of APIs that provide developers access to some of the functionality behind the site. We will create our own API to allow developers to interact with Dino Space.

In this chapter you will learn:

- What an API is
- What other social networks expose through their APIs
- What we should expose through our API, and who we should expose it to
- Methods of creating APIs
- How to develop a RESTful API
- How to deal with authentication through the API
- About the implications of creating an Applications API

Let's get started and add an API to our social network!

What is an API and why should we create one?

An Application Programming Interface (API) is an interface that allows developers and other applications to interact with the application, exposing data and facilitating certain operations (such as create, edit, and delete) on data.

By providing an API, we offer a number of benefits to our users:

- Reducing their concerns about "Vendor lock in"—if, for whatever reason, they choose to leave Dino Space for a competitor, the API provides access to their data

- Other developers and websites can enhance what we offer by extending our functionality or providing additional benefits to our users on their sites

- If we develop an application framework API, we could even allow third-party developers to directly extend what is available on our site

APIs in social networks

Let's take a look at what APIs other social networks offer developers, and what they do.

Facebook

Facebook provides a range of APIs to allow different types of applications to interact with their platform. This includes:

- **Website Integration**: Integrating Facebook with your own website, including authentication, Single Sign-On, liking external content, and displaying Facebook network information within a page

- **Mobile Integration**: Incorporating Facebook into mobile applications

- **Facebook Applications**: Extending the functionality of Facebook by developing third-party applications, which operate from within the Facebook site

The range offered by Facebook is used not only to enhance what is available on the Facebook site, but also by integrating Facebook across other websites, it helps increase its popularity, almost making it an essential tool to get the best experience out of other websites that make use of its website integration APIs.

More information is available on the Facebook developer's site: `http://developers.facebook.com/docs/`.

MySpace

With a similar API offering to Facebook, MySpace provides APIs to:

- Develop games and applications for integration within MySpace using the Games and Apps APIs

- Allow MySpace users to log in to your website using the MySpace ID APIs

- Share third-party content with their MySpace network using the Share on MySpace APIs

- Integrate with the stream with the Real Time Stream API

More information can be obtained from the MySpace developer website: `http://developer.myspace.com/wordpress/`.

OpenSocial

While not technically a social network, this is a suite of APIs used on a number of different social networks.

Google, MySpace, and a number of other social networks worked together to develop OpenSocial (`http://www.opensocial.org/`), a collection of common APIs for use on social networking sites. The idea behind it was to make it easier for developers to create applications for many social networks, with them only having to develop with one API. It also provides an easy way for social networks to allow developers to interact with their sites.

Sites which support third-party applications written using the OpenSocial API are called OpenSocial Containers. More information about developing containers is available on the OpenSocial website: `http://www.opensocial.org/page/building-an-opensocial`.

Some planning

Before we can start implementing this feature, we need to think about what information it needs to be able to return, access, view, edit, and delete. We also need to think about who can do what with the API, as well as how we will structure the API.

What should it do, and who should be able to do what?

Let's look at the main areas of functionality within Dino Space, and list the operations within that we may wish to open up to our API. Depending on the operation, it may be restricted either by:

- **User**: The user themselves—editing data they themselves created
- **Users**: Any users within the site

- **Connections**: Connections of the user the data relates to

Area of Dino Space	Feature	Description	Who
Profiles	List	List user profiles	Users
	View	View details of a specific user's profile	Connections
	Search	Search for user profiles	Users
	Edit	Edit your own user profile	User
Statuses	List	List the statuses of your connections	Connections
	Create	Create a new status	User
Stream	List	List the stream from your network	User
Relationships	List	List relationships from your connections	Connections
	Create	Create a new connection with another user	User
	Delete	Delete a connection with another user	User
Events	List	List events within your network	User
	View	View details of a specific event	User
	Edit	Edit the details of an event you created	User
	Create	Create a new event	User
	Attend	Change your attendance status on an event	User
Groups	List	List groups you are a member of, or all public groups	Users
	View	Get details about a specific group	Users
	Join	Join a group	Users
Messages	List	List your inbox messages	User
	View	View a message	User
	Create	Create a new message	Connections
	Reply	Reply to a message	User
	Delete	Delete a message	User

How should it work?

Now that we have an idea of what information and which features we would like to expose to our API, we need to think about how it can work; in particular, what sort of architecture or standard should we use when developing our API.

How could it work?

There are three commonly-used methods for an API to work:

- REST: Representational State Transfer
- RPC: Remote Procedure Call
- SOAP: Simple Object Access Protocol

Let's look into what these are.

REST

Representational State Transfer (REST) is an architectural style, when used in an HTTP application; it utilizes existing HTTP features (URIs, response codes, and request methods—GET, POST, PUT, and DELETE) to work out what the API user (consumer) is trying to do.

REST: The quick pitch

David Megginson has posted a useful definition and overview about REST on his blog: `http://quoderat.megginson.com/2007/02/15/rest-the-quick-pitch/`.

RPC / RMI

Remote Procedure Call (RPC) or **Remote Method Invocation (RMI)** is a way of remotely executing specific functions (or methods) on a remote server. This generally works by the client application calling a stub, a local version of the method accepting appropriate parameters. The stub then calls the server's version of this method and the response is then passed to the local stub, and back to the caller of the stub.

There is a library available for the PHP implementation of XML-RPC: `http://phpxmlrpc.sourceforge.net/`.

SOAP

Simple Object Access Protocol (SOAP) is a stateless, one-way message exchange system that uses XML to transfer data between the client and server, confirming to certain specifications. A brief tutorial on using SOAP with PHP is available on the Apple developer website: `http://developer.apple.com/internet/webservices/soapphp.html`.

Let's go with REST

REST is now a very popular API architecture, with most social networks providing REST-based APIs. The way RESTful APIs rely on descriptive URIs for providing access to data makes them very easy for consumers to utilize, as the URIs provide information on what the request does, and what data it will return. Some implementations, such as the Twitter API even make it possible to change the format of the data returned, simply by changing a part of the URI.

Requests

Requests to a RESTful API use HTTP verbs to describe what the consumer is trying to do. The API requests are made to specific URIs, which define the resource that the consumer is trying to perform the action (determined by the verbs) upon.

HTTP verbs

The HTTP verbs and their usage are described as follows:

Verb	Description
GET	Retrieve information
POST	Create records
PUT	Update records
DELETE	Delete records

Resources

RESTful APIs relate URIs to resources. Below are some examples:

- `http://ourdomain.com/profiles`: To list or create profiles
- `http://ourdomain.com/profiles/1`: A specific user's profile

 Our RESTful API will be based within an API controller, thus prefixing all URLs with `api/`, which goes slightly against the REST concept of a resource.

Resources and verbs—the requests

Let's look at how resources and verbs combined result in API requests.

API operation	HTTP verb	Resource
Creating a user	POST	http://ourdomain.com/api/profiles
Listing users	GET	http://ourdomain.com/api/profiles
Viewing a user's profile	GET	http://ourdomain.com/api/profiles/1
Updating a profile	PUT	http://ourdomain.com/api/profiles/1
Deleting a profile	DELETE	http://ourdomain.com/api/profiles/1

 In the above resources, the number 1 represents the ID of a user's profile.

Responses

The response to an API request is generally made up of two parts. The first part of the response is the HTTP header containing an appropriate status code. Some examples of HTTP status codes are below:

HTTP status code	Meaning
200	OK
201	Created
400	Bad request
404	Not found

Within PHP, HTTP status codes are set as follows:

```
header("HTTP/1.0 404 Not Found");
```

The second part of the response is the data itself; for instance, if the API request was for a list of users, the response would be the list of users. Commonly, response data is sent as XML or JSON. Some APIs allow the consumer to request the format of the response by supplying the format to the API. We are going to use JSON. If we have an array of data that we want to return as JSON, we simply do the following:

```
echo json_encode( $users_list_array );
exit();
```

Further reading

There are numerous resources available regarding web services and REST. Following are the resources you may find particularly useful.

RESTful PHP Web Services

Packt has a book dedicated to creating RESTful APIs in PHP—*RESTful PHP Web Services*, by Samisa Abeysinghe, `https://www.packtpub.com/restful-php-web-services/book`. This book details the concepts of a REST architecture, how to make use of existing RESTful APIs in your framework, how to create a RESTful API for other applications to interact with, as well as debugging information and case studies.

Conference talks

Lorna Jane Mitchell (`http://www.lornajane.net`), a widely-respected developer and conference speaker on PHP-related topics, has recently spoken at a number of conferences on the subject of web service design. Slides from related talks are available online: `http://www.slideshare.net/lornajane/best-practices-in-web-service-design`, `http://www.slideshare.net/lornajane/php-and-web-services-perfect-partners`.

Implementation

Now that we know what sort of API we are going to develop, we can move onto the implementation. In this chapter we will only implement a small sub-set of the API's functionality. Feel free to extend this to match the entire functionality of Dino Space, if you wish.

Data format

Most commonly, RESTful APIs either return their data in XML format or as JSON. Some APIs allow the consumer to specify the return type by adding `.xml` or `.json` to the end of the URL. For the purposes of our implementation, let's stick to JSON, as it is simpler to convert data to JSON (simply by passing the data to the `json_encode` function).

API controller

Our API controller itself won't do very much; instead it will pass control to delegate controllers, which contain logic specific to the various sections of the site.

```php
<?php
/**
 * API Controller
 */
class Apicontroller{
```

To indicate which files are available for control to be delegated to, we should maintain an array of allowable API controllers. For our work in this chapter, we will create the `profiles` delegate.

```php
/**
 * Allowable API Controllers, for control to be delegated to
 */
private $allowableAPIControllers = array( 'profiles' );

/**
 * Request data
 */
private $requestData = array();
```

The object's constructor simply sets the registry object, gets the value of the API delegate that should be used, and calls the delegator method (`delegateControl`).

```php
/**
 * API Controller Constructor
 * @param Registry $registry the registry
 * @param boolean $directCall
 * @return void
 */
public function __construct( Registry $registry, $directCall=true )
{
  $this->registry = $registry;
  $apiController = $registry->getObject('url')->getURLBit(1);
  $this->delegateControl( $apiController );
}
```

The `delegateControl` method checks that the delegate controller is within the allowed delegates. If it is, then it includes the appropriate controller, instantiates it, and passes the registry and the API controller object to it. There are a number of methods that will be common to all API delegates. These methods are stored in this object, and called by the delegate referencing this object. If the requested controller is not allowable, then we generate an appropriate HTTP status code; in this case: `404 Not Found`.

```
/**
 * Pass control to a delegate
 * @param String $apiController the delegate
 * @return void
 */
private function delegateControl( $apiController )
{
  if( $apiController != ''  && in_array( $apiController,
    $this->allowableAPIControllers ) )
  {
    require_once( FRAMEWORK_PATH . 'controllers/api/' .
      $apiController . '.php' );
    $api = new APIDelegate( $this->registry, $this );
  }
  else
  {
    header('HTTP/1.0 404 Not Found');
    exit();
  }
}
```

A shared method is required by our delegates. This is called if a delegate requires the API user to be an authenticated user on the site. It generates a basic authentication prompt (this is presented to users viewing the site in their browsers, but for API users the username and password are passed as part of the HTTP request).

Alternatives to basic authentication

Basic authentication isn't the best option in terms of security, especially if many websites begin offering services utilizing our API. Our users' passwords could be stored (with their permission) within these websites, putting reliance on the integrity and security of those sites and their owners. An alternative is **OAuth**, where the API provider deals with the authentication, and provides consumers with an API key for their users. If a user then wishes to stop a third-party service utilizing their account via the API, they can simply revoke access. We will discuss this option more in the security section of this chapter.

If the authentication fails, then the `401 Unauthorized` status code is issued.

```
/**
 * Request authentication for access to API methods, called by
   delegates
 * @return void
 */
public function requireAuthentication()
{
  if( !isset( $_SERVER['PHP_AUTH_USER'] ) )
  {
    header('WWW-Authenticate: Basic realm="DinoSpace API Login"');
    header('HTTP/1.0 401 Unauthorized');
    exit();
  }
  else
  {
    $user = $_SERVER['PHP_AUTH_USER'];
    $password = $_SERVER['PHP_AUTH_PW'];
    $this->registry->getObject('authenticate')->postAuthenticate(
      $user, $password, false );
    if( ! $this->registry->getObject('authenticate')-
      >isLoggedIn() )
    {
      header('HTTP/1.0 401 Unauthorized');
      exit();
    }
  }
}
```

PUT and DELETE data (technically, there should never be DELETE data sent on a DELETE request) cannot be accessed through super globals as POST and GET data can ($_POST and $_GET), so we need a mechanism to get the request data, regardless of the type of request.

```php
/**
 * Get the type of request
 * @return array
 */
public function getRequestData()
{
  if( $_SERVER['REQUEST_METHOD'] == 'GET' )
  {
    $this->requestData = $_GET;
  }
  elseif( $_SERVER['REQUEST_METHOD'] == 'POST' )
  {
    $this->requestData = $_POST;
  }
  elseif( $_SERVER['REQUEST_METHOD'] == 'PUT' )
  {
    parse_str(file_get_contents('php://input'),
      $this->requestData );
  }
  elseif( $_SERVER['REQUEST_METHOD'] == 'DELETE' )
  {
    parse_str(file_get_contents('php://input'),
      $this->requestData );
  }
  return $this->requestData;
}
}
?>
```

php://input

php://input is an input stream wrapper in PHP, which allows us to read raw request data. More detailed information is available on the PHP website: http://php.net/manual/en/wrappers.php.php/.

Wait—no models?

That's right; we don't need to create any models for our API. All of the functionality our API needs to provide already exists through the various models we have created. So instead of creating API-specific models, we will create some additional API controllers, which work with the pre-existing models to get the data and present it to the consumer.

Authentication

Keeping with the RESTful way of leveraging HTTP, we can make use of HTTP authentication to authenticate the user. This is where authentication details are passed as part of the HTTP request from our API consumer. You will have seen examples of this if you have ever visited a web page, and your browser has opened a pop up prompting for authentication details before loading the page. In this case, your browser reads the server's request for authentication, and then requests login details before sending the authentication request to the server.

> **More information**
> You can read more about HTTP authentication with PHP here:
> `http://php.net/manual/en/features.http-auth.php`

Sessions lead to unREST!

REST is a stateless architecture, which means all of the information required for a particular operation or request should be included within that request. It shouldn't rely on information from a previous request or other information such as sessions and cookies. To that end, we should amend our `authenticate` registry object and our `index.php` file.

Amending the authenticate registry object

We need to amend the `authenticate` registry class (`registry/authenticate.class.php`) to only set `$_SESSION` data if that is required, so that we can indicate, from our API controller, that we don't want `$_SESSION` data to be created.

We should add an optional parameter to the postAuthenticate method to indicate if $_SESSION data should be set, with a default value of true so it doesn't impact on other aspects of our site, which we have already implemented.

```php
public function postAuthenticate( $u, $p, $sessions=true )
{
$this->justProcessed = true;
require_once(FRAMEWORK_PATH.'registry/user.class.php');
$this->user = new User( $this->registry, 0, $u, $p );
if( $this->user->isValid() )
{
  if( $this->user->isActive() == false )
  {
    $this->loggedIn = false;
    $this->loginFailureReason = 'inactive';
  }
  elseif( $this->user->isBanned() == true )
  {
    $this->loggedIn = false;
    $this->loginFailureReason = 'banned';
  }
  else
  {
    $this->loggedIn = true;
```

If the sessions parameter for this method has been set to true, then we set the appropriate session. If it has been set to false (for example, by our API controller), then it is not set.

```php
    if( $sessions == true )
    {
      $_SESSION['sn_auth_session_uid'] = $this->user->getUserID();
    }
  }
}
else
{
  $this->loggedIn = false;
  $this->loginFailureReason = 'invalidcredentials';
}
}
```

Amending index.php

Our `index.php` file by default checks for `SESSION` data for authentication.

 See Chapter 2, or take a look at the `index.php` file to refresh your memory.

```php
<?php

session_start();
DEFINE("FRAMEWORK_PATH", dirname( __FILE__ ) ."/" );
require('registry/registry.class.php');
$registry = new Registry();
// setup our core registry objects
$registry->createAndStoreObject( 'template', 'template' );
$registry->createAndStoreObject( 'mysqldb', 'db' );
$registry->createAndStoreObject( 'authenticate', 'authenticate' );
$registry->createAndStoreObject( 'urlprocessor', 'url' );
$registry->getObject('url')->getURLData();
// database settings
include(FRAMEWORK_PATH . 'config.php');
// create a database connection
$registry->getObject('db')->newConnection( $configs['db_host_sn'],
  $configs['db_user_sn'], $configs['db_pass_sn'],
  $configs['db_name_sn']);
```

Firstly, we need to move the line that sets the controller variable to just before authentication is checked. We then wrap the authentication check line in an IF statement, so that it is only executed if the controller being requested isn't the API controller.

```php
$controller = $registry->getObject('url')->getURLBit(0);
if( $controller != 'api' )
{
  $registry->getObject('authenticate')->checkForAuthentication();
}

// store settings in our registry
$settingsSQL = "SELECT `key`, `value` FROM settings";
$registry->getObject('db')->executeQuery( $settingsSQL );
while( $setting = $registry->getObject('db')->getRows() )
{
  $registry->storeSetting( $setting['value'], $setting['key'] );
}
```

```
$registry->getObject('template')->getPage()->addTag( 'siteurl',
  $registry->getSetting('siteurl') );
$registry->getObject('template')-
  >buildFromTemplates('header.tpl.php', 'main.tpl.php',
  'footer.tpl.php');


$controllers = array();
$controllersSQL = "SELECT * FROM controllers WHERE active=1";
$registry->getObject('db')->executeQuery( $controllersSQL );
```

Next, we need to change the code that gets active controllers from the database. Previously, it set the $controller variable for temporary use. This wasn't a problem initially, because we reset the variable to the active controller after this. However, now it is overriding our default controller. This is simply altered by changing $controller to $cttrlr.

```
while( $cttrlr = $registry->getObject('db')->getRows() )
{
  $controllers[] = $cttrlr['controller'];
}
```

The final change is to only add authentication-related template bits to the view, if the active controller isn't API.

```
if( $registry->getObject('authenticate')->isLoggedIn() && $controller
  != 'api')
{
  $registry->getObject('template')->addTemplateBit('userbar',
    'userbar_loggedin.tpl.php');
  $registry->getObject('template')->getPage()->addTag( 'username',
    $registry->getObject('authenticate')->getUser()->getUsername() );
}
elseif( $controller != 'api' )
{
  $registry->getObject('template')->addTemplateBit('userbar',
    'userbar.tpl.php');
}

if( in_array( $controller, $controllers ) )
{
  require_once( FRAMEWORK_PATH . 'controllers/' . $controller .
    '/controller.php');
  $controllerInc = $controller.'controller';
  $controller = new $controllerInc( $registry, true );
}
else
```

```
{
   // default controller, or pass control to CMS type system?
}

$registry->getObject('template')->parseOutput();
print $registry->getObject('template')->getPage()-
   >getContentToPrint();
?>
```

Delegating control: API controllers for our features

With the basic API controller in place, we can now add delegate controllers for the features on our site. As discussed earlier, in this chapter we will only look at adding support for profiles; however, it is easy to extend should you wish to.

Profile's delegate

Our delegate controller simply needs to store the registry and caller objects, and then depending on the nature of the user's request, either output a list of data, output the data from one instance of a model, update a record via a model, or delete a record via a model.

In this instance, we can't process create or delete requests, as creating a profile is done on signup, and this feature requires a logged-in user. Deleting a user has lots of implications, and shouldn't be done easily — it should be something the user can do via the site itself, after a number of confirmations.

```php
<?php
/**
 * API Delegate: Profiles
 * Proof of concept
 */
class APIDelegate{

   private $registry;
   private $caller;
```

The constructor sets the `registry` and `caller` objects if a profile ID has been passed, and then it calls the `aProfile` method. If no profile ID has been passed, it calls the `listProfiles` method.

```
public function __construct( Registry $registry, $caller )
{
  $this->caller = $caller;
  $this->registry = $registry;
  $urlBits = $this->registry->getObject('url')->getURLBits();
  if( isset( $urlBits[2] ) )
  {
    $this->aProfile( intval( $urlBits[2] ) );
  }
  else
  {
    $this->listProfiles();
  }
}
```

The `listProfiles` method first calls the APIController's `requireAuthentication` method. If authentication fails, that method will exit, preventing the rest of the method from being executed. Since we can't create a profile, we should prohibit submission of POST data. If the request is valid (and there isn't any POST data), then we can query the profiles table, convert it to JSON, and display it for the consumer. This method should either be optimized to allow pagination or filtering (based on searching for a user's name) or just to show members a user has a connection with (otherwise it could return a lot of data).

```
private function listProfiles()
{
  $this->caller->requireAuthentication();
  if( $_SERVER['REQUEST_METHOD'] == 'POST' )
  {
    // we can't create a profile as we already have one!
    header('HTTP/1.0 405 Method Not Allowed');
    exit();
  }
  else
  {
    // ideally, we would paginate this, and/or put some filtering
    //   in i.e. filter by name starting with A,B,C, etc.
    $sql = "SELECT user_id, name FROM profile";
    $this->registry->getObject('db')->executeQuery( $sql );
    $r = array();
```

```
      while( $row = $this->registry->getObject('db')->getRows() )
      {
        $r[] = $row;
      }
      header('HTTP/1.0 200 OK');
      echo json_encode( $r );
      exit();
    }
  }
```

If the URL dictates that the consumer is doing something with a specific user profile, then the aProfile method is called. As with the listProfiles method, it first requires authentication, and then includes the profile model path.

```
    private function aProfile( $pid )
    {
      $this->caller->requireAuthentication();
      require_once( FRAMEWORK_PATH . 'models/profile.php' );
      if( $_SERVER['REQUEST_METHOD'] == 'PUT' )
      {
```

If the request method is PUT, it assumes the consumer is trying to update the profile. It verifies the logged-in user owns the profile, and if they don't the appropriate HTTP response code is issued. If they do own the profile, the validity of the profile is checked, and then the profile is updated based on the PUT data.

```
        if( $pid == $this->registry->getObject('authenticate')-
          >getUser()->getUserID() )
        {
          $profile = new Profile( $this->registry, $pid );
          if( $profile->isValid() )
          {
            $data = $this->caller->getRequestData();
            $profile->setName( $this->registry->getObject('db')-
              >sanitizeData( $data['name'] ) );
            $profile->setDinoName( $this->registry->getObject('db')-
              >sanitizeData( $data['dino_name'] ) );
            // etc, set all appropriate methods
            $profile->save();
            header('HTTP/1.0 204 No Content');
            exit();
          }
          else
          {
            header('HTTP/1.0 404 Not Found');
            exit();
```

```
        }
      }
      else
      {
        header('HTTP/1.0 403 Forbidden');
        exit();
      }
    }
    else
    {
```

If the request method isn't PUT, then it simply checks that the profile is valid, and returns the profile data to the consumer. Depending on privacy settings, and the relationship between the logged-in user and the user profile, we may want to restrict the data that is presented.

```
      $profile = new Profile( $this->registry, $pid );
      if( $profile->isValid() )
      {
        header('HTTP/1.0 200 OK');
        echo json_encode( $profile->toArray() );
        exit();
      }
      else
      {
        header('HTTP/1.0 404 Not Found');
        exit();
      }
    }
  }
}
?>
```

Tweaking the profiles model: validity and data

One thing our profile model doesn't do at the moment is provide any indication if a particular profile was found within the database. This can be changed with a new variable, a change to the constructor, and a getter method to return if it is valid or not.

It also doesn't have a simple method for returning all of the properties in an array, which can return to the consumer from our API.

Revised controller

The additions to the model are highlighted in the code below:

```
/**
    * Profile constructor
    * @param Registry $registry the registry
    * @param int $id the profile ID
    * @return void
    */
public function __construct( Registry $registry, $id=0 )
{
  $this->registry = $registry;
  if( $id != 0 )
  {
    $this->id = $id;
    // if an ID is passed, populate based off that
    $sql = "SELECT * FROM profile WHERE user_id=" . $this->id;
    $this->registry->getObject('db')->executeQuery( $sql );
    if( $this->registry->getObject('db')->numRows() == 1 )
    {
      $this->valid = true;
      $data = $this->registry->getObject('db')->getRows();
      // populate our fields
      foreach( $data as $key => $value )
      {
        $this->$key = $value;
      }
    }
    else
    {
      $this->valid = false;
    }
  }
  else
  {
    $this->valid = false;
  }
}
```

New getter: isValid()

We use a simple getter method to return the value of the valid variable.

```
/**
 * Is the profile valid
 * @return bool
 */
public function isValid()
{
  return $this->valid;
}
```

New getter: toArray()

This is almost a copy of the `toTags()` method:

```
/**
 * Return the users data
 * @return array
 */
public function toArray( $prefix='' )
{
  $r = array();
  foreach( $this as $field => $data )
  {
    if( ! is_object( $data ) && ! is_array( $data ) )
    {
      $r[ $field ] = $data;
    }
  }
  return $r;
}
```

 Depending on privacy settings, we may want to filter the information that is returned to the consumer, depending on their status.

An Application Framework API

The API we have developed allows other websites and web services to interact with our social network; it doesn't allow any provisions for our users to interact with third-party applications within our site. Let's briefly discuss what would be involved in creating such an API, and the practical implications it presents.

To allow third-party developers to build functionality that runs on our social network, we would either need to provide a mechanism for them to upload code to our servers (which is a big security risk, and should never be done), or a way for them to host their code externally, but for our site to interact with it, communicating login information between the two systems, taking the output generated and rendering it through the Dino Space social network.

Even by having the code hosted externally, there are still security implications: we would have to ensure no sensitive data (such as passwords) was passed to the application. This would require an alternative method of authentication within the API, either one using API keys or something like the OAuth standard. The developer could also add in malicious HTML or JavaScript, such as code to trigger download of a virus on the user's computer, something to trick the user into entering their password, or any number of other things.

Social networks like Facebook get around this problem by allowing two methods of integration:

- **iFrame**: The application is embedded through an iFrame. However, the use of JavaScript is restricted.

- Alternatively, the code is written to generate special markup, which Facebook then parses (ensuring it is clean).

The other problem with providing such a system is that developers would only use it when the site starts to become popular. Until the site has proven itself developing applications for it will be seen as a waste of developer's time, as there is no guarantee that the site would be successful.

One solution: use OpenSocial

One potential solution is to use the OpenSocial API we discussed earlier. Because the API is standard across all sites which use it, developers only need to develop their application once, allowing it to be installed and used on any website that makes use of the API. The API also provides a common way to authenticate and access data.

Consuming

As we have learned from this chapter, creating an API is a very large topic, one which is covered in greater detail in a number of books dedicated to the subject. Let's look at how we can quickly consume our new API using cURL (`http://www.php.net/manual/en/intro.curl.php`).

With cURL, we can pass our username and password, and it will handle passing the appropriate values to authenticate against the basic authentication we have in place.

```php
<?php
```

First, we need to set our username, password, and the URL we wish to connect to.

```php
$username = 'michael';
$password = 'password';
$url = "http://localhost/api/users";
```

Next, we initialize a connection to the URL.

```php
$ch = curl_init($url);
```

We then set a number of options, including the username and password, and if we wish to have the headers returned to us.

```php
curl_setopt($ch, CURLOPT_USERPWD, $username.':'.$password);
curl_setopt($ch, CURLOPT_VERBOSE, 1);
curl_setopt($ch, CURLOPT_NOBODY, 0);
curl_setopt($ch, CURLOPT_HEADER, 1);
curl_setopt($ch, CURLOPT_FOLLOWLOCATION,1);
curl_setopt($ch, CURLOPT_RETURNTRANSFER, 1);
curl_setopt($ch, CURLOPT_HTTPHEADER, array());
```

We then execute the cURL request and assign the data returned to a variable.

```php
$response = curl_exec($ch);
```

We then store any additional information and close the cURL connection.

```php
$responseInfo=curl_getinfo($ch);
curl_close($ch);
?>
```

In the code above, we have chosen to store the returned headers. For us to be able to process the data returned from the API, we would need to strip out the headers and process them accordingly. Since we use mod_rewrite to make search engine-friendly URLs, we have a redirect header set before the API's header. So we would want to ignore the first header, and then process the second header. Everything after this would be the response data to the request.

If we just want to work with the data returned, we can change the CURLOPT_HEADER option to 0.

POSTing data to our API with cURL

To send POST data to our API using cURL, we simply build an array of the POST data we wish to submit, convert the array into a suitable string, and then pass these variables to our cURL request, as illustrated by the following code.

First, we set our POST fields:

```
$fields = array( 'field' => urlencode( 'some data' );
$fields_string = '';
foreach( $fields as $key => $value )
{
  $fields_string .= $key.'='.$value.'&';
}
rtrim($fields_string,'&');
```

We then pass the POST fields to our cURL request:

```
curl_setopt($ch,CURLOPT_POST,count($fields));
curl_setopt($ch,CURLOPT_POSTFIELDS,$fields_string);
```

Summary

In this chapter we have looked into the APIs that other social networks offer, and discussed the advantages in providing APIs to our users. We then discussed the various types of APIs available, before settling on REST as an API architecture and developing our API in a RESTful way. Finally, we discussed the implications involved in creating a third-party application API and how OpenSocial, an API we discussed earlier in the chapter, could be used to integrate third-party applications.

12
Deployment, Security, and Maintenance

With Dino Space complete and functional, we are now ready to put the site online so that we can begin to attract users, and grow our website. As well as putting the site online, we need to keep the security and maintenance provisions in mind, to ensure our site stays secure and well maintained should anything go wrong.

In this chapter, you will learn:

- How to deploy Dino Space to the Internet, including looking at domain names, hosting providers, and the manual deployment process
- How we might automate the deployment of our site
- How to keep our site secure
- How to maintain our site
- How to back up our site, and restore it should the worst happen

Let's get started by deploying Dino Space to the Web!

Deploying the site

There are quite a number of stages to go through to put Dino Space online, so that it can be accessed on the Internet. Typically, this will involve:

- Choosing and registering a domain name
- Signing up with a hosting provider
- Setting the nameservers for the domain
- Creating a database on the hosting account

- Exporting our local database
- Importing our local database to the hosting account
- Changing some of our database records
- Changing our database configuration options
- Uploading the files for our site
- Testing

Choosing a domain name

Hopefully, by this stage, you will have already decided on the domain name you wish to use. With a site such as Dino Space, we could either combine the two names as one word, or we could hyphenate the name, this gives us more options should the TLD (top level domain for example, .com) for our name be taken.

Sites such as `DomainTools.com` have whois lookup tools on them, which allow you to check whether a particular domain name has been taken. Most domain name registrars also have these. They are an ideal starting point to check domain name availability.

Some website owners have taken advantage of international TLDs to form a part of their web address, for example, `dinospa.ce` (.ce isn't a valid TLD, however), so this is another option if there is a relevant TLD, though for country-specific TLDs, sometimes, there are restrictions on who can register a domain through them.

Registering a domain name

Once we have found a domain name that suitably represents our site, and is available, we can register it through a domain name registrar.

For around 10 dollars, you should be able to register a .com domain name for a year, or a .co.uk domain for two years.

Popular domain name registrars

There are a number of popular domain name registrars, including:

- NameCheap (`www.namecheap.com`)
- GoDaddy (`www.godaddy.com`)
- 123-reg (`www.123-reg.co.uk`)

Signing up with a hosting provider

Signing up with a hosting provider generally involves choosing a hosting provider, selecting a suitable hosting package from their offering, supplying personal information, and supplying billing information to pay for the hosting.

Once signed up, most hosts send over a welcome e-mail including login details within an hour or so, once they have activated the account.

Choosing a web hosting provider

Hosting is a very big market on the Internet, and there are a large number of hosting providers available. There are also a number of different types of hosting providers available, including:

- Shared hosting—lots of customers have space and resources on a single server, for example, A Small Orange.

- Virtual Private Servers—a small number of customers have access to dedicated resources on a single server, in the form of a dedicated virtualized instance of the server, giving the customer complete control, for example, SliceHost.

- Cloud Hosting—Similar to VPS hosting, in that it is a virtualized server, except that the resources are generally spread over many machines, and the resources are not dedicated, allowing the hosting to use as much or as little resources as required, by making use of more physical machines, for example, Amazon EC2.

- Dedicated Servers—an entire machine dedicated to one customer/website, with complete control to the customer, for example, Rackspace.

- Co-location—the same as dedicated servers, but where the customer purchases their own equipment, and rents space in a data centre to house the servers and connect them to the Internet, for example, The Planet.

As our social network will be starting off small, it is advisable to start with either a shared hosting package, a small VPS, or a cloud hosting. These should allow us to start with a small amount of server resources, for a low cost, and increase the resources as our site becomes more popular. Normally, with shared hosting, accounts can be upgraded to include more space or bandwidth, though not additional processing power; with VPS and cloud providers, the specification of the server, and the processing power allocated can often be upgraded and downgraded as necessary.

We will discuss VPS and cloud hosting in more detail in *Chapter 14, Planning for Growth.*

When looking at potential web hosting providers, the following factors should be taken into account:

- The amount of web space offered — we need to at least cover the space for our files, and have a reasonable amount left over for user uploads.

- For VPS/Dedicated servers, the amount of dedicated memory we have access to is also important, because when all of the RAM is used up, servers make use of the SWAP space on the disk, which is much slower.

- The amount of bandwidth required (data transferred from the web server to customers and other visitors per month) — the amount we need will depend on the traffic to our site, but it's important to see what happens when you exceed your bandwidth. We also need to check whether this bandwidth is for upload and download — some providers include unlimited upload bandwidth, so updating our site won't use any of our bandwidth limit.

- Any service level agreements in place, such as a guaranteed uptime, or turn-around time for hardware replacement.

- Minimum contract term — how long are you tied in for?

- Acceptable usage policy, to ensure they don't prohibit any of the functions of our social networking website — some hosts limit outgoing e-mail traffic to prevent spam, this could affect some of our notification e-mails.

- To have software installed on the server, we obviously require PHP, MySQL, sendmail, and Apache with the `mod_rewrite` module.

- If we have full SSH root access (essential for VPS/dedicated servers so that they can be fully managed).

- What level of support they offer (some hosts even lend a hand if a script isn't playing nicely on their servers).

- Cost and any benefits for paying monthly or annually.

Web-based control panels, such as cPanel or Plesk are included with most standard web hosting accounts. This makes many administrative tasks easier, including:

- Setting up and managing e-mail accounts
- Setting up and managing databases
- Viewing statistics, access, and error logs
- Performing backups, restoring from backups, and so on

One of the most common control panels is cPanel, and is included with most shared hosting and **Virtual Private Server** (**VPS**) providers. Some aspects of this chapter contain instructions specific for cPanel (manual deployment, and backing up and restoring), as well as alternative instructions for power users using the command line (assuming SSH access is enabled on the hosting account; this can normally be requested for shared hosting accounts, as for VPS/Dedicated servers, check that you are given full root access via SSH).

Packt Publishing has a book available specifically for cPanel, should you be interested in learning more about it: *cPanel User Guide and Tutorial* by *Aric Pedersen* (`www.packtpub.com/cPanel/book`).

Considerations for hosts of social networking websites

Here are a few additional considerations worth keeping in mind, specifically for social networking websites:

- Are websites backed up regularly, automatically? If they are not, you could always write your own backup cron job script (SSH access would be helpful for this).

- What security measures are in place?

- Do the hosting accounts scale nicely?

- Can you pre-purchase additional bandwidth in advance of exceeding a limit?

- How many concurrent users can the hosting account cope with?

Popular web hosting providers

Some popular web hosting providers include:

- Slicehost (`www.slicehost.com`) is a Virtual Private Server provider, designed for developers with functionality to easily upgrade and downgrade server capacity.

- A Small Orange (`www.asmallorange.com`), also provides shared hosting accounts, virtual servers, and dedicated servers.

- MediaTemple (`www.mediatemple.net`) is a provider of scalable virtual servers, with a control panel to make things as simple as with standard shared hosting accounts.

- VPS.Net (`www.vps.net`)

- 1&1 Internet Inc. (`www.1and1.com`), provides shared hosting accounts, virtual servers, and dedicated servers for larger websites and web applications. However, be careful as their lower-end shared hosting accounts don't support databases, such as MySQL.

Research hosting providers

Web Hosting Talk (`www.webhostingtalk.com`) is a popular discussion forum focused on discussing the web hosting industry, containing many reviews and comparisons. It is worthwhile taking some time to research for the different providers before signing up with one.

Setting the nameservers for the domain

Once we have our domain name registered, and a hosting account set up, we need to change the nameservers of our domain to those of our hosting provider. This ensures that any traffic to our domain name is directed to our hosting account.

When signing up to a hosting provider, their welcome e-mail will generally include a reference of their nameservers; these are the addresses to servers that translate DNS requests for that particular domain name, into IP addresses of the servers the site is hosted on. They are typically of the form `ns1.hostingproviderabc.com` and `ns2.hostingproviderabc.com`. Some domain registrars require the IP address of the servers as well as the hostname.

Full information on how to set the nameservers can be obtained from your domain name registrar, and changes made to nameservers can take up to 24 hours to take effect.

Creating a database on the hosting account

Let's look at the two most common ways to create databases on a hosting account; firstly using the popular control panel cPanel, and secondly using phpMyAdmin when logged in as a user with suitable permissions (permissions to create users and databases, such as the root user).

With cPanel hosting control panel

This section assumes that a hosting account with cPanel is installed.

The first stage is to log in to our control panel (this is usually, `www.yourdomain.com/cpanel`), and within the **Databases** section click on the **MySQL® Database Wizard** icon. This will allow us to create a database and a user with permissions to access this database.

Next, we enter a name for the new database; this is normally then combined with the hosting account's username, so the database name `network` would become `dinospac_network`. Once we have entered a name, we need to click on **Next Step**, to move on to the next stage of the database wizard.

Then, we need to create a user within MySQL, who will connect to the database server to access the database we have just created. It is important to use a secure password; for this, we'll use the **Generate Password** button to have cPanel automatically generate a secure password for us.

Once we have entered the username and password, we need to click on the **Next Step** button.

Now that we have a database and a database user, we need to grant permissions for that user to be able to manage the database. Let's check the **ALL PRIVILEGES** checkbox and click on the **Next Step** button again.

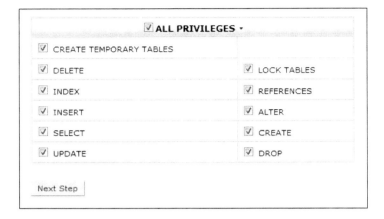

We now have a database on the server and a database user who can access the database. These are the details we will need for our configuration file.

With appropriate privileges on phpMyAdmin

Assuming we have suitable permissions, allowing us to create a database and a database user, we can use phpMyAdmin to create a new database and a user with permissions to use it. We will create a new user for MySQL, and set it to have its own database. We need to click the **Privileges** tab first, as shown in the following screenshot:

On the privileges screen, we need to click the **Add a new User** link, as shown in the following screenshot:

From here, we give the user a username, select the host from which the user can connect (normally, **localhost**), and set a password (or we can use the **Generate** button to generate a secure password randomly for us).

We should select the **Create database with same name and grant all privileges** option under **Database for user**; this will create a database called dinospacenetwork, and give the dinospacenetwork user privileges to use it. The following screenshot shows the create new user form:

Once we submit the form, we have our new database and our database user. The reason we want a new database user, as well as a new database, is that should we have a vulnerability in our code, which would allow a user to access our database, it would only allow them access to this one database. Similarly, if there was a vulnerability in another application, they couldn't get to our database (unless of course, we used the root database details).

Exporting our local database

With our database set up on the server, we now need to export the database we have on our local development installation. This can be done by selecting the database and then clicking on the **Export** tab in phpMyAdmin.

From here, we can select which tables we wish to download, and have the option of either exporting the database as SQL, or as a download containing SQL, as shown in the following screenshot:

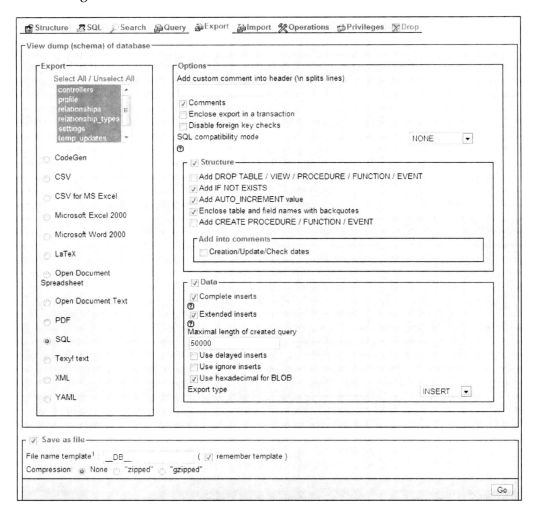

Importing our local database to the hosting account

With a copy of our local development database exported, we can import it into our hosting account using the **Import** tab on the server's phpMyAdmin, where we simply upload the SQL file (if we exported as text, we would use the **SQL** tab to paste the SQL into it and import the database).

In most cases, there is a 2 MB limit on file uploads. This can cause problems when importing a large active site, however, we are only importing our skeleton database—so, this shouldn't be a problem. For importing and exporting large databases, you should use SSH, as discussed later in this chapter.

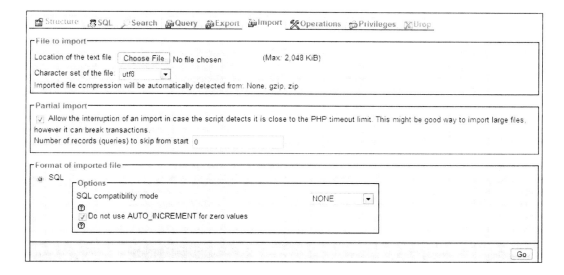

We now have our database set up and working on the production server!

Changing some of our database records

Some of our database records might have been specific to our local development version of Dino Space. Most of these should be contained in the settings table, such as the `siteurl` setting, which at present points to our local installation. We will need to update this record to reflect our live site.

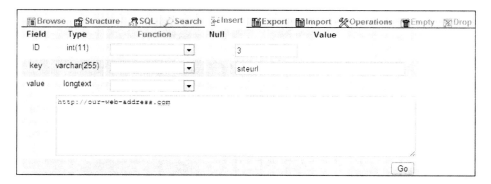

Changing our database configuration options

As the production database is on the production server, we will also need to update our `config.php` file to point to the database on the server, as opposed to the database on our local machine. The details required for this file were established when we created the database and database user on the server earlier in this chapter.

```php
<?php

$configs = array();
$configs['db_host_sn'] = 'localhost';
$configs['db_user_sn'] = 'dinospacenetwork';
$configs['db_pass_sn'] = 'dinospacenetwork';
$configs['db_name_sn'] = 'Ac932w4dheJDbFfd';


?>
```

Uploading the files

With the configuration file updated, and the live database set up, we can now upload all of our files to the server. To upload the website files from our development environment to our production environment, we need to use an FTP client. One such example of an FTP client is FileZilla, a free FTP client available for download.

Within FileZilla, we simply enter the web address of the site, and our FTP username and password and then click on **Quickconnect**.

Secure FTP

If you have SSH access, instead of leaving the port field blank, you can supply port number 22. This would force the connection to be secure, using SSH.

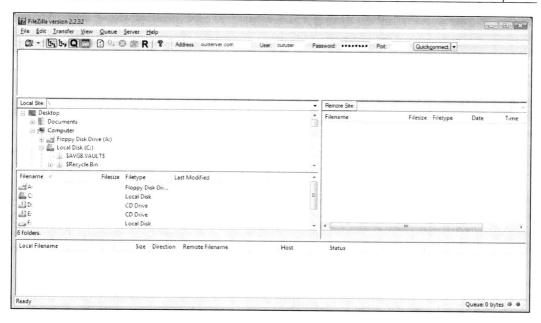

Once the FTP client is connected, we simply drag the files from the relevant folder on our development environment in the **Local** site pane on the left to the relevant folder within the **Remote** site pane on the right. Commonly, the folder on the server would be either `public_html` or `htdocs`, and files within these folders are generally made accessible to the public through a web browser.

Permissions on certain folders, such as the `uploads` folder, will need to be changed to allow write access.

Testing

We now have a domain name, a suitable hosting environment, our codebase in our hosting environment, and a live database. The next stage for us is to visit the live site in our browser to check whether everything is working as intended.

Automating deployment

When we next update our social network, we won't have to do most of the initial deployment process again; however, we will be presented with a new challenge – downtime.

If we take our website offline to make an update, we lock out our users, which may cause them to go elsewhere, and put off any user who is new to the site. One solution is to automate the deployment process; this can get rid of the downtime problem, and because it is automated, the deployment process will be fast.

To make use of automated deployment, we would need to make use of version control, to keep a centralized copy of our code, which the deployment system can access, and within the version control, we would need copies of our development configuration (that is, files pointing to our local database) and production settings. We would then have a deployment script which:

- Moves the live site to a new location and updates the Apache virtual host to point to the new location.
- Exports the sites code from version control (for example., from a Subversion repository).
- Places the code where we previously had the live site.
- Removes development configurations and updates them to live configurations.
- Updates file permissions.
- Updates the Apache virtual host so that new visitors to the site go to the new codebase.
- The old codebase shouldn't be deleted just yet, as some users who visited the site before the virtual host change, will be using that codebase. Instead, we should set our deployment script to remove old copies before running, which means we always have the live site, and the previous iteration, on the server at any one time.

The exact setup of this is beyond the scope of this book, however, the above information should provide a good starting point. I've discussed this topic in more detail on my personal blog, which provides an example shell script for automatic deployment, which may be of use if you are considering automated deployment, `http://www.michaelpeacock.co.uk/blog/entry/svn-deploy-script`.

Security

Security is a very important aspect with any website, though with a social networking website it is extra important, as we will store personal information of lots of users, so we need to ensure we keep this data secure.

Data Protection legislation

It may be worth investigating the Data Protection legislation in the country you reside in, and in the country your website is hosted in. As well as mandating how data must be kept secure, some countries, such as the UK, also have a register of Data Controllers who are responsible for data protection in a particular organization.

Server Security

The security of the server itself is one aspect that needs consideration. This can be broken down into two primary areas:

- Server software
- Firewall and network traffic

With shared hosting environments, there are some other considerations that we will discuss.

Software

Almost all software contains security vulnerabilities; once a vulnerability has been discovered, it is important to ensure that the software is upgraded or patched to prevent malicious users from exploiting these vulnerabilities. With managed hosting, we don't need to concern ourselves with server installed software, as our hosting provider should keep that up to date. However, if we want to concern ourselves with the software on our server (and check our provider is up to date), or if we are operating on unmanaged virtual or dedicated servers, we need to keep updated on security developments with:

- PHP
- MySQL
- Apache
- The FTP server software
- The SSH server-side software
- Operating system versions and kernel updates

This could be done by subscribing to any mailing lists found on the sites for those projects.

Any other software we install, such as bulletin board systems, chat rooms, and so on, will also need to be regularly checked for available upgrades and security updates.

It is important to check with your hosting provider that they update and patch software quickly, to ensure it is secure.

Securing the site with a firewall

Software and hardware firewalls can help protect our website from attack; these generally work by blocking access to certain parts of the server from certain computers (for example, allow anyone to access the website stored on the server, except users we explicitly banned, but disallow anyone to access aspects such as FTP or SSH unless explicitly permitted). Most web hosts can advise on their firewall setup, and documentation is available for firewalls that can be used on virtual and dedicated servers.

Shared hosting precautions

With shared hosting, there are other considerations, in that other hosting customers have access to the same machine; it is worth checking if the following security provisions are in place when using shared hosting:

- Open_basedir restrictions — these ensure that code (for example, PHP code) only interacts with code in a customer's home directory, and certain shared areas, preventing another customer's code from interfering with ours
- Jailed Shell — this prevents a user from leaving their home directory when connecting to the server via SSH
- Jailed FTP — this prevents a user from leaving their home directory when connecting to the server via FTP

Passwords

As the website owner or administrator of a site, our passwords unlock not only administrative areas of websites we manage, but also hosting accounts, databases, e-mail systems, statistics systems, and in some cases root access to servers. Because of this, it is important we use a range of secure passwords.

Passwords that are not secure can be obtained by users' guessing, automated dictionary attacks where a computer goes through a list of words trying them as the password, or by social engineering.

Strong passwords are one of the easiest ways to prevent user accounts from being compromised, or guessed by dictionary or social engineering attacks. These involve either going through a list of common passwords until the system logs the hacker in, or by researching the user and trying to guess passwords based off memorable information, such as dates of birth, names of friends and family, and so on. Some suggestions for making a strong password are as follows:

- Use both letters and numbers

- Make use of special characters, such as @, /, \, #, *, &, and so on

- Make all of your passwords unique, otherwise, if someone guesses your administrator password, they may be able to gain access to your personal e-mail, other websites you are a member of, and so on if the passwords are all the same

- Include spelling mistakes to make the word harder to guess

- Don't include personal information such as dates of birth, names of family, and so on

- Make the password as long as possible, longer passwords require more combinations for dictionary style attacks

- Consider using numbers in place of some letters

Error reporting

If we have errors in our code, these will be displayed to the user when they view our site and it encounters the error. Depending on the level of error reporting set, the error could reveal information about our site that we don't want to make public, such as folder structures, database structures, potential vulnerabilities, and so on.

To prevent this, we can set the `error_reporting` directive using the `error_reporting` function; we simply call the function and pass 0 as a parameter, and this disables error reporting. We would simply set this in our `index.php` file.

```
error_reporting(0);
```

More information on error reporting in PHP can be found on the PHP website: `http://php.net/manual/en/function.`

```
error-reporting.php.
```

Directory listings

We would also want to disable directory listings; this is where if a user visits the URL of a directory, they can see a list of the files and folders within. In particular, we wouldn't want this on folders containing user uploads, photographs, and profile pictures.

We can disable directory listings by adding the following line to our `.htaccess` file:

```
Options -indexes
```

SPAM

With SPAM becoming increasingly common on the Internet, we would want to take precautions to prevent this. SPAM can clog up our database with thousands of fake comments and fake user profiles, as well as making our social network less appealing to search engines and other users. We can prevent this by implementing a CAPTCHA system, which helps determine whether it is a genuine person and not a machine trying to access the site.

There are a number of SPAM protection APIs that we can send user submitted content such as comment forms, through to check if they are SPAM. Two popular services are Akismet (`http://akismet.com/`) and Mollom (`http://mollom.com/`), both of which are well documented and have PHP implementations available.

Maintenance

There are a number of maintenance options for us to consider and implement once our site is online.

Backing up and restoring your social network

Backing up and restoring our site is one of the most important maintenance tasks to do, because if something goes wrong with our site, server or host, we would want to be able to restore the site quickly. Ideally, backing up should be automated, if you have purchased backup provisions with your hosting account, you may have automated backup options available in addition to the ones listed below.

With cPanel

Within the main cPanel interface, in the **Files** section, there is a link to the **Backups** area:

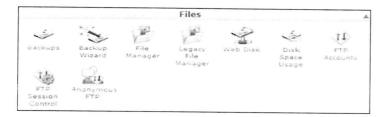

We can download a copy of our **Home Directory** (all of the files and most of our settings), and also a copy of the database from this section. Simply clicking on the relevant backup buttons will prompt us to download the backup files from the server.

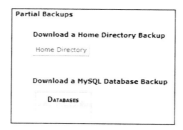

It is essential that we keep these files stored somewhere safe and secure.

Restoring the site and database

To restore from a backup we need to ensure we are logged into cPanel, and then click on the **Backups** button to go to the backups section, as we did when backing up the site.

On the right-hand side of this screen are the options to **Restore a Home Directory Backup** and to **Restore a MySQL Database**.

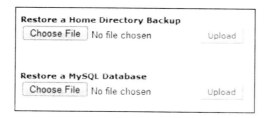

To restore from the backups, all we need to do is browse for the file we wish to restore from, and then click on **Upload**.

 When restoring, any existing database or home directory content will be removed, so only do this if you really need to. If you need to gain access to a specific file that you need to back up, decompress the home directory backup, look for the file, and upload it to your site using an FTP client.

Using the command line

An alternative method to back up and restore our site is by using the command line.

Command Line Access and PuTTY

Most shared hosting accounts won't provide command line (SSH) access by default, but many will enable it on request for your account. Simply file a support ticket with your host to request this, and if they allow it, they will provision it for you.

To connect to the server using SSH, you can either use the terminal interface on a Mac or Linux, or on Windows use a program such as PuTTY, a free SSH client available from: http://www.chiark.greenend.org.uk/~sgtatham/putty/.

Backing up the site and database

Once connected through SSH to the server, we need to navigate to the location of our site. In most cases, this will be /home/ourusername.

```
cd /home/dinospac/
```

Then, we can compress the public_html folder to a single file, using:

```
tar cvzf backup.tar.gz public_html
```

With the folder compressed, we need to move it to within the public_html folder, so we can download it by visiting oursite.com/backup.tar.gz:

```
mv backup.tar.gz public_html/backup.tar.gz
```

The following command exports our database to a web-accessible location on our server, where we can download it using a web browser:

```
mysqldump -u username -p databasename > /home/dinospac/public_html/
backup.sql
```

After executing this command, we will be prompted for our password, and then we can download the file from our browser.

Once downloaded, it is important that we remove the database and site downloads immediately, so that it is not downloaded by anyone else.

Restoring the site and the database

Assuming we upload the `tar.gz` file into our server, we can decompress it with the following command:

```
tar -xvf backup.tar.gz
```

Assuming we upload the SQL file onto our server, we can import it with the following command:

```
mysql -u username -p databasename < /home/dinospac/backup.sql
```

Do they work?

Backing up the site, and knowing how to restore it in an emergency is only half of the battle; we also need to ensure that our backups work! We can test our backups by extracting them and setting them up on a localhost machine; this should be done regularly to test the integrity of backups.

Access logs and statistics

We should regularly keep an eye on our access logs and statistics, particularly for things like:

- Errors generated by our site
- 404 (file not found) requests—to allow us to fix broken links on the site, or put in suitable redirects, making the experience better for our users—reducing the amount of broken links they find
- Examining bounce rates and leaving pages, so we can improve the content, design and structure of certain pages to reduce the number of users who leave the site.

Summary

In this chapter, we took our development code, and set up a suitable production environment so that our site can be accessed on the Internet by the public. Along the way, we looked at hosting accounts and domain name registrars, how we might automate our deployment process, and the fiddly settings that needed to be changed so our code would work in a production environment.

We then looked at security options and provisions, to ensure our site stays secure, before looking at maintenance options, focusing on backing up, restoring and testing backups of our site, to ensure we are prepared should something go wrong. We are now ready to look at generating traffic for our site, through marketing and search engine optimization.

13
Marketing, SEO, User Retention, and Monetization Strategies

With Dino Space up and running, we now need to get members to our site, because without members our social network will fail (unless we were setting up Dino Space for a select group of people whom we know). Let's look at useful marketing, search engine optimization, and user retention concepts, to help us increase our user base, and keep our users.

In this chapter, you will learn:

- How to promote sites online using:
    - Pay Per Click campaigns
    - Advertising space
    - Newsletters
    - Social marketing

- How to keep the search engines happy
- On-site and off-site search engine optimization
- Some customer retention tips
- Some tips to help make money from the site

It is important to note that this isn't a technical chapter, and the contents covered can (and do) fill several books. The purpose of this chapter is to give you some valuable insight, hints, and tips, which can help you increase the performance of your website in the search engines, and to promote the site through other ways, to help ensure it is a success.

Marketing

Marketing can range from some simple online marketing, advertising, or PPC campaigns. Let's take a look at some of the marketing methods available to us.

Online advertising

There are a number of different online advertising techniques available for us to take advantage of, including:

- Pay-Per-Click advertisements
- Purchasing advertising space
- Newsletter advertising

Pay-Per-Click

Pay-Per-Click (PPC) advertising only costs us each time a visitor clicks on an advert and goes through to our site. When looking at or negotiating cost-per-click rates with advertisers, it is important to work out how many of these visitors are likely to join Dino Space (our conversion rate), so we can decide how much we wish to invest in a PPC campaign.

If we had a monetization strategy in place for our site, for example, paid advertisements on the site, we could work out how much each user earns us, which would help us to establish how much we could invest in PPC, combined with our conversion rate, to ensure we don't lose money. Of course, with this type of site, in the early stages, it is essential to build up the user base, even if it doesn't earn us any money initially.

Most PPC services allow us to set daily and monthly budgets, so that when a daily maximum is reached, our advert is no longer displayed until the next day, when a new daily limit is in effect.

Let us now take a look at how most PPC services work:

- We sign up to a PPC network.
- We provide information about our site, and some personal information.
- We provide billing information, either a credit card number, or we make payments in advance.
- We select the keywords we wish to target (for example "dinosaur breeding tips". These are words that visitors may type into a search engine, or the page may have content related to these keywords for adverts displayed on pages, triggering our adverts), as well as any information on the visitors we want to target (for example, UK users).

- Finally, we set a budget for how much we would be willing to pay for each click, the maximum we would be happy spending in a day, and so on.

Once the campaign is up and running, we can generally log in to a control panel and see how much of our budget has been spent, and how much we are paying on average per click. The monthly budgets mean if we don't pre-pay, and instead provide credit card information, we are never billed more than we have agreed to.

One thing that advertisers are often concerned about is the possibility of fraudulent clicks. For example, a competitor can perform a search to find our advert, and then repeatedly click our advert. This would cost our campaign budget, and not give us a return, because the clicking was not by a potential new sign up. To prevent this from affecting advertisers, and ruining the reputation of advertising networks, most of them have systems in place: tracking duplicate clicks and crediting the accounts of advertisers when this occurs. It is important to ensure that the PPC network we chose has provisions for detecting fraudulent clicks, so our money isn't wasted!

Search engine PPC networks

Many search engines also provide their own PPC advertising network, three of which are listed below. The algorithms employed by many of these search engines determine how much a click is likely to cost, based on the site itself, and its position in the natural search engine rankings.

A site that is completely unrelated to dinosaurs (and more specifically unrelated to supplies, breeding tips, health care tips, and so on for keepers of dinosaurs), would probably need to pay more than a relevant site for the same (dinosaur-related) keywords with search engines.

Three of the most popular Search Engine Advertisement Networks are:

- **Google**: (`http://www.google.co.uk/intl/en/ads/`)
- **Yahoo!**: (`http://sem.smallbusiness.yahoo.com/searchenginemarketing/index.php`)
- **Microsoft**: (`http://advertising.microsoft.com/search-advertising?s_int=277`)

Most search engines also allow their advertising networks to be used on third-party sites, so apart from appearing as a sponsored link on search engine results pages, the site will also display on websites, which decide to display adverts from that particular advertisement network, and also contain relevant content to the advertisement.

One important thing to remember about competing sites is that most PPC networks allow us to enter sites where we don't want our advert to appear, so if a competitor displays adverts, and ours appear on theirs, we can detect this through their control panel, and add them to the list to prevent our advert displaying, hopefully increasing our return on investment.

Pay Per Action—a look to the future

Pay-Per-Action is a new scheme being investigated by a number of PPC networks, where you only pay when a visitor performs a certain action on your site. This can involve registering for an account, entering their e-mail address in a newsletter box, or making a purchase. This is still very much at the research and development stage for most networks; however, it is worth keeping an eye on the progress in this area.

For Dino Space, the bonus for us would be that we only paid each time a user registered on our site and created a profile. Of course, we would pay more per action than we would pay per click, but in theory, we should only pay when we get results, giving us guaranteed return on investment.

The downside to PPA schemes, is for sites that display such advertisements, they may not necessarily make as much money (for example, sites currently displaying Google Adwords) because there may not be any actions performed, despite a large number of clicks.

Advertising space

A number of websites offer advertisement space, generally, on a monthly basis, which can often be a great way to generate new traffic and bring new customers to a site. There are a few simple points to take into account when considering renting advertising space from a site:

- Does the site you are looking to advertise on compete directly with your own site? If so, they probably wouldn't accept your advert, nor would it be an ideal place to advertise. The visitors have already clicked through to their site, and would probably not be inclined to go elsewhere. Thinking back to our Dino Space social network, this means we wouldn't want to advertise on fictitious sites such as:
    - Dino Net
    - Dino Planet

- Is the site relevant to ours? If the site is relevant (but non-competing), then we are more likely to get clicks through to our site, as visitors will be interested in the area we work in.

- Is the site we are advertising on reputable? If the site has a bad reputation, that reputation will come to us by association. Visitors will see we are associated with the site, and that will affect their view of our site. It is important to spend some time checking a site's reputation; it may even be worth contacting the owner of the site to find out some background or history about the site and the owner.

- What are the statistics for the site like? If the site does not get many visitors, then it isn't worth us advertising on it. It is important to find out statistics from the website owner, including visitor numbers and preferably some information on the demographics of user. If the site has a small number of visitors, then it would be important to ensure that payment is for a certain number of impressions or clicks, as opposed to a set period of time. Services such as Google Analytics provide this information; however, there are many providers available who can process the raw log files on the hosting server, and generate statistics from that.

Warning: keep the search engines happy!

Search engines hold a lot of power when it comes to promoting websites, as they run a number of advertisement networks, and list websites organically in their search results pages. We need to ensure we stay on their good side, and keep them happy, otherwise, we will feel their wrath and have our rankings in their results pages penalized.

Getting penalized by the search engines

Page listings in **Search Engine Results Pages** (SERPs) are determined by search engines by a number of different metrics, including age of domain name, content on the site, and also the number of incoming links to a site. With Google, this link factor, along with some other metrics, makes up a page rank. Depending on a site's page rank, the links the site has to other sites (outbound links) can gain page rank from this. Links from one site to another are classed as a vote, and it assumes that the site owner was happy to display that link, and that they approve of the site, and wish to attribute a vote to it, improving its page rank.

In some cases, paid advertisements are seen as a way to buy increased page rank, which search engines see as a way of "spamming" their search index. Many search engines, including Google, have anonymous online reporting tools, where users can report paid links on websites, which are then investigated. The sites involved are penalized with regards to their rankings in the SERPs.

Keeping them happy

The sale and purchase of links and adverts isn't wrong on the Internet — it is just the sale or purchase of links to adjust page rank that is, so most search engines take into account some additional information within a link that indicates that the site owner does not wish for the link to receive their "vote" when calculating page rank. This attribute should be used for any paid advertisements or links, to ensure neither the site selling nor the site buying the adverts are penalized for this. The solution is to add `rel="nofollow"` to the link, so we would end up with a link such as this:

```
<a href=http://www.packtpub.com rel="nofollow">Packt Publishing</a>
```

This does not mean that we need to add this attribute to all of our outbound links, only links that are paid for.

Here are some useful tips to ensure you stay in the good books of the most popular search engines:

- Don't buy or sell links; only buy advertising space from reputable sites (and ensure the advert has the `rel="nofollow"` attribute)
- Ensure that all adverts on your own site contain the `rel="nofollow"` attribute
- Be wary of e-mails offering to place advertisements on your site

Hopefully, by following these tips, and taking a common sense approach, you won't jeopardize your search engine rankings.

Newsletter advertising

There are a large number of online newsletters available, many of them targeting specific niche markets. It would be useful to advertise our stores within e-mail newsletters that are relevant to our store; for instance, an e-mail newsletter that is sent to all prop managers at theatre companies.

This method involves quite a lot of research, finding suitable newsletters, and discussing with the owners of the newsletters to negotiate advertising pricing.

 Don't forget to consider the points we discussed earlier, with regards to advertising space, when looking at advertising on newsletters. The tips apply to both forms of advertising quite well.

Newsletters

There are a number of newsletter systems available, which we can use to send newsletters to our customers or interested parties. Visitors to our site can leave their e-mail address to indicate they are interested in our site, but are perhaps not ready or convinced enough to join our site, and instead would like for us to e-mail them every now and then with new information on what is happening with our social network.

One particularly popular newsletter system is Campaign Monitor; this not only makes it easy to manage many lists of subscribers, but also provides advanced tools to track the success and performance of newsletter campaigns, with metrics such as:

- How many users opened the e-mail?
- How many times users opened the e-mail?
- Which links were clicked on, by whom, and how many times?
- Which e-mail clients were used?
- Who, or how many users, unsubscribed from the newsletter, forwarded it to a friend, or reported it as spam?

These metrics are not accurate, as the techniques used to detect how many times an e-mail has been opened rely on images within the newsletter, thus requiring the user to set their e-mail client to display images. However, they are useful as a basic indication of minimum statistics.

It is also possible to integrate the newsletters with stats programs such as Google Analytics. One final feature worth mentioning is that Campaign Monitor, MailChimp, and many other newsletter systems, also allow us to preview the contents of the newsletter in various different e-mail clients to ensure the newsletter will look as intended. For all of our subscribers, along with this, it can also run the e-mails through spam filters to detect if they are likely to be flagged as spam.

Social marketing

While it may seem contradictory, it makes sense to also make use of other, non-competing, social networks to promote Dino Space. Most existing social networks have provisions for user and business information as well as profile data including website addresses. Examples of this include creating a Facebook fan page for our site, adding the site's URL to our Facebook and MySpace profiles, and to our Twitter accounts. These extra links can help with additional promotion, and even if they only bring one or two new members, it is still worthwhile.

It is important, however, to not use competing social networking sites to promote our site on, as such promotion is likely to be removed, and does not help our reputation. Sites such as Facebook are large and generic, so provided we are promoting a site such as Dino Space, which is specific and targets a niche market, we would be encouraging users to also join our site, and not encouraging them to abandon the site for ours.

Viral marketing campaigns

Viral marketing is a relatively new marketing concept, which revolves around utilizing social networks. One particular example of viral marketing is utilizing video sharing websites such as YouTube and promoting videos within which we advertise our site, for instance spoof or gimmicky videos that engage the viewer, and encourage them to either join our site or help us promote our site.

This technique is probably more suited to large social networking sites with large marketing budgets who are trying to promote a brand. Information on using YouTube in particular was recently posted on a technology blog called TechCrunch, and can be found at `http://www.techcrunch.com/2007/11/22/the-secret-strategies-behind-many-viral-videos/`.

Twitter

We can use Twitter, a social network that aims to tell your friends and followers what you are doing, to keep up to date with our users. One potential method is to create an announcement Twitter account to post news, updates, and feature releases, in addition to keeping an eye out for comments or feedback from customers on the social network, and responding to them, perhaps taking into account their ideas or suggestions for new features for us to implement.

RSS feeds

Many websites offer content to their users through **Really Simple Syndication** (**RSS**), which allows them to read the content, such as blog articles, latest products, recommendations, and reviews and so on, off-site in their favorite RSS reader.

For Dino Space, we can use this to display the latest public content that has been posted to our site, or a list of new updates to the site, or if we wanted to be really clever, we can give each user a custom RSS feed link that contains the latest additions to their status feed, though this could hinder any monetization options that involve on-site advertisements. One potential counter to this is displaying advertisements within RSS feeds, something that is slowly becoming more common, and is certainly worth investigating.

Services such as Google's FeedBurner allow us to monitor our users' usage of RSS feeds, and gather statistics from them.

Search engine optimization

One way to increase traffic to our website is through **Search Engine Optimization (SEO)**. This involves ensuring that the content and the structure of our site are well optimized for search engines, making it easier for them to access our sites, and digest the important content. The other aspect is with regards to inbound links to our site.

Therefore, search engine optimization can be broken down into two primary areas:

- On-site search engine optimization, focusing on changes to the actual website itself
- Off-site search engine optimization, focusing on building up a reputation for the website through reputable, high quality, inbound links

Let us take a brief look at these two methods.

On-site SEO

On-site SEO requires us to ensure that the website itself is suitably structured, and the content is appropriate and up to date, encouraging search engines to index the site, and helping them realize which content is most relevant within the site.

Headings

Properly structured pages make use of appropriate headings to break down the content of the document into sections. The content within these headings is also considered highly by search engines. It is important that we don't fill them with too much content—three to seven words should be sufficient, keeping with the feel of a heading. The different levels of headings indicate their importance within the page (heading level one is most important, level two less so, and so on). There is much discussion on the web design community about what a first level heading should contain—either the name of the site, or the name of the page. Personally, I find the name of the page more appropriate and more relevant in terms of optimization too. There should only be one instance of the `h1` tag on a page, however, there can be any number of lower level headings.

Links

Having links to other pages within the site is a very simple and useful way to improve search engine performance. The trick is to make use of relevant sentences, using the relevant keywords as hyperlinks, and also ensuring that the titles of the link are suitably optimized. Take the example of a novelty hat category page. A poorly optimized link would be:

```
To see Dino friendly restaurants our members have
    reviewed <a href="dfr/">click here</a>
```

The link has no context to search engines, and contains no meaningful information. A more meaningful, and therefore, search engine friendly link would be:

```
Why not view our members reviews of <a href="reviews/
    dinosaur-friendly-restaurants/" title="Reviews of Dinosaur
    friendly Restaurants made by our members">Dinosaur
    friendly restaurants</a>
```

All these small changes do make a difference!

Up to date, relevant content

One of the most important things about a website is its content. Visitors like content to be fresh and up to date. By the same token, search engines also like this, as it shows the site is related to the user's search, and that it is relevant because it is regularly updated.

Page metadata

An older method for search engine optimization was to take advantage of the Meta tags within an HTML document. Because this was widely abused, it isn't as effective as it once was; however, it is still a useful technique. Some sites have their description text in search engine results pages showing as the text from their description Meta tags.

The two important Meta tags are `keywords` and `description`. The `keywords` tag allows us to associate a number of keywords with our content, and the `description` tag allows us to associate a friendly, easy-to-read description to the page. Because search engines penalize sites that hide some content from their users (with the purpose of it being shown only to the search engines, to make the search engines think the site was more relevant for certain phrases or keywords), this technique was abused as a legitimate way to have text that was unrelated to the page (or repetitions of related content) to try and boost rankings, and as such the search engines don't put as much emphasis on these now.

The Meta tags are contained within the `<head>` section of an HTML document. Example of the `keywords` and `description` tags in use is as follows:

```
<meta name="description"
   content="Dino Space is a vibrant, buzzing community for keepers of
   Dinosaurs, sharing health-care, breeding and leisure tips" />
< meta name="keywords"
   content="dinosaur, keepers, help, community, health, reviews,
   friendly, leisure, supplies" />
```

While the search engines don't take these into account too much, it is still important not to overuse them, as that indicates to the search engines that the site is trying to abuse the Meta tags and their purpose.

Site speed

One very new edition to the list of factors to a sites ranking in search engines is the speed of the site, as announced by Google in April 2010. Sites that take a while to load are penalized. More information can be found on the Google blog: http://googlewebmastercentral.blogspot.com/2010/04/using-site-speed-in-web-search-ranking.html.

There are a number of tools available to help monitor and improve the speed of your website. Some potential tools include:

- YSlow from Yahoo!: http://developer.yahoo.com/yslow/
- Page Speed browser plugin: http://code.google.com/speed/page-speed/
- Articles on speeding up your site: http://code.google.com/speed/articles/

Search engine goodies—sitemaps and tools

Many search engines provide a number of tools to help webmasters improve the performance of their sites in the search engines, and to help webmasters with the best practices. Google has a number of webmaster tools—a collection of tools geared towards helping webmasters manage the errors within their site, and see how Google sees their website—has been developed by Google, and is available for use, freely. Webmasters can also create a sitemap in XML format, to tell Google of all of the pages within our site, their importance within the scheme of the site as a whole, and how frequently they are updated, to help them decide when to return to re-index the updated content.

The webmaster tools in general, outline errors such as duplicate content, duplicate metadata within pages in the same site, as well as broken or forbidden links. More information can be found on the following pages:

- `https://www.google.com/webmasters/tools/home?hl=en`
- `http://www.google.com/support/webmasters/bin/answer.py?hl=en&answer=40318`

Off-site SEO

Off-site SEO relies on promoting the website on various other websites through inbound links, which is why it is referred to as off-site SEO. This is a particularly large area, and some companies spend very large amounts of money on this, though of course, this is all relative to the amount of return they get on their SEO investment. Off-site SEO is particularly useful for gaining rankings for specific keywords within the search engines.

Inbound links are, as we discussed earlier, an important metric in determining the ranking of websites within the SERPs. One of the easiest ways to generate inbound links, is with existing social networks, or social websites (forums in particular), by adding a link to the website within our personal signatures on discussion forums. This needs to be done carefully and considerately. If we were to sign up just to promote our link, we would be seen as a spammer, and most sites would deactivate our accounts. Posting comments on relevant blog entries or articles with a link back to our site is also useful, provided the comments are appropriate, relevant, and our own site does not compete with the article or blog in question.

Some examples of services which SEO agencies offer as part of an off-site campaign include:

- Writing articles for relevant blogs or article networks with links back to our site
- Guest blog posts on other blogs
- Online distributed press releases
- Link baiting (articles, content, or applications designed to generate many comments, blog trackbacks, forwarding, and linking to; often, this is done by posting on controversial topics within a specific niche, or by viral marketing)
- Link building (building high-quality, relevant inbound links)

What to look for in an SEO company

Search engine optimization is very much an art as opposed to a science. Here are some useful tips to consider if you do wish to use a company to manage SEO strategy:

- Nobody can guarantee results — so watch out for companies that claim they do.

- SEO is a long term investment. However, watch out for minimum terms imposed by the companies; but by the same token you should appreciate that results take time, so small (3-6 month) minimum terms are acceptable.

- SEO and PPC are not the same — some companies claim to offer SEO, when all they do is set up Google Adwords.

- Find out about their link-building campaigns to ensure they build relevant links, which won't have a negative effect in the long term.

- Audit trails — do they provide a log of work they do, links they acquire, webmasters they contact, on-site changes? Most won't give much information, as it is what is paid for, but make sure you get some indication of work performed.

- Reports — ensure you are updated regularly with search engine performance, and the effect their work is having on the rankings.

User retention

Another important aspect of marketing, is marketing with existing users, keeping them coming back to the site to make the site more useful and relevant for other users.

E-mails for the user's action

Regular e-mails can remind users about the site, if they have forgotten about it, or not had time to visit for a while. We don't want to send them lots of emails to nag them into returning; however, we can e-mail them with relevant updates. For example, when someone tries to connect with them on the site, or when they receive a message through the site, we e-mail the user to notify them of this.

This also doubles as a reminder to our users, and if the user connecting with them is of interest to them, it may help members who have lapsed in their interaction with the site, to return.

User feedback

By asking the user for feedback and ideas for improvement, they can feel more engaged and involved in the site. This also gives us feedback to use, ideas to discuss, and new features to implement.

Hello there!

As we discussed earlier, newsletters are a great way to remind a user that our site is still around, without there being a specific reason. Perhaps just to tell them what they have been missing out on, or to ask for feedback on why they haven't participated in a while, or to tell them about new developments and features on the site.

Monetization options

One other important consideration is how to monetize our site. While Dino Space hasn't been designed to make a profit, it may be useful to try and recuperate expenses such as hosting fees. Some simple options to get you started:

- Cafepress.com/Spreadshirt—create merchandise with your site's logo on, and earn a percentage from sales. This can be prominently promoted on the site.

- Google Adsense—Advertisement blocks from Google on the site earn money on a per-click basis; alternatively, integrating a Google search feature provides a less obtrusive form of advertising.

- Affiliate Marketing—Become an affiliate of sites such as Amazon, where relevant products can be promoted on the site and a commission earned.

Final tips: web stats

We can monitor the statistics and performance of our site, using a number of stats tools that are available. One such product is a very powerful statistics and analytics package called Google Analytics, available from Google, completely free of charge. This is useful for us to see which pages our visitors are using, and which pages are being ignored, allowing us to either promote them more heavily, or to focus on the more popular areas of the site.

There are also ways to integrate Google Analytics with e-commerce installations, to try and help us to determine average income per visitor—this is particularly useful when making use of PPC marketing, as it links in with Google's own PPC network, AdWords.

We can sign up for Google Analytics on `http://analytics.google.com/`, where we are supplied some HTML code to insert into our site's footer template, so that it can begin tracking our statistics.

We can also use tools like this to monitor Bounce Rates, to see how and why our users leave our site and from which pages they decide to leave. We can also see where the visitors come from, so we know which advertising sites or sites we have links on are helping us. Statistics on error pages can be useful to help us find links that are broken, or incoming links that are outdated, so we can either correct the broken link, or put a redirect in from an outdated inbound link to the new location of a moved page.

Summary

In this chapter, we looked into effectively marketing and promoting websites and social networking websites with online marketing techniques, search engine optimization, and user retention strategies. We also looked briefly into how we may wish to monetize our site.

Now, not only do we have a great framework to use for our projects, but we are placed to market and promote them effectively, hopefully generating a great return on investment for ourselves with our own projects, and for client projects.

14
Planning for Growth

Thanks to the groundwork from *Chapter 13, Marketing, SEO, User Retention, and Monetization Strategies*, we are well on the way to making Dino Space a success. However, as we get more and more users, and our site becomes more and more popular, we have a new set of challenges: growth and scalability.

As site usage increases, more resources are consumed on the server — depending on the hosting provisions and resources we have at our disposal, this can lead to slower experiences for some of our users, server failure, or some users being unable to access the site. We can rectify this by looking at how we can get the most out of our hardware by improving our site, and how we can scale by adding more resources (not just by adding more servers).

In this chapter, you will learn:

- Why code performance is important, and how you can improve code performance
- How to scale websites using cloud hosting solutions and adding additional servers to your infrastructure
- What caching systems are and how they can help get the most out of our hardware
- About Content Delivery Networks
- How to use message queues to process tasks behind the scenes
- When to use third-party services to make things easier

Let's look at how we can improve performance, get more out of our resources, and plan for growth! The information contained within this chapter should either provide a starting point for improvements and options available, or provide some food for thought for further research.

Code performance

One of the most important factors when it comes to the speed, performance, and scalability of our site, is our code. By improving the performance of our code, it consumes fewer resources, allowing us to get more out of our current hardware. Thankfully, because we have used the Model-View-Controller architecture, our code is already maintainable, extendable, and flexible, which is a big advantage, particularly with regards to plugging in new features further down the line.

So, what can we do to improve our code performance?

- We can profile our code to look for problems
- We can look for slow MySQL queries that we can optimize
- We can compress our output

Code profiling

We can profile our code to find bottlenecks in our code, so that we know which aspects need improving or refactoring. Profiling tools, such as xdebug (http://xdebug.org/index.php), are integrated into PHP to run as our scripts run, logging performance information to a file, which we can analyze using another suitable tool (with xdebug, we can use tools such as KCacheGrind or WinCacheGrind).

Slow queries

MySQL can be configured to log slow queries, so that we can see which queries are taking too long to run, so that we can investigate them, improve the queries or improve the database scheme itself, that is, by adding more suitable indexes. To enable the slow query log, we simply add the following line to our MySQL configuration file (`my.ini` file):

```
log-slow-queries = dinospace_slow_queries.log
```

Once enabled, the query log by default logs queries that take longer than 10 seconds to complete; we can change this by adding the following line to our configuration file:

```
set-variable = long_query_time = 2
```

Compression

By compressing our website's output, we can reduce network latency between the server and the user, and reduce bandwidth usage, making the site load faster. While the code won't be generated any quicker, it should be received by the user faster.

This can be done either with some Apache configuration, or by tweaking our PHP installation. The Apache option involves installing and enabling the `mod_deflate` Apache extension. More information on this can be found online, see `http://httpd.apache.org/docs/2.0/mod/mod_deflate.html` and `http://www.howtoforge.com/apache2_mod_deflate`.

The PHP option involves using zlib (`http://php.net/manual/en/book.zlib.php`), this isn't installed with PHP by default on Linux installations, but can be installed fairly easily—contact your web host for further information.

Once installed, there are a number of different ways in which it can be enabled to compress the output; we can either enable it directly in our `PHP.INI` file, or if we have suitable access, we can dynamically set/override the ini file's value in our PHP script, with the following line of code at the top of our `index.php` file:

```
ini_set('zlib.output_compression', '1');
```

alternatively, if we are not able to set INI file values, we can use object buffering to not send anything to the browser initially, buffering the output instead. Once all the output has been buffered, the compression handler is called to compress the output and send it to the browser. To do this, we simply put the following line of code at the top of our `index.php` file:

```
ob_start( 'ob_gzhandler' );
```

Useful tools and resources

Mainly related to improving client-side performance, Yahoo! YSlow is an add-on for the Firebug extension for the Firefox web browser, which offers suggestions for improving the performance and speed of the page load, as well as providing tools, information, and statistics relating to the page to help us improve the speed of the page.

`http://developer.yahoo.com/yslow/`

As part of the Yahoo! Developer Network, they also have a number of helpful hints and tips for improving page performance, `http://developer.yahoo.com/performance/rules.html`. Some of the hints include:

- Putting JavaScript at the bottom of the page
- Cache information in AJAX calls
- Don't use HTML to scale images
- Minimize HTTP requests

There are also some useful tips in the following ComputerWorld article: `http://www.computerworld.com/s/article/9140234/Five_ways_to_improve_Web_site_uptime_`.

Server performance

So far, we have looked at improving the performance of our code. Our code runs on services that are highly configurable, including Apache and MySQL, our PHP installation can also be customized through various configuration files. We can change the settings of these services too.

Apache

Our Apache configuration file (name and location depend on the setup of the server) contain settings related to how many connections can be accepted, timeout period, and so on.

The maximum number of clients who can connect to the server at any one time is set by the `MaxClient Directive` in the configuration file; this can be increased to allow more connections to the server, provided we have sufficient resources to allow this of course. More information is available here: `http://httpd.apache.org/docs/2.0/mod/mpm_common.html#maxclients`.

The length of time a process can take before Apache times out the request is set in the `Timeout Directive`, and we can reduce this to prevent processes that are likely to time out from consuming as much processing time. More information is available here: `http://httpd.apache.org/docs/2.2/mod/core.html#timeout`.

Apache has some useful performance tuning information on their website to help get a higher performance out of the server. More information can be found on: `http://httpd.apache.org/docs/2.0/misc/perf-tuning.html`

MySQL

We can optimize MySQL for high availability and performance. Packt have published a book on this topic, *High Availability MySQL Cookbook*, by Alex Davies, https://www.packtpub.com/high-availability-mysql-cookbook/book.

Alternative web servers

An alternative to increase the performance of our web server is to use a different web server, such as lighttpd or nginx, which are light-weight web servers, designed for speed and performance:

- http://nginx.org/

- http://www.lighttpd.net/

Scaling

With our code optimized, and our server's resources being utilized as best as they can, we now need to look into how we can scale our systems to easily provision more resources as and when we need them. Options available include:

- VPS Cloud Hosting, which generally involves either:
  - Adding more resources to a virtualized server, or
  - Paying for only the resources we use

- Adding additional servers for certain functions

VPS Cloud Hosting

Cloud hosting is generally a form of VPS (Virtual Private Server) hosting, where one or more physical machines have one or more virtual servers running on top of them. In most cases, a high specification server has a number of virtualized servers running on top of it, each with dedicated and guaranteed resources available, acting as far as the customer is concerned, as their own dedicated server. When we start our website, we won't need too many resources, so we can happily share the resources with other users on the same server; as the site grows, we can upgrade our account to use more resources. Some cloud solutions also allow a VPS instance to run on several physical machines, either for redundancy (should one go down, others kick in), or to provide more resources. By virtualizing the server, we don't need to spend money on new hardware when we need to upgrade, or wait while a technician upgrades or replaces hardware.

A number of cloud hosting providers offer ways to upgrade the resources required dynamically, so should the site experience a spike in traffic, more resources would be provisioned. Two examples of such providers are Amazon with their EC2 service (Amazon Elastic Compute Cloud) and VPS.NET.

With Amazon EC2, we will only be charged for the resources our website uses, be it storage space, bandwidth, or CPU time, which has the advantage of growing and shrinking to meet our needs. VPS.NET has auto-provisioning functionality, so that if load, storage space, or memory usage exceeds certain thresholds, it can automatically, add more resources. The main difference here is that you are charged based on a set dedicated amount of resources.

By starting with a scalable VPS provider, we can have our website up and running with generous resources at a low cost, and can add and remove resources as and when required easily, and if we wish, automatically.

Additional servers

Either in addition to VPS/Cloud hosting, or with dedicated servers, we can add additional servers to the infrastructure, with each server performing certain operations, for instance, a dedicated MySQL database server, a dedicated Apache server, a dedicated server for sending outgoing e-mails, a Memcached server, and so on. The advantage is that each server can be specially optimized for the services running on it, as well as providing more resources for each aspect. The downside is that it introduces network latency, as database query results and so on, will have to be transferred over a network to the web server, and then sent to the user. If MySQL is hosted on a separate server, then it should be located on the same network with a low latency link (hardware and data center permitting).

Caching systems

Caching systems can reduce the number of database and file system calls our code needs to make, by caching (creating a more easily accessibly copy of) commonly used data in the systems memory.

When we needed to access the contents of a commonly used file or frequently accessed database record, we would have the information cached, and simply check the cache when we need to access the data. For example, static pages (such as the about page, contact page, policies, and so on), as well as some of the templates used for these pages, are not going to change frequently.

We can adjust our system to update the cache every time we make a change to the page or template, and have the code that accesses the data simply check for it in the cache.

Memcached

Memcached is a popular caching system, and with some minor configuration, can be integrated with PHP. Below is some example code showing how you would connect to a memcached server, and get content associated with the home_page_content key. If there was no content, then we fall back and perform a database query.

```
$m = new Memcached();
$m->addServer('localhost', 11211);
If( ! ( $pageContent = $m->get('home_page_content' ) ) )
{
  $sql = "SELECT * FROM pages WHERE reference='home_page_content' ";
  $this->registry->getObject('db')->executeQuery( $sql );
  $data = $this->registry->getObject('db')->getRows();
  $pageContent = $data['content'];
}
```

Available caching systems

There are a number of other caching systems available, including:

- XCache
- Memcache
- APC—which supports PHP Opcode caching; this means our PHP code itself doesn't need to be interpreted each time a page is loaded

Redundancy

As Dino Space becomes more popular, the consequences of downtime become more severe. Each second of downtime is time that new users are turned away from the site, leading them to potentially look elsewhere. It is also a time when existing users may be put off from the site, and may look into alternative sites that may be more reliable. This point is emphasized by the media coverage and public reaction each time a popular social website, such as Twitter or Facebook, goes offline.

Redundant systems should help reduce or eliminate downtime, by providing backups of everything, including:

- Replicated database servers—so if our primary database server goes offline, a back up server kicks in. The data on this backup is up to date because it would constantly replicate from the primary server.

- Redundant network connections to the data centre, so should one particular connection become congested, or suffer failure, another provider's connection can be used.

- Redundant web servers should one suffer an outage.

Most redundancy options are dependent on the services available from the data centre the servers are hosted within. Provided we have access to shared IP addresses, provided by the server provider/data centre, we can set up a fallback server using Heartbeat—the primary server sends a heartbeat to the secondary server; if the secondary server doesn't receive a heartbeat in a certain time limit, then it activates and traffic is routed to the secondary machine instead. More information is available on the project's website at `http://www.linux-ha.org/wiki/Main_Page`.

Slicehost has an excellent tutorial on setting up Heartbeat (the only slicehost-specific aspect is requesting a failed over IP address) at `http://articles.slicehost.com/2008/10/28/ip-failover-slice-setup-and-installing-heartbeat`.

Content Delivery Networks

A content delivery network is a network of servers with a number of different geographic locations. When a user visits a website that uses a CDN, static files such as user downloads, images, stylesheets, and JavaScript libraries are downloaded from the visitor's closest server on the Content Delivery Network. This reduces the number of connections to our primary web server, and increases the speed at which the site loads for the user (while, in most cases, it won't speed up the PHP processing or the HTML transfer, the images, and other supporting files, are usually larger and take longer to download).

Akamai (`www.akamai.com`) is one CDN provider that offers more than just a content delivery network. The following case study shows some of the benefits in a real world situation: `http://www.akamai.com/html/about/press/releases/2009/press_071509.html`.

Message queues

Message queues can be used to make a record of any non-critical processing that needs to be done, so that either another server can perform the processing, or we can process it when resources are available.

A message queue stores a list of messages being sent either between computers or servers, or between services running on a server. Example message queue systems include RabbitMQ and Beanstalkd.

Message queue versus database table

If we have the need to store and retrieve a lot of messages in a queue, this can cause table locking if a database table was used (though this can be prevented using the InnoDB storage engine), whereas a message queue system is designed specifically for this sort of thing, as well as providing extra support for distributing the work from the queues across physical nodes.

What can we queue?

So, how can we benefit from a message queue? There are a number of tasks and processes that our website does which are not critical. Examples include:

- Resizing images—when a user uploads a photograph, we may resize it to a number of sizes, such as a thumbnail, profile picture size, standard size, and keep a copy of the original

- Sending e-mails—when a user signs up, invites a friend, or initiates a relationship, we send them an e-mail

- Deleting data—if a user removes themselves from the site, we would need to remove their profile, and any references to them, such as relationships, images, comments, and so on. This would involve a number of queries, and file system processes (to remove images, and so on.)

Processing queued tasks

When we come to a situation where we need to add something to our queue, such as a resize operation, e-mail sending, or SQL query, we can either store it as a URL that we will call, such as: /resize/image-file-name/new-x-size/new-y-size, some text, or some serialized data.

If we store a URL, the processes we have running to process the queue simply needs to call the URL, which would handle that specific request. If we are sending e-mails, we probably need to pass a fair amount of information, so it would be best to serialize the data, and have our process detect that it needs to send an e-mail, and use the serialized data to construct and send the e-mail.

These tasks can be performed by servers that are not busy serving pages to our visitors.

No SQL

There are a number of database systems available that are schema-less, useful for storing large amounts of data that doesn't need to relate to other data, such as logs, pages, documents, and so on. Examples of systems available include MongoDB and CouchDB. Generally, each individual record defines its own structure and fields, allowing such systems to be flexible to the data they are needed to store.

It may be useful for us to bear this type of system in mind as we extend our site, as we may add features that would benefit from such a system, in addition to using MySQL for the rest of our site's functionality.

A large number of companies, including a number of social website companies, make use of MongoDB and have listed on the MongoDB website what they use such a database system for, `http://www.mongodb.org/display/DOCS/Production+Deployments`.

Learn from the experts

Facebook and other social networking websites develop their own systems for certain situations they encounter, either to work faster than existing solutions, be more flexible, or because there wasn't anything available that fit their requirements. With Facebook, a number of these have been released to the community as Open Source projects at `http://developers.facebook.com/opensource/`.

One such project that has recently been launched is HipHop for PHP, `http://wiki.github.com/facebook/hiphop-php/`, which converts PHP source code into optimized C++ to help make the code execute faster. For most uses, the performance difference won't be very noticeable, but for a very popular site, even a small saving of CPU time means we can get more from the same resources.

Farm it out

Where possible, we can look to use third-party services for non-essential functions. For instance, we are going to want to have e-mails at our Dino Space domain name. By managing and receiving these e-mails on our server, we are taking resources from our primary function — the website. We can either offload e-mails onto another server, though this is adding additional cost, or we can look at utilizing a third-party service, such as Google Apps — their hosted e-mail solution.

By doing this, we no longer need incoming e-mail services running on our server, and additional resources are freed.

We don't have to just farm out non-web services, we can make use of various APIs — as we discussed in *Chapter 12, Deployment, Security, and Maintenance,* SPAM is an common problem for websites. We can either build functionality into the site to check content against SPAM filters, and build CAPTCHA systems to generate images for users to read to verify they are human, or we can make use of existing APIs to do this for us, making use of their processing resources, and reducing the work our own hardware does.

Summary

In this chapter, we have looked at how we can improve the performance of our code and our servers to get more out of our hardware. We have also looked into a number of hosting and scaling options to give us more resources when needed, should our site become more popular, or have a temporary traffic spike. Caching systems can be used to reduce database and file system calls, by keeping some information in memory, and as we saw, this can be integrated into a PHP application. We also looked at speeding things up for the user with Content Delivery Networks, and queuing processes into a message queue, which can be processed when convenient, or by another server with resources available.

We now have our social network developed with a wealth of features, hosted online, optimized for search engines, and attracting traffic through online marketing, and finally, optimized in terms of performance and scalability. Where our social network goes next is really up to you; extend it to meet your needs, improve it, and hopefully, your site will prosper. I look forward to seeing your new social networking sites on the Web!

Index

Symbols

$_GET variable 53
$last variable 34
1&1 Internet Inc.
  about 377
  URL 377
123-reg
  URL 374
.htaccess file 58

A

access logs 393
addTemplateBit method 171
administrators
  system events stream 197
advertising spaces
  purchasing 398-400
affiliate marketing 408
Akamai
  about 418
  URL 418
Akismet
  URL 390
Amazon EC2 416
Amazon Elastic Compute Cloud. *See* Amazon EC2
Apache 414
APC 417
API
  about 347
  adding, to social networks 348
  benefits 347, 348

API controller
  about 355
  example 355, 356
API, implementing
  API controller 355
  data format 354
API, methods
  REST 351
  RMI 351
  RPC 351
  SOAP 351
Application Programming Interface. *See* API
A Small Orange
  about 377
  URL 377
authenticate registry object
  amending 359, 360
authentication
  404 Unauthorized status code 357
  about 357
  POST authentication 67
  registry object 65, 67
  SESSION authentication 68
authentication controller
  password reminder, implementing 94, 95
  username reminder, implementing 92, 93
authentication object
  about 90
  authentication method, calling 91
  database, connecting 90
  logout request, verifying 91
  remember me option 92
  user status, verifying 91

Thank you for buying
PHP 5 Social Networking

About Packt Publishing

Packt, pronounced 'packed', published its first book "*Mastering phpMyAdmin for Effective MySQL Management*" in April 2004 and subsequently continued to specialize in publishing highly focused books on specific technologies and solutions.

Our books and publications share the experiences of your fellow IT professionals in adapting and customizing today's systems, applications, and frameworks. Our solution based books give you the knowledge and power to customize the software and technologies you're using to get the job done. Packt books are more specific and less general than the IT books you have seen in the past. Our unique business model allows us to bring you more focused information, giving you more of what you need to know, and less of what you don't.

Packt is a modern, yet unique publishing company, which focuses on producing quality, cutting-edge books for communities of developers, administrators, and newbies alike. For more information, please visit our website: www.packtpub.com.

About Packt Open Source

In 2010, Packt launched two new brands, Packt Open Source and Packt Enterprise, in order to continue its focus on specialization. This book is part of the Packt Open Source brand, home to books published on software built around Open Source licences, and offering information to anybody from advanced developers to budding web designers. The Open Source brand also runs Packt's Open Source Royalty Scheme, by which Packt gives a royalty to each Open Source project about whose software a book is sold.

Writing for Packt

We welcome all inquiries from people who are interested in authoring. Book proposals should be sent to author@packtpub.com. If your book idea is still at an early stage and you would like to discuss it first before writing a formal book proposal, contact us; one of our commissioning editors will get in touch with you.

We're not just looking for published authors; if you have strong technical skills but no writing experience, our experienced editors can help you develop a writing career, or simply get some additional reward for your expertise.

PHP 5 CMS Framework
Development - 2nd Edition

ISBN: 978-1-84951-134-6   Paperback: 416 pages

This book takes you through the creation of a working architecture for a PHP 5-based framework for web applications, stepping you through the design and major implementation issues, right through to explanations of working code examples

1. Learn about the design choices involved in the creation of advanced web oriented PHP systems

2. Build an infrastructure for web applications that provides high functionality while avoiding pre-empting styling choices

3. Implement solid mechanisms for common features such as menus, presentation services, user management, and more

Drupal 6 Social Networking

ISBN: 978-1-847196-10-1   Paperback: 312 pages

Build a social or community web site, with friends lists, groups, custom user profiles, and much more

1. Step-by-step instructions for putting together a social networking site with Drupal 6

2. Customize your Drupal installation with modules and themes to match the needs of almost any social networking site

3. Allow users to collaborate and interact with each other on your site

Please check **www.PacktPub.com** for information on our titles

CPSIA information can be obtained at www.ICGtesting.com
Printed in the USA
LVOW050200250212

270388LV00003B/52/P

9 781849 51238